Satisfied
with God
Alone

Satisfied
with God
Alone

PAUL F. GORMAN

TRUE VINE BOOKS
Redondo Beach, California, USA

*For I say unto you, I will not drink of the fruit of the vine
until the kingdom of God has come.*

Luke 22:18

Rise in consciousness – this is the entire secret.

As consciousness rises, detaching from and leaving
behind false belief, ever greater degrees of heaven
are visible through the unconditioned mind.

"As in heaven so on earth."

The earth and all its people, creatures and conditions
are witnessed unconditioned, whole and harmonious,
love and union of all emerging through the fog
of false sense.

Indeed, "As in heaven so on earth" emerges as the one
reality – the bondage of false material sense dispelled,
the unconditioned experience of Man, Earth and Universe
harmonious, peaceful and free, in love.

Edited by M.L. and W.U.

My deepest gratitude for your steadfast work on this text. You have both labored at it with nothing but love, a love which glows from every page.

Your devoted attention to every detail and nuance has lifted this work into a realm of clarity and beauty I could not have imagined.

Thank you!

Satisfied With God Alone

First edition 2014

Copyright © 2014 by Paul F. Gorman

Published by True Vine Books
An imprint of Giving Self, Inc
2110 Artesia Boulevard 109, Redondo Beach, CA 90278

www.miracleself.com

ISBN-13: 978-0692026366
ISBN-10: 0692026363

Set in JansonURW 11/13
Printed by CreateSpace

Available worldwide from Amazon and all other book stores

CONTENTS

1

The Truth Principle

॰

The dawn of a spiritual vision first received during the summer of 2012, on a trip to St. Tropez, France has given rise to a beautiful awakening among spiritual devotees. A great dispelling of material belief has taken place in consciousness; the light of truth has sparked a new, global awakening. Individuals and whole groups are rousing from the sleep of false sense to truthful identity. Freedom and unity of being is rising in consciousness.

The vision provides the world with a subtle yet profound spiritual clarity, a clarity which is dissolving long-standing difficulty in understanding the 'outer' or 'material' experience we call 'this world' versus the 'inner' or 'truth' experience we call 'God'.

The fruitage of this vision, and the clarity it brings, is now liberally shared in the pages of this book. It is set to clear the blockage of collective consciousness — at least the consciousness of those who are reaching up to true spiritual awareness (thousands if not tens of thousands of students, awakening souls) — in a way that we have not witnessed before. Spiritual understanding has perhaps never been quite as clear.

This probably is the blockage that has prevented what should be far greater fruitage — spiritual fruitage — among the hundreds of thousands of devotees awakening to truth. Yet that fruitage, after more than one hundred fifty years of contemporary truth clarification, is not evident. Student consciousness is so very wanting of tangible fruitage. Much confusion still exists, and because consciousness is experience, confusion results in a lack of fruit.

You Are Ready

You are reading these pages because you are ready to hear this clarity and then go live it. Welcome! You are among many friends around the earth, a great 'surging through' of illumined consciousness worldwide. Along with this surging or pushing through of illumined consciousness comes much struggle and pain. Never believe that 'outer' appearing discord of any sort is the cause or effect of anything real. It is not. Outer discord is a picture certainly, but out of *every* seeming discordant experience there is the blossoming or the pushing through of a greater degree of truth.

That is *why* the outer looks discordant; that's always why. Discord and disharmony never are what they seem to be. Never. And that goes for the entire scope of human suffering: pain, lack, limitation, loneliness, immorality, greed, war, atrocity — it doesn't matter what it looks like; the actual 'reason' for any and all disease, discord or disharmony is consciousness rising. As consciousness rises (spiritualizes), it 'pierces' the dark of awareness. By the degree of pain experienced, you can know the degree of spiritual consciousness you are attaining. Spirit is pushing through harder than ever. It is that 'pushing through' that seems like discord for awhile, just as light piercing the dark of night could be 'painful' to the dark.

If only all students would be aware of this, therefore leave the discordant experience alone for the 'nothing' it *of its own self* is, and turn to spirit alone, they would have much faster so-called healings. More than faster healings, they would rise in spiritual consciousness, therefore harmonious experience, far, far more easily and far, far more quickly.

Be Open

Be open as you read and absorb the message in these pages. It is very important that you not try to understand the truth you are about to discover. Do not put truth into the intellect. It doesn't work. Let it flow *through* the intellect, yes. You will hear it, and you will begin to feel it. The truth you read and feel an affinity with is not being put into you, but is emerging or blossoming *as the truthful you*.

A Few Preparatory Suggestions

Truth is before the intellect, before thought. Truth has nothing to do with the intellect or thought. So keep the intellect — thought — empty of 'understanding'. Don't be like Nicodemus who tried to intellectualize truth. It cannot be done. The mind is a faculty of awareness, not a faculty of understanding, thought and word. Simply be aware, behold, let. Then the light of truth becomes evident.

Keep your conversation in heaven. If you think, think about heavenly things. If you talk, talk about heavenly things. Be careful also not to talk to anyone about what you discover in these pages. If you start talking about what you hear, you lose it. Talking about truth is to leak it and to watch your body of truth wither just as a balloon leaks air and withers if it is punctured. Truth must 'build up' in you — in and as your conscious awareness — until it bursts forth as the good and rich fruitage of experience. Be a beholder, not an intellectualizer. Witness rather than think; let rather than do.

Let truth do the work. Do you think, for one moment, that you can assist God, spirit, truth in its presence and expression as you? Do you think you, as a human sense, are involved? We often do think we're involved. We think we're assistants to God. It's the funniest thing in heaven – the thought that we're assistants to omnipresence and omniscience. "Let me help you, God, because I need to pay the rent in a few days, or this painful body is really becoming too much to bear. Let me help truth through the machinery of my mind. Surely that's what's missing. That'll heal me, comfort me, pacify me; that'll enable me to experience health instead of illness, disease, injury; that'll bring me a sufficiency of dollars."

Forget it. Omnipresence is not absent of some of itself where you are or where your need is. But *you* make your *experience* absent of omnipresent good if you believe there is omnipresence 'and' local presence, infinity 'and' finiteness, incorporeality 'and' corporeality, God 'and' matter, or if you leak truth that has not yet sufficiently 'built up' within and pushed through as fruits on your branches of life.

Redefined Truth Principles

We are to hear a redefined set of truth principles. God is principle — whatever we are going to call God: spirit, consciousness, I, presence. That infinite *something* is principle not caprice. God is absolute truth, not variable, not unreliable, not personal, not conditional; but absolute, invariable and unconditional principle or law.

In the same way that we must understand any principle in order to experience the fruits of it, the good or 'truth' of it, even more so we must understand the principle that is God, the principle of truthful experience. Otherwise we cannot experience its treasure, its harmony, its wholeness. And if you think you've heard enough of principle, then realize that until the day that, wherever you are on earth, you witness unconditional wholeness blossoming — love and life, abundance, happiness and freedom, peace and harmony for all — then actually you haven't heard anything of principle. As soon as truth is truly heard, there it is, perfectly evident and real in experience. Always realize that hearing truth and evidencing it are one and the same thing. *Awareness is experience.* Truthful awareness does not 'produce' truthful experience. Truthful awareness *is* truthful experience; whereas untruthful consciousness is untruthful experience. All is one. There is not consciousness 'and' experience. Consciousness *is* experience, because only *one is*. It is simply a matter of what individual consciousness is being: untruthful or truthful. Whether untruthful or truthful, whatever individual consciousness is being, there it is as individual experience.

God Is

God *is*, period. There is none but God, and because God is infinite and omnipresent, there is no 'inner' versus 'outer'. God, truth, spirit does not *produce* good experience and then send it from an 'inner' to an 'outer'. There are not different departments in God, oneness. There is not a cause department creating effect. There is not an invisible versus a visible, or an intangible versus a tangible. Oneness is one, not two. Omnipresence is fully present at and as every point of itself simultaneously. The conceptual experience we call 'this world' including absolutely everything everywhere in it and of it is how oneness appears to be, or appears as, as we observe it through the three dimensional and five-sense mind.

There is no time and there is no space. Again, oneness, I, God, truth appears to consist of time and space as we experience it through the senses of mind, but mind — sense — does not change God. Nothing can change God because God is the only. God does not, nor ever can, change its substance, its form, its presence, its amount, its type, its category. If it did or if it could, then that change would leave something other than, or lesser than, God, something other than oneness. But God is one, spirit is one, truth is one, presence is one, not two. Again, oneness does not have, nor can have, different departments in which substance changes, or presence changes, quality or amount changes, to become some other substance, presence, quality or amount. *God is*, period, and because God is incorporeal, infinite, omnipresent and eternal, *all* is incorporeal, infinite, omnipresent and eternal, there being "none other".

As you hear this now, stay restful, open and receptive. Drop all ideas or beliefs you may be holding onto. Be open, be receptive. Hear this truth as if it were the very first time you've heard truth.

The First Principle

Let's begin with the first principle, the greatest, actually the only, the one true principle: *Only God is.*

You use any synonym you like — only spirit is, only truth is. *Only* truth is. There is nothing, under any circumstance, anywhere in or of infinity, right here, right now, anywhere, everywhere, that is not God, spirit, truth. Only God is. Only spirit is. Only truth is — *only*.

Spirit is, God is *the* infinitude, infinity itself. Therefore nothing 'else' is. If infinity is, then nothing *else* can be; otherwise infinity wouldn't have been infinity in the first place.

Only infinity is, only God is, only spirit is. God *is* infinity. Infinity *is* this *something* we are calling God or spirit or truth or I or consciousness or presence. Nothing can exist outside of the infinitude, and indeed does not. You cannot have infinity 'and' something else. So all of infinity is of itself alone because there is nothing but infinity. Only infinity is, only God is, only spirit is.

There are no exceptions. The mind does not change the fact that only God is, only spirit is, only infinity is. And if only infinity is, then the entire kingdom, the entire being-hood — all beings, all things, all places, amounts, circumstances, conditions — actually, despite appearance, have to be, and are, infinity, God, spirit because only infinity is.

Do not be concerned at this moment about why, or how, infinity appears to be finite, and omnipresence appears to be objectified and local presence. For this moment, keep your awareness on the first principle, the first and greatest truth: *only God is, only infinity is*.

Now, with your eyes closed, go and visit a dozen places of your experience, and rename those beings, those places, those circumstances, those objects, those amounts as infinity. *You are actually infinity, spirit, truth because only infinity is.* Do not try to use the mind in any way other than observer. Do not try to understand. Just observe, just behold but without belief, without opinion, without what you think of as understanding. There is he, she or it, and actually that he, she or it, is infinity, spirit, truth because only infinity is. "If you see me, you see the Father [infinity] that sent [is] me."

I live and move and have my being in, and as, God, infinity, spirit. Infinity lives and moves and has its being as me — but not the me belief wants to identify with: but *me*, infinity itself. Infinity lives and moves and has its being as itself as what belief has believed as being you and me, a human, finite, temporal self. But no, only God is, only infinity is. Therefore, yes, I live and move and have my being as and in infinity, spirit, God; and infinity, spirit lives and moves and has its being as itself as I.

If you put this truth into the intellect, you've lost it. You have 'you' back, and I have 'me' back. And having you back and me back instantaneously finitizes experience, separates from infinity and oneness your and my tangibility of experience. Everything of experience instantaneously finitizes, separates, becomes many, the pairs of opposites, of both good and bad. Truth has not changed one iota, but experience has. So do not put truth into the intellect. Never try to intellectually understand truth. And don't think about how not to do that! "My ways are not your ways, and my thoughts are not your thoughts."

Recognize that everything everywhere, without exception is, despite the way in which it appears or acts, infinity *being* everything everywhere. Only infinity is. I live and move and have my awareness singing *Only infinity is.* I walk with it, I sleep with it, I conduct my business with it as my living awareness: *Only infinity is, only God is.* God is here as this very observed him or her or it or condition, circumstance, activity, amount. *Only God is.* Make that your song: *Only spirit is, only infinity is.* Sing this song all day long and very soon you'll feel it singing you.

The Second Principle

The second principle, a principle every great master gives us, is that we must treat our brothers and sisters as ourselves. If you are infinity, if all that is, is infinity, God, spirit, which indeed *all is,* then we must treat — which means we must recognize our brothers and sisters, our world, our conceptual experience, and the whole of it, not omitting a single breath, a single fiber or grain, a single step, a single moment — *all* as the same despite appearance. Dismiss appearance. "Judge not by the appearance, but judge righteous judgment." All is God alone, spirit alone, infinity alone.

Now, what is the nature of God? What is this thing we call truth? The first thing to realize is that God, infinity is *omnipresence. The whole of infinity is present at every point of itself simultaneously.* There are no departments, no different states or experiences in or as, or happening in or as God, omnipresence. The whole of God is omnipresent as all presence. It doesn't matter what 'we' call that presence, the truth is that the whole is present as the one. Nothing of infinity is missing from this very place, wherever that place is. And because all is God and God is consciousness, this 'place' is a place of consciousness, of awareness — your awareness, your consciousness (more about this later). The whole of God, the whole of infinity and everything of infinity is fully present at every point of itself simultaneously. One doesn't feed another. One doesn't supply another. There is not a department of love versus a department of life versus a department of relationship versus a supply department, and then a peace department. *The whole of infinity is present at every point of itself simultaneously.*

God Is One, Omnipresent, Indivisible

God is indivisible. God is one. There is nothing but oneness, and oneness does not have twoness. One is *all*. One is the all-inclusive, self-inclusive whole of the one, God, infinity, spirit. The whole of infinity, God, is embodied in, and as, your consciousness. God is finished, and because God is all, all is finished, whole, complete, already fully manifest and demonstrated. There is no 'unfinished, unmanifest or undemonstrated' God. Nothing is 'going to' happen because all already is. Yes, *in experience* much is going to happen — everything is going to happen — as we experience three-dimensionally and with five senses because experience contains a sense of time and space, a sense of evolution, progress, a start, a middle and a finish, cause and effect, attainment and achievement. But experience and everything of it *in and of its own self* is nothing. It is *sense* alone, and sense never has been reality. Only God is; therefore only God is real, and God is whole, complete, and finished; therefore all is whole, complete and finished. Never judge (believe) the appearance as being something of its own self. Keep your attention on truth itself, infinity itself, God itself.

Infinity is omnipresence being omnipresent. Wherever you are, there is the omnipresence of infinity, the omnipresence that *is* infinity — the one and the whole of the one, omnipresence being omnipresent *as* this very moment, this very experience, this very him, her or it, this very amount, condition or circumstance. And what is infinity, omnipresence? Love. Infinity is love; therefore, love is omnipresence; therefore, love is the only consciousness, the only awareness, the only actual form and expression, place and condition, amount and state.

The Truth Principle

Aspects of Love

Aspects of love are life, good, harmony, peace, limitlessness, freedom of being, purpose and fulfillment. Love *is* infinity, *is* omnipresence, *is* omniscience and omnipotence, *is* unconditional experience, *is* the presence of God itself, *is* truthful experience itself.

Love is omnipresence being omnipresent; therefore there is none but love. There is no such thing as love 'and'. There are not degrees of love just as there are not degrees of oneness, love and oneness being the same one. There are not degrees of God, degrees of infinity, degrees of omnipresence. Can you imagine degrees of infinity or omnipresence — less here, and more there? Such an idea is utterly false, utterly nonsensical. Infinity *is*. Omnipresence *is*. Infinity, omnipresence is omnipres*ent* at and as every point of itself at the same time.

Indeed, there are no degrees of God, degrees of infinity or omnipresence, and because love *is* God, *is* infinity, *is* omnipresence, the whole of love is fully manifest and demonstrated at and as every place and point within and of infinity. There is nothing else, nothing different; there are no degrees. Only the whole of God – good – is.

God Is Unconditional

There are no conditions to truth. Where in omnipresence would or could a condition exist? Belief believes you have to be good in order to experience love, that you have to earn love, that you have to pray or meditate to experience love. Really? Where is such a condition happening in the infinitude, in omnipresence, in oneness, in God, in love as all, therefore as you and your experience? It is believed you have to make some sacrifices to experience love, to experience truth. Jesus says, "The only sacrifice God requires of you is the sacrifice of self". So do we not have to sacrifice before we can experience truth? There is a sacrifice to make, yes. But it's not the kind of sacrifice you may have thought you need to make. For this moment, keep in awareness that only God is. There are no conditions and no exceptions to only God is: only infinity is, only love is, only omnipresence is, only the one principle is — period.

SATISFIED WITH GOD ALONE

God Is Omniscience

Only omniscience is, only divine intelligence is, only illumined awareness is. All of God is being everything of experience. There is no other. Omniscience is the very presence of infinity, fully manifest, fully demonstrated, fully present at and as each point of infinity simultaneously. There is nothing other than infinity itself, omnipresence itself, omniscience itself. There is no other body, presence, form, experience, amount, or activity. God is forever embodied; there is no 'unembodied' God. Therefore all that God is, is all that all is, all embodied. And because God is indivisible — the whole being the only — all is the whole of omnipresence, the whole of infinity, the whole of omniscience. Nothing of the whole is lacking, separate, divided. The whole is here, being all, being one. "Son, I am ever with you, and all that I have is yours." "I and the father are one."

Remember, you cannot have infinity 'and'. There is no 'and', no 'other', no different state or substance or body. All of experience, all of life, all of presence is divine intelligence itself, infinitely greater than any intelligence we know of, or can be. All is divine wisdom, the all-knowing one presence, fully manifested as everything in your immediate consciousness, and as every point of infinity, simultaneously. Realize the whole of God awareness — omniscience — is fully embodied *as* all, as every moment, every form, every activity, simultaneously. Therefore, you are that.

Now let me ask, how many times do you find yourself reaching up to God, screaming, "If only I had a little more awareness, if only I knew more truth." Yet the whole of God awareness itself, the whole of omniscience, is 'happening' as individual consciousness. God consciousness is the only consciousness. There is no other type or category or degree of consciousness. How could omnipresent God consciousness — the only — somehow become a different type or category or degree as your consciousness or mine? What power could or would make that change when God is the only power, fully being itself alone? Only God is, only God consciousness is; therefore, only omniscience itself is consciousness. Yet how many times do we scream to God, wishing to know more truth? The very belief that we do not have sufficient awareness is the consciousness that keeps experience absent of that which we think we do not possess.

The Truth Principle

God Is Omnipotence

God is omnipotence, the one almighty power that is God itself, the only power, there being "none else". That one power is love, is life, is harmony, is peace, is oneness, is omnipresence, is what consciousness is.

Do not put this into the intellect. Do not attempt to understand it intellectually. Rather, *feel* its truth. If you try to understand truth with the intellect, you'll forever be trying to understand the truth of untruth, and that is impossible. You cannot understand the truth of matter because there is no matter. Matter is simply a material *sense* we are having of spirit. In this way, if you try to understand the one power, omnipotence, to be the truth of what seems to be many powers, you're lost before you begin.

The many powers experienced in 'this world' are nothing but many false beliefs about the one power, God, omnipotence. Those false beliefs are witnessed as an infinite variety of what appears to be different powers, some good, some bad, some terrible, some destructive, some beautiful, some positive. Lift above false belief — belief in that which appears to be. Stay with *God alone is.*

God Alone Is

God alone is; therefore only omnipotence is. Only good is — omnipresence, omniscience, omnipotence. Only infinity is; therefore all amount, all thing, all consciousness is nothing but infinity. Put this truth into the intellect and into thought and you thrust your experience into finiteness. The intellect *is* finiteness; thought *is* finiteness and because the intellect and thought are just very low *senses* of truth, and because sense is experience, experience is limited by, and as, that which is sensed. False sense makes infinity appear to be finite, whether that 'finiteness' is one pebble, one blade of grass, one dollar, or a million pebbles, a million blades of grass, a million dollars or a billion or trillion — it doesn't make any difference.

Put infinity into the intellect, into thought, and suddenly you have, in experience, finiteness — a never-ending degree of amount, both large and small, abundant and lacking, rich and poor. All the time, present exactly where the false experience of variable amount is, is the whole of perfectly visible and tangible infinity. But it takes spiritual consciousness to experience infinity as all.

All Being Is God Being

All being is God being, spiritual being. Every he, she, every animal, insect, plant, mineral, cell, atom and subatomic particle is God, the whole of God, appearing through the mind as that which appears as experience. All life, all color, all fragrance, all activity, all condition, all circumstance, all place, all cause and its seeming effect, all time, all space is *actually* and *only* God because there is none else. All measure is *actually* infinity. All presence is *actually* omnipresence. All opinion, judgment and idea is *actually* omniscience. All activity is *actually* omnipotence. Absolutely everything everywhere is, despite the way he, she or it appears to be — either good or bad — is actually and only God, only spirit and truth because absolutely nothing anywhere at any time is anything but God, the only, the one.

God Does Not Give or Withhold

Because God is, and because God is finished, wholly manifest and demonstrated already and forever, nothing can be added, nothing can be taken away, and nothing can be withheld. *Is* cannot 'give' more of itself because all of *is* already is. There is not a single grain of *is* left to give. And *is* cannot withhold any of itself because *is* is indivisible and inseparable. Indeed, God does not give, God does not withhold. All already *is*.

Awareness moves, yes. Awareness moves, God does not. All already is. The whole of infinity, the whole of eternity is fully present at every point of itself simultaneously. The whole of infinity, the whole of eternity is fully present as the you you are. There is no other being or presence you can be. Only the one is. Nothing of God, good is or ever can be withheld from you. Nothing of God, good can be added to you. You already are and have all that God is, which is all that infinity, omnipresence and eternity is.

If omnipresence is omnipotence, which it is, then the being you are is the only power your consciousness, mind and world is and has. There is no power outside of you. Nothing is acting upon you either to give or withhold. Nothing is acting negatively; nothing is holding back good from you; nothing is blocking you from, or delaying utter freedom and fulfillment of your being. Only God is, only infinity is, only omnipresence is, only omnipotence is. Therefore, only aspects of God are present and happening in, as and through you as experience. Only love, life, abundance, peace, harmony, joy, completeness *is*, all being indivisible, inseparable, undisturbable, with nothing to gain, nothing to improve, nothing to harmonize, heal or pacify. You cannot, nor would you ever need to change omnipresence, change God, change paradise. Only God is, only bliss is, only fulfillment is.

Two Things to Do

Can you do two things from here onwards? One, can you keep your mind on only God is, only spirit is? And two, can you not think about that, not analyze it, not try to understand it, but just accept it as the truth?

Without thinking, be aware that everything — every he, she, it, place, activity, every experience you have, every thought — is God, spirit, truth alone. Your attention may dart to your home, your business, your practice, your neighborhood, your loved one, your family, your finances, your country or world.

Attention loves to do just this, belief also, darting back and forth, thinking about its sense of experience and what it believes about it. How is my life doing? How are my finances? Is everything okay? What about the decision I have to make by this afternoon? What about that phone call? What about that condition, that circumstance?

So every time you catch your attention or belief misbehaving in this way, simply bring it back and tell it to think only of God. Think of spiritual things, not material things. Think — be aware — without understanding, without attempting to witness magic tricks. Fill your attention, your interest, your awareness with *only God is.*

SATISFIED WITH GOD ALONE

*I live and move and have my being in and as God alone, Spirit alone —
incorporeality, infinity, omnipresence and eternity alone.*

2

God Witnessed

❦

What does *only God is* mean? We have heard that only God is, only infinity is, only one and oneness is, only omnipresence is — only the *incorporeal* is. But what does this mean, not only in what we label 'truth terms' but in every day, practical terms? You have intellectually heard a thousand truths, I am certain, but I will say to you that unless fruits of health, wealth, harmony, love and peace fill the branches of our life, we have heard no truth whatsoever. The reason this is true is that the presence — the true hearing — of truth itself *is* the fruit of experience.

God is oneness, God is omnipresence. What does this mean? *God is.* What does that mean? *God is love.* What does that mean? *God is life, God is infinite manifestation, infinite form. God is peace* — "My peace I give unto you." What does that mean?

We know the words. We intellectually know and can probably repeat from memory every truth we've heard. But the world is still full of the pairs of opposites, good and bad. We still have our aches and our pains, problems to deal with, struggles to get through. We still battle disease, poverty, injustice, cruelty, greed. Many countries of the world are still, or newly at war with each other. And so what does all the truth we've studied mean? What has truth to do with practical experience? Indeed, what is experience itself — what is 'this world'?

Let us clarify this quandary once and for all. There must never again be confusion about experience, about this world, and about the apparent pairs of opposites — the good and bad — that make up human experience. Also let us be certain: it is absolutely true and real that *only God is*. Every other truth statement is also absolutely true and real. We could carry on hearing, discussing and repeating truth statements for the rest of our lives — indeed the instruction and discussion of truth has been going on for eternity:

God is. . . God is the only.
God is omniscience, omnipresence and omnipotence. God is incorporeal. . .
God is infinite. . . I am the Lord, and besides me there is none else.
I am that. . . I am. . . I.
I and the Father are one. . . Where the presence of the Lord is, there is liberty.
The whole of the infinite, God, exists at every point of itself at the same time. . .
I am ever with you, and all that I have is yours.

All this truth is wondrous, inspiring and encouraging. But if it remains in the intellect alone — in memory alone — it is one hundred percent impotent and invisible in terms of practical experience. It is wondrous to read and meditate on. It lifts us and provides hope. But not one percent — not one millionth of one percent — of truth is evidence-able in, or as, or by the intellect.

God Is

God-is means one thing, and until this one thing is happening as you — in, and as, your all-inclusive consciousness — then God-is is not visibly happening as your experience. The fact that God-is is absolute and practical truth will not be evident — visible and real — in and as your world.

God Witnessed

The one thing *God is* means is God *felt happening as you.* That is the only *God is,* the only omnipresence, the only infinity, the only power, the only intelligence. That is the only truth of presence, the only truth of life. That is the only oneness of life, the only wholeness and freedom. That is the only body, the only mind. You see, God-is has nothing to do with the intellect. God felt happening within, or as you, is the only world, the only love, the only relationship, friend, amount, activity: God or spirit or truth or presence — that divine something — *felt* stirring within, *felt happening* within, *felt welling up* within, a 'something' we are creating ourselves, that we are not responsible for experiencing.

We can say it is happening 'to us' or 'for us' — to or for our sense of being. A divine something which has nothing to do with our effort or design is being experienced, is *felt happening within.* It is not by mental effort. It is not by thought that this is being experienced. All the thinking and all the personal effort in the universe will not witness one second of God felt happening within, anymore than thinking and effort will produce a sunrise or a sunset. The sun rising and setting has to be *experienced happening,* not thought or made effort for.

All the reading, all the meditating and contemplating, all the memorizing of truth statements, all the teachings of Jesus, Buddha, Isaiah, Paul, John, Elijah, Moses, Nanak, Mohammed, Shankara — all of them — all the sitting and listening to all these great lights will not, even if we sat and listened for an eternity, evidence one grain of truth. Be clear: truth, God, spirit, the whole of the infinite fully manifest at every point of itself simultaneously (every point of your consciousness simultaneously); omnipresence, omniscience, omnipotence; peace, love, life, harmony, abundance, joy and freedom — all of truth! — is you and yours in the most practical and real ways, and in all departments of life *only* as it is *felt happening within,* filling you, stirring within, welling up within and overflowing into your experience.

How Is God Felt Happening?

How is God witnessed? Let us be crystal clear about how God-is is witnessed. It is in the *nothingizing* of the personal sense of being. It is the taking away of that which is the ego, the sense of you, the sense of me. It

29

is the withdrawing of our attention, our interest, our fixation, our effort, from the whole of what's happening as us, the whole of the sense of personal or human being.

We withdraw attention from the whole of what's happening in and as our sense of awareness, our sense of consciousness. Why? Our — the human or material — sense is made up of false belief. We are living a false sense of being, a false identity. And because consciousness, or sense, is experience, the false sense we live is the false sense we experience as our mind, body and world. Sense *is* experience; experience *is* sense. All is one omnipresent experience, not causal sense 'producing' an effect we call 'experience'. All is one, period, whether the one we are individually being is untruthful or truthful. We cannot escape the consciousness we are being. Whatever we are experiencing is the consciousness we are being, the 'one' and the 'other' being the same one.

God Is Not Evidence-able in the Human Scene

God is not evidence-able in the mind. There is no God in the human scene, in the human picture. Well, the human scene, the human picture, is the mind — the degree of consciousness we have named 'human' or 'this world'; one of the "many mansions in my father's house".

If only God is, only infinity is, only spirit is, only omnipresence is, then the entirety of you and your world, your universe is spirit and spiritual, not human or material.

You are spiritual, yet you think and believe materially. You act materially. You pursue material achievement, recognition, reward and fulfillment. You make material effort for material result. You study materiality, you learn material skills, you build material houses, businesses and practices. You guard and protect yourself materially. Yet it is this very material belief, thinking and pursuit that blocks from experience the fullness of truth you inherently are and have. The freedom, the bliss of spiritual being, heaven as earth, with all the true fulfillment and joy that comes with it, is invisible to experience *even though it is fully manifest and demonstrated already, fully existent all around you.*

God Witnessed

The Truthful You

Realize now, that what feels like 'you' is a mental and physical sense of being. You are used to sensing your life, your being, through idea and belief about who you are, where you came from, and what you 'have' in intelligence, skill and ownership. You believe you are physical, material, human. You believe you, all beings, and all things exist in a world of matter. Yet what and who you *actually are*, and what you *actually have*, is one hundred percent spirit and spiritual. You are the one, the only presence, the whole of God, the whole of the infinite — inseparable, indivisible, always whole and omnipresent.

Remember now, the whole, the *whole* of God is the only God. God is indivisible, the whole being the literal presence at and as every point of infinity simultaneously. God is here, omnipresent as you, being an individual and unique expression of the whole of itself (infinity, spirit) already fully manifest and demonstrated. There is no un-manifest God. There would have to be two departments of God if there were an un-manifest God over here, becoming a manifest God over there. God is one, God is omnipresence, spirit, the *whole* of spirit, the *whole* of infinity. Therefore, what is actually you is the whole of God, truth, fully manifest, already finished and complete, already demonstrated and perfectly visible and tangible.

Nothing of God Is Separate

Nothing of God, nothing of truth, is separate from you this very minute, ever. The miracle, the fully manifest perfection and completeness of life ("earth as it is in heaven") — all the miracles of the masters we've ever read about and witnessed, and all that we *will* read about, hear about and witness — is this minute fully embodied in and as your consciousness. The feeding of the four thousand, the feeding of the five thousand, the feeding and healing of millions is fully manifest and already demonstrated in and as your consciousness this minute.

Do not take thought about this. Simply become aware: God is one, indivisible. God is life, consciousness; therefore, God is your consciousness; infinity is your consciousness; all the miracles of healing, the miracles of food, abundance, love, peace, safety, union, accomplishment, harmony — all of this is fully, infinitely and eternally embodied in and as your consciousness.

There is no God outside of you somewhere, anywhere; there is no truth, spirit, outside of you; therefore, there is no life outside of you, no love outside of you, no peace outside of you. You are that.

There is no abundance outside of you, no power outside of you, no presence outside of you — separate from you, acting upon you, for you. No, no. You are that — not the believed version of you. Forget that; it isn't true. It isn't what you are and it isn't what your world is. Your sense of you and your world is such an infinitesimal grain of what you really are. Forget it. Cease from pursuing more of it or different from it or better of it. It will fail you, quickly or eventually. It is not your truth. You are the very infinity of spiritual being — God being — itself.

Where Is Your Truth?

How do you find you? How do you find this infinity, this literal infinity of being, the infinitely free being, with the freedom of the infinite, which, remember, is the freedom of love, life, good, boundlessness, effortlessness, happiness, accomplishment, plenty and purpose? Where is this found? How is it witnessed?

Number one, always bring your awareness to your withinness. I can tell you, it is virtually a waste of time to ponder truth while awareness is still in the outer. Bring your awareness to the deep place within, where *feeling* exists. This is what we're interested in, *feelings*, where love wells up, joy wells up, happiness wells up, freedom wells up into conscious awareness, as conscious experience. You know that place, deep within your being, deep within your consciousness — the place before thought, before the sense of matter clutters your senses. It is not a physical place within; it is the place of withinness, the 'place' of pure consciousness. For beginner students 'within' may appear to be a 'physical' within — in the center of the physical sense of body — and that's fine. Even if it remains being a physically sensed withinness forever, that's fine too.

Do it now. Bring awareness within. Forget the outer sense of mind, the outer sense of body or thing or activity or condition or world. Bring your awareness to your deep within. "The kingdom of God is within." It is of no use, really, even pondering the kingdom of God if our awareness is still 'out there' somewhere. Remember, God cannot be found in matter, in the 'outer', in 'this world', in 'humanity'. While you're immersed in or transfixed by that which appears to be, or by belief, you can never witness God. If you are 'in' matter (in belief) you are only able to witness that which is *of* matter — the pairs of opposites: some good, some bad, some large, some small, some happy, some unhappy, some healthy, some unhealthy or diseased or injured, some loving, some hating, some just, some unjust, some peaceful, some argumentative, some warring, some disagreeing, some difficult. All of this is of belief. We'll hear more about belief shortly.

So it is utterly useless — let us understand this once and for all — pondering truth while attention is still in matter, 'out there' somewhere, among the forms, the names, the amounts and the conditions. Remember Lao Tzu: "If you can name it, it isn't it." It is of belief, it is 'out there'. So if your belief and attention is 'out there' and you think, "Well, the first thing I must do is ponder truth, keep my mind on God, contemplate and fill myself with truth", you're practically wasting your time. You cannot start with untruth and find truth. You have to go to where God is, then experience God. You must immediately start with truth, carry on with truth and end with truth. *Only truth witnesses truth; only truth consciousness witnesses truth as experience.*

Bring attention to 'in here' – again, not with understanding but with non-understanding, a non-knowing. Just bring attention, without knowing, to within. We can do anything we wish to with our attention. There is no condition attached. Just bring your attention here, within. You do not have to pay a dollar, you do not have to sacrifice anything, you do not have to pray, you do not have to meditate, you do not have to be good or stop being bad. Bringing attention to within is free and unconditional. Just do it. Bring your attention *here, within* . . . .

Now you are in the right place, or state, of consciousness. Now start pondering truth. What truth? What shall you ponder? Slowly, deliberately:

God is life . . . God is life . . . God is life . . .

God is love . . . God is love . . . God is love . . .

SATISFIED WITH GOD ALONE

Do not at this moment ponder in terms of thing, object, amount, body. Simply ponder the truth that *only God is, only omnipresence is, only spirit is.* Never meditate (ponder) in terms of anything of this world. Leave 'this world' completely out of your meditation. Meditate on God alone *for* God alone.

> *Set your mind on the things that are above*
> *[the spiritual things, the incorporeal things],*
> *not upon the things that are on the earth.*
>
> *Ye shall seek me, and find me, when ye search*
> *for me with all your heart [all your being].*
>
> *Of him, and through him, and to him are all*
> *things.*

Do you see any 'human being' or any of 'this world' in these truth statements? All is God being itself, as itself, to and for itself — because there is none other. Therefore, ponder God as God for God, never for anything 'else'.

Now witness how quickly, with attention within, pondering only God is, only spirit is, only omnipresence is — without understanding — you feel peace or warmth or light or a sense of release welling up within and filling your universe.

Infinity is this I that I am . . . . Do not put it into the mind. *Infinity is this I that I am, this being that lives as I.*

Something is now *happening within*, isn't it? *Something.* Actually that something is indescribable. We attempt. We say it is 'peace', we say it is 'warmth' or 'light' or 'heat' or 'harmony' or 'relaxedness', a welling up of 'joy', a sense of release, a sense of safety, a sense of bliss, euphoria, boundlessness, spaciousness. You literally feel free, complete, whole. All that has happened to bring this experience to our conscious awareness is the withdrawing of attention from the 'outer' and the bringing of attention to within, where truth, reality exists. The intellect is still operating. We're not speaking of stopping the intellect, stopping thought.

That is impossible. Thought continues, but now thought is centered or 'used for' truthful awareness rather than untruthful.

In God consciousness we still observe the world just as everyone else does. When we open our eyes from meditation, we observe the room we are in, along with everything it contains; we recognize the world; we can still find our car, we haven't lost it, nor have we lost the ability to find it. So the intellect is still perfectly operative, in fact more keenly so. All we have done is withdraw our attention, our belief, our interest and fixation from the outer sense, and brought it to the inner sense. That 'inner' is what and where God is, and where we feel the actual experience of truth happening. Remember, God is always happening as you, as me, as all. There is never a moment in each twenty-four hours when God is not the fullness of our being and experience. *But our awareness is not there.* Our awareness has gone out into the world of appearance, of matter, of false sense. It has been seduced by sense. As Charles Fillmore whimsically stated, "There is a church service going on inside you twenty-four hours a day, *but you're not there*".

God is, and God is happening — the whole of the infinite, fully manifest, fully demonstrated, fully tangible— as you, as the only truth of you, twenty-four hours a day, eternally. But it is all a matter of *conscious awareness*. Where is *your* awareness, versus mine, versus Gautama's, versus Jesus', versus Shankara's, versus Moses'? Where is your awareness? If you learn to bring and rest your awareness *within* instead of tangled up *without* — and worse than tangled up, interested, even fixated on what it's tangled up in — then you're in the place, or state of conscious awareness where God is felt happening.

The Inverse Way of Being

Practice the inverse way of being, with your awareness always seeking within:

I want to feel God happening; I don't want to feel the world happening; I've had enough of the world in and of its own self. I want to feel, I want to be aware of, God.

35

SATISFIED WITH GOD ALONE

This is what we seek and how we seek it. We've been seeking truth in books, audios, classes, and truth statements, while all the time the fullness of God, fully manifest, is happening twenty-four hours a day as you, as me, as everything everywhere.

Awareness has been in the wrong place, so it does us no good *in tangible experience* that God is the only presence, fully happening as us. God happening as the entire world, the entirety of infinity — peace, bliss, love, life, infinite form, the freedom of being, the boundlessness of expression, union of (and among) all being and all of the world — is, this minute and forever, the only being and presence, the only world, fully manifest and tangible, never intangible, never a mystical 'tomorrow world' that one day we will go to, probably after 'death'. No. Right here, right now the only being is the spiritual being, the being of infinity, omnipresence, God, eternity. There is no life that is not eternal life. There is no birth, no death. There is one, omnipresent, eternal, constant, self-complete, infinite, effortless life. That *is the one and only life* that is your life, my life, all life. There is no 'other'.

All life, all form, all supposed inanimate as well as supposed animate, all place, condition, circumstance — everything everywhere — is the one whole of eternal life. But this truth *alone* does us no good in experience. Why? Our attention is elsewhere. Our attention is entangled in that which appears rather than that which *is*, and all belief does of this one, omnipresent, eternal, effortless life — self-complete, perfect, pure, joyous — is finitize and limit the experience of it. It doesn't finitize God. You cannot finitize God; you cannot change the one and only substance, being, type, category, amount and quality that is God, truth. But belief infallibly finitizes and limits the tangible *experience* of truth.

No Power But God

Can you imagine, for one second, belief having the power to change God from infinity to finiteness, from eternality to temporality, from incorporeality and omnipresence to corporeality and locality? Can you imagine that? Do you think God can be changed from omnipresent harmony and peace to locally present disharmony, disagreement, war and atrocity — whether between men or nations, cells of the body, or dollars in the bank? If that were possible (and it is not), it would make belief more powerful than God, the one power. Nevertheless, if our attention is tangled up in that which is believed, then our experience — because consciousness is experience — becomes finite, limited, of both good and bad.

God Is 'Before' Thought and Word

God is 'before' thought and word. The mind presents oneness as multiplicity. In and of its own self, the mind and its formation — the universe, the world, and everything in it and of it — is innocent and impotent. The mind is unconditioned, therefore all form *of its own self* is equally unconditioned because all form is mind-form.

We'll hear more about this in following chapters, but for now, all you need to know is that God — truth — is before thought and word; hence, do not think about truth. Do not put truth into the intellect and try to understand it, try to bring it to bear, bring it to a witness-able state of being or form or amount or condition. Never attempt to do that. The only result will be failure. Truth is not there, and never available there. Truth is before thought and before word. Truth is consciousness, pure consciousness. As awareness rises — spiritualizes — that more truthful awareness *is* more truthful experience. Conscious awareness rises and there *is truth* as experience. Thought has nothing to do with truth, and thought has nothing to do with the evidence of truth. In fact, thought has everything to do with the non-evidence of truth.

Before You Think, Truth Is

Realize: before you think, truth is. Truth already is, before the mind, before thought. Therefore, mind is not involved in truth and thought is not involved in truth. "Take no thought for your life."

One thought, just one — in other words, one step into the intellect or belief or thought — *is* the personal self. *Thought — the intellect, the ego, belief — is the personal self.* Thought or belief therefore is itself the form of both good and bad — good and evil as it's referred to in the Bible.

'Good and bad' — what does this actually mean? *God and matter.* As soon as we've stepped into the mind and its formation (the universe, the world, and everything in it and of it) and believe it as being something *of its own self,* something different from God, we are entertaining a false sense of truth. We've called that false sense matter, physicality, materiality, this world. The entire false experience *is itself* that of the pairs of opposites, both good and bad happening as that very point of matter, that very point of awareness, that very thought.

Every Thought Has an Opposite

Every thought has an opposite, and that proves that thought is the personal sense. Each and every single thought has an opposite: this is good and that is bad; this is black and that is white; this is healthy and wealthy and that is unhealthy and poor. And of course each good and each bad has an infinite number of degrees in between the two — healthy and sick; happy, unhappy; here, there; much, little; safe, unsafe; home, no home; good clothes, cheap clothes; love, hate; peace, war.

Every thought has an opposite. Give me one thought — one in any language you like and from any country in the world — that does not have an opposite. You can't find one — and don't be smart and give me, *I !* The whole race is living the opposite of *I !*

You see that as soon as we enter the mind and believe what we experience as being something of its own self, something other than or different from God alone, as soon as we become entangled with and fixated on appearance, we've entered an experience that has no God in it, nor can have. Yet what is the first truth, the only truth? What does all awareness eventually come home to? *Oneness. Only oneness is, only God is.* As soon as we are consciously living oneness, all belief disappears. Thought and conversation dissolve.

Only God is.
God is infinite, and because God is infinite, there is nothing 'else'.

God does not think, so the moment we have one thought, we are separating ourselves from God in experience because we are being something other than God presence. We have introduced an 'and', an 'and' that doesn't actually exist — God 'and' matter, good 'and' evil as described of old. I've never liked the word 'evil' — good and bad, positive, negative, variable experience, unreliable experience, separation — these are better words.

The very thought itself is the separation — one thought. We are not attempting to stop thought; we do not need to. But we do have to be aware that if we believe what the mind presents, if we're judging, if we have opinion and desire instead of using the intellect and thought truthfully to recognize that only God is and to let the presence of God be *felt*, be experienced spiritually as a *feeling happening within*, then we are not in truth and therefore unable to witness truthful experience.

This is why Jesus told us, "Judge not by the appearance, but judge righteous [truthful] judgment". Judge truthfully. Be aware truthfully. What is the truth? The truth is that only God is, only infinity is. You cannot have infinity 'and' — God 'and'. The 'and', in experience, is belief.

Now go back within. This is always the first thing to do. At every opportunity, one hundred times a day, get back within:

Let me turn within. Let me not be interested in 'out here'; let me not get tangled up in opinion, in judgment, in idea, in belief, in the pursuing of anything of the 'outer' world, in thinking I know what 'is' and what 'is not'.

I do not, nor ever can, know a single thing of truth. "I of my own self am nothing. . . My thoughts are not your thoughts, my ways are not your ways." Therefore, how could I of my own self know something, or have the ability to truthfully judge something? What opinion can I possibly have if I of my own self am nothing? I can only have a false opinion.

So here within, with attention withdrawn from the outer, we contemplate these things of truth, and as we do, while we remain in the right place — the kingdom of God within — then we quickly start feeling that magical *something* stirring within. That felt happening is the only *is*. That *is* the only tangible experience of God, of infinity, of omnipresence. That is the only form of experience of God, truth, spirit; therefore, that is the only body.

You experience your true body only when you are feeling truth happening within. You call it intangible, which means belief calls the feeling intangible. That just proves how little belief knows. God is the only tangible, the only body. The intellect doesn't understand; it's a little baby. It does not possess the faculty of truthful awareness.

God Felt Happening Is Life

As you feel God happening within, you *have* life. You do not need healing when you're feeling God happening within— you *have* life, you *are being* life itself.

The feeling is happening *as you*, is it not? It is yours rather than mine. It is not separate from you; it is happening *as you*. Therefore you *have* life. Forget belief's idea of body. This felt happening within, this life felt happening *is* the wholly healthy and vital body. The felt happening does not produce a healthy body, it *is* the healthy and vital, strong and perfect body. There is no other body. But hear this carefully: if you try now to bring the experience of this life — the only life, God — that you are now feeling happening within, into the physical sense of body to heal it, you lose it.

On the other hand, if you realize that this felt happening within *is* the life and health itself, and if you never forget that all of God is fully embodied (there is no unembodied God), then this life and health quickly becomes your tangibly experienced embodiment (body) of life, and the 'healing' is witnessed. But realize, all 'healing' is really a healing — an illuminating — of *sense*, not physical body. The physical body is nothing more and nothing different from a physical *sense or belief*, a corporeal, material *sense* of that which is one hundred percent incorporeal, spiritual.

Personal Sense Is Infantile Sense

The intellect has only the faculty or capacity to experience truth with a very infantile sense, or awareness. That is why when you remove the intellect — remove thought — you quickly witness whole and truthful embodiment. Belief has named its sense of body 'physical'; the intellect has cut its sense of body open, taken a look, and witnessed its sense of organs and functions of body. Forget this. Forget what the intellect reports.

Do not believe appearance. Again, "Judge not by the appearance". If you realize that this *felt happening within* is the only and the whole and the eternality of the life, uniquely and individually embodied as you and your world, and you rest there, *satisfied with that experience alone*, not looking for anything else of life (because in looking for anything 'else', you realize you're looking for a false and limited sense of life. Why would you do that?); if you tenaciously stay with the one life fully embodied as the you you are, and the tangible experience of it as the felt happening within, then you watch how the infantile physical sense springs up so quickly — "quickly and sharply and powerfully" — in the fullness of life, in full vitality, in beauty, in joy, in harmony and with purpose, shaking itself free, saying, what happened there? I dreamed I was sick, limited and unhappy, but no, I am full of life and energy.

The Only Tangible and Visible God

God is only in your experience and mine — tangibly and visibly — when God is *felt happening within*. That's it. That experience *is* the truth of you, the infinity of you, the omnipresence of you, the truth of all form in your world; there is nothing 'else' of you nor your world.

Yes, when you look through the mind, everything is fragmented in experience — not in reality, but in experience, in or as sense only. Everything seems separate, of many and of variability. There seems to be a physical body; there seems to be a world of physical beings, mental minds, material matter, of both good and bad, time and space, cause and effect, varying amount, different condition — each with its opposite. None of this is truth, and is — *in and of its own self* — unconditioned, innocent, impotent appearance, imagery, sense.

Yet, as you realize what has been revealed in this chapter, and you live it — live by the *felt happening within* as your one and only life; when you live that one truthful life, one truthful body, one truthful world realizing that that is itself infinity, omnipresence, omniscience, omnipotence; and as you no longer take thought for matter, no longer search for truth in the mind or in the world, no longer try to bring truth to bear through the mind or in or for the world; when and as you live that one experience only (God *felt happening within*) — then you have the miracle of truth in your hands, and witness it fully and naturally embodied as the good of life in all ways.

SATISFIED WITH GOD ALONE

Ignore the Way God Appears Through the Mind

Ignore the way God, oneness appears to be when observed through the mind. Ignore it. Withdraw, come within, live within. *I live and move and have my being in God.* Understand now, that you do not "live and move and have your being in God" unless you are living and moving and having your being *here within, feeling God happening.* When you do, then what unfolds as your life, and all of it — your world, your family, your success, your creativity, your talent, your home, your peace, your safety, your joy of life, effortlessness of truthful life — is heaven. "In earth as it is in heaven." Heaven is not found anywhere else other than the felt happening of it within.

When You Are and Have God

When you are feeling this blissful presence happening within, you have the power of the infinite; you *are* and *have* the presence of God itself; you *are being* and *have* the infinity of all being, all form, all activity. You *are* and *have* peace as and throughout the infinity of you, the entirety of your consciousness.

When you do *not* feel God happening within, you do *not* have life, you do *not* have infinity, you do *not* have peace and joy and love in tangible experience. You've cut yourself off from God in sense, in experience, and because sense is experience — consciousness is experience — that empty-of-God experience is yours. Life depletes, success depletes or is variable at least. Happiness, love, relationship is variable at least, unreliable at least, and at worst, crumbles. Peace is not evident. By some degree at least, disharmony and discord are experienced. *We* have cut *ourselves* off. We've cut ourselves off from the very love we wish in our lives, from the healthy life we wish to experience, the satisfying relationships we wish to enjoy, the abundance we wish to experience, the very happiness, the skill, the talent, the wisdom we wish we had. Then we pick up a truth book and hope we'll find it there.

God Witnessed

We Cut Ourselves Off

We cut ourselves off by believing in something other than God. We've gone back into belief, into what appears to be, and unfortunately in this way cannot experience God, which means we cannot feel God happening, feel the very presence of truth happening while our belief, attention, interest and effort is in the outer. We've cut ourselves off, we've pulled the cord from the power socket, from the truth, and our whole life depletes.

Our whole life instantaneously falls into God 'and'. Our life gradually or rapidly runs out, dries up and withers, just the same as if we pull the lily from the ground, or we pull the fan from the electricity, or we take a body of water from the ocean and separate it. What happens? It withers and dies, it evaporates, it shrivels, it is suddenly 'on its own' having an experience something other than its truth. There's the 'and', there's the separation. We do it to ourselves when we take our awareness away from our within-ness. We go back into the mind and start operating, thereby cutting ourselves off — in sense, in experience — from God. We're never actually cut off from God in truth. God is the only presence, but because consciousness is experience, sense is experience (whichever term we wish to use), then that separated sense is our experience.

'Separated' from God Experience

Do you see what is meant by 'separated'? We have taken attention away from God; we've separated our awareness from God felt happening within. We're no longer attentive to, and feeling God happening within. There's the separation. Do you see that?

It's all about consciousness. The whole key is wrapped up in that word consciousness, or awareness. By separating ourselves in consciousness — by having an 'and' in consciousness, a belief in something other than God alone — we then are presented with every experience but God. We're experiencing everything but the actual and only truthful experience of God felt happening within. It is then no use believing that by *thinking more* about God instead of the multitude of 'this world' things will evidence the harmony and wholeness we desire.

Thinking alone — even of God — will do us no good whatsoever, apart from frustrate us more, because all the effort of thinking will not and cannot *evidence* one single grain or moment of God itself in experience. Only God *felt happening within*, by no effort of our own, is God visibly and tangibly *experienced*.

Receiving Truth Non-Intellectually

By now, you are able to receive truth without churning it through the intellect. You are able to simply rest with the truth you are hearing, simply beholding it being presented to you, simply receiving it and accepting it without having to understand it. Only God is, therefore only God is understanding. Let God be your understanding, just as you let the sun be your sunrise.

Let truth be received with a non-understanding. The being who doesn't attempt to understand truth *but rests its personal sense of self and beholds that which is*, is the being who witnesses truth.

It is perfectly logical that only by withdrawing sense from the outer, and coming within, do we find truth, God, spirit. We've been told it for thousands of years: The kingdom you are searching for, the truth you are searching for, is within. It does not have names. "If you can name it, it isn't it." So we come within, and we ponder truth until we feel what we are really seeking — truth itself happening within. You cannot name that. You can try your best, but actually you cannot name or quantify or capture it. You can *feel* it, experience it happening within, feel the presence alive within. That's it. That is the miracle of truth witnessed or demonstrated — truth evident as actual, real experience.

~

A quite profound revelation took place December, 2012, which we are to hear about next, including its subsequent fruitage. You are ready to receive it now that you have the one, first principle: *God is, period*, and now that you know what 'God is' means — the *felt happening within*.

You know that if God is not felt happening within, there is no God to be found as visible and tangible experience — there is no fruit on the vine. In that case, God is intellectually but not *actually* known (experienced). This is the entire reason for a lack of 'result' in an individual's — and the world's — experience.

3

What Is Experience?

❦

T he first thing we must understand about *experience* — that which we call 'human, physical, material, conceptual, this world' — is that it of its own self, *before belief is introduced*, is one hundred percent good. "And God saw every thing that he had made, and, behold, it was very good."

Degrees of Awareness

God is one, and because God is all, all is one. God is consciousness, and again, because God is all, all is consciousness. Experience is simply a *degree of conscious awareness* — a degree of illumined awareness or awakening. Spiritual teachings have often referred to human experience as 'a degree of consciousness' (and maybe we sometimes have too) but this is incorrect. There are no degrees of consciousness. Consciousness is God, and God has no degrees anymore than math or aerodynamics has degrees. Only the *whole* exists. God is one, forever whole, omnipresent, omnipotent, infinite — *the* infinitude itself — incapable of being anything 'less' or 'different' or 'partial'. God is eternal — eternity itself — incapable of being temporal, 'different' or 'other than' eternality itself. Therefore, in the whole of God there is not one grain or flicker of consciousness other than the *entirety* — omnipresence itself being all, that 'all' always being the whole. *Always the whole.* Nothing 'less' exists. Therefore, your consciousness is the *whole* of consciousness, the *whole* of God here, now and forever.

However, there are degrees of *awareness* of the whole — infinite degrees. *Awareness* is experience; awareness is *what* experience *is*. I can be standing a foot behind you, but you may not be *aware* that I am. That doesn't mean I'm not there, it just means you are not *aware* that I am there. In this way, the whole of God is what you are — what your consciousness is. Remember, the *whole* is the only. The whole of God is fully existent, fully manifest and demonstrated, fully visible and tangible in and as your consciousness this minute, and forever. The whole of God!

Think about that! Yet your *experience* is the degree, or 'amount' of God you are individually consciously *aware* of being. Each individual experiences his or her individual level or degree or amount of *awareness* of God, the whole. The more illumined or spiritualized individual awareness becomes, the more of God — the whole — becomes visible, tangible, real as experience. The whole of God already and forever *is* perfectly visible, tangible and real — the *only* visibility, tangibility and reality. But now, as awareness lifts, illumines, spiritualizes, ever more of the whole becomes witnessed as experience, just the same as when you become aware that I am standing behind you, I become visible and tangible as your experience.

The whole of God *is*. That *is* is consciousness, the one consciousness, *your* consciousness, and that of all. Simply become ever more consciously *aware* of that truth of you — your truthful identity, the truthful identity of all (despite its given name or nature) — and your experience becomes ever more full of God alone as mind, body and world. Awareness *is* experience.

SATISFIED WITH GOD ALONE

Understanding Mind and Form

This excerpt from the *7 Spiritual Steps** beautifully explains mind and form:

All formation is of mind. Mind 'and' form are one and the same 'thing' or presence or 'happening'. There is no 'and', there is just *is*. Mind *is* form; form *is* mind. Form is not an entity in and of its own self. Mind does not observe or experience form; mind *is* form. Form is not being observed by mind; form *is* mind, mind *is* form. The question, therefore, is *what is mind?* Once we know what mind is, we also know what form is because mind *is* form; form *is* mind.

As always, the first thing to do is get immediately back to God – pure God: *Only God is.* Only God is, and God is unconditionally whole and omnipresent; therefore God is *all, without exception*. We must take "God is all, without exception" literally. Then our consciousness is open to hear and receive truth.

Here's that truth, a truth known by only the few enlightened beings of each age, now given to you. If you can truly hear this – if you have "eyes to see and ears to hear" – if you have sufficient spiritual discernment, you will discover the greatest secret of the ages. To paraphrase the Master, "Whoever discovers this truth will be untroubled by that which appears to be, will live free in truth, will witness fulfillment of all, and not taste death."

There is one consciousness: God. Yet there are infinite degrees or levels of *individual awareness* of the one – just as there is only the one math yet infinite degrees of awareness of that one.

The Master gave us the secret of consciousness: "There are many mansions in my father's house," followed by, "If it were not so, I would have told you." The "many mansions" are the many (infinite) degrees of *conscious awareness* of God, of truth.

Right where you are is the infinity, is the omnipresence, of God – the almighty truth of being and experience – *being the very you you are*. Despite this great truth, our awareness of God as individual being determines – *is* – our individual experience.

Consciousness *is* experience. Our degree of conscious awareness *is* our tangible experience. Experience, both good and bad, appears convincingly real to us. It is false *sense* of the real, not reality itself, yet every degree or level of consciousness appears to be real at and

* *The 7 Spiritual Steps To Solving Any Problem* by Paul F. Gorman

to its own level. As our consciousness becomes ever more *spiritual,* our experience becomes ever more beautiful, bountiful, harmonious and fulfilled.

And so by the degree we individually are either unaware or aware of God as the only, *is the degree of truth* – health, wealth, love, harmony, peace and fulfillment – we experience as the 'reality' of life.

The degree we call 'human' awareness is the one 'human collective' mind, consisting of what has been named 'mentality and matter'. It is what we call 'this world, the physical, material world' – everything in it and of it – experienced as five senses and three dimensions.

Each degree of awareness – each of the "many mansions in my Father's house" – is infinite in and of its own degree, excluding none of infinity. *Every* degree including the 'human' degree of consciousness is infinite because only infinity is. "The whole of infinity exists at every point of itself (degree, level of awareness) at the same time." It is for this reason that we can have as much of 'humanity' and all the things and conditions of 'this world' as we wish to have. Nothing is limited, nothing is separate, nothing is apart. All is infinite and omnipresent and because all is God, the truthful infinity and omnipresence we are and have is good alone. "And God saw every thing that he had made, and, behold, it was very good."

You may believe that today you lack something of health or wealth or love or peace or harmony or safety. Yet the whole of God, the whole of the infinitude, is right where you are, *being* what you are and what your world experience is. This means that all of life, abundance, love, harmony and utter fulfillment of being – all that God is – is where you are this minute, fully tangible as the need fulfilled. As we know the truth, as we fill our consciousness with truth morning, noon and night, we discover our truthful identity: the "man in Christ", the spiritual being who toils not, neither does he spin, yet "Solomon in all his glory" was not arrayed as beautifully and bountifully in all the world's goods. When we understand that 'this world' is nothing but God appearing as our experience with five senses and three dimensions of mind, we have awakened to the truth and treasure of heaven as earth.

Mind is simply a faculty of experience. Mind happens to, at the 'human' degree of awareness, consist of five senses and three dimensions. But the five senses and three dimensions *do not change God.*

Mind is not a power. Only God is power. Mind does not *change* God into different form, substance, characteristic, presence, truth. All form is one hundred percent God, and *of* God, utterly unchanged and unchangeable because nothing but God is. Just because the mind forms God into five-sensed and three dimensional experience does not in any way 'change' God. Nothing including mind can change God, the one and only power.

Throughout the ages, the quandary of 'this world' has fooled most truth students, thereby keeping them out of truthful experience. *How can form which appears to be corporeal, finite, local, variable and temporal consisting of many different powers of both good and bad be God when God is the only – incorporeal, infinite, omnipresent, invariable, eternal and of one power alone?* The key is found in three of the Master's statements:

"I am in this world but not of it."

"Judge not by the appearance, but judge righteous judgment."

"Know the truth, and that very truth will set you free."

I am in and experiencing the world of form ('this world') just as you are and as the whole of humanity is. *But form is not what it appears to be.* It is God alone – unconditioned, unchanged, pure and whole – because nothing can condition or change God. *Only God is.* There is nothing but God, therefore nothing that could 'condition' or 'change' God even if it were possible, which it is not!

The mind simply forms of God, of oneness, five-sensed and three dimensional experience (images). But that experience or appearance does not make it *of its own self* real anymore than the experience (appearance) on the movie screen makes it of its own self real. The images on the movie screen are nothing of their own selves. They have no 'truth' in and of their own selves. Their 'truth' is whatever the reel of film is and contains. Neither the light nor the screen have power to change the 'truth' of the film, it's character, nature, activity, plot and conclusion. In this way we realize that the images of life, that which we call the 'this world' experience, are nothing of their own selves. Their truth is God and everything God *is* and *has*, and nothing 'else'. There is none else! Their actuality here and now is God. Nothing has to 'change' before form becomes truth because nothing has been changed in the first place. Their substance, presence, form and activity are all God. Remember: the only visible presence is God. The only, *only* is God! The only 'he, she or it' that can present itself to you is God.

What Is Experience?

Because form *appears to be* a real entity in and of its own self – a real 'he, she or it' of either good or bad quality and nature – does not make it so. "Judge not according to the appearance, but judge righteous judgment."

Why "judge not by the appearance"? Hear this closely: because God *is*, and is unconditioned and unconditional (principle); and because God is mind, mind is as equally unconditioned and unconditional. God 'and' mind are one, not two – not two different things or states or presences or activities. And because mind is form, form is as equally unconditioned and unconditional. God *is* mind (one of the many mansions in my Father's house) *is* form – all one.

Whatever or whoever you observe is God-mind-form: all one, all unconditioned and unconditional God, simply observed or experienced as five senses and three dimensions at our level of consciousness *but never 'changed', never 'different'* because nothing – *absolutely nothing* – has the capability of changing God.

All form – this entire universe, world and absolutely everything everywhere in it – is nothing in or of its own self, is innocent and impotent. Form in and of its own self has no power, no law, no principle, nothing to uphold it in or of its own self. Of its own self it has no substance, no power, no law, no principle, no body, no ability either of good or bad.

The World Is Not Erroneous

The world is not erroneous; mind and body are not erroneous. Human *belief* is erroneous, and because belief is experience, the world *appears to be or contain or include* error in it. There is no error 'out there' in concept, in form, in the world *in and of its own self.* All error is 'in here' in belief. We have false belief about that which *is*.

If the world were error, and if that error were real, a real entity — something different or other or less than God alone (which is impossible) — the 'healing' of error could never occur simply by it being bathed in truth consciousness, just as if darkness were a real entity, it could not be 'healed' simply by being bathed in light. Darkness is not an entity but simply a lack of light. In this way, disease, discord, lack and limitation are not entities but simply a lack of God consciousness — a lack of living God awareness. Only that which is *unreal*, therefore insubstantial — not being an entity in and of its own self, therefore unable to offer resistance — can be revealed as real simply by bringing reality to it.

Think!

If the world were error, every illumined consciousness would be unaware of it. Error — false belief, materiality — is non-existent in illumined (God, spiritual) consciousness. The world would not exist in such a consciousness. No saint, seer or prophet would be seen here, nor the miracles each demonstrates, and in turn, the world would be unable to see *them and their miracle works*. Yet Jesus and every illumined being lived, and lives today right here among us, experiencing the conceptual world just as everyone does. Indeed, the world and every being, thing and condition in it, and of it, is perfectly true and perfectly good (God) — "one of the many mansions of my father's house".

The key is to be not *of the world* — not to be of the belief that the world, matter, is an entity in and of its own self, a being, body or other form separate from or different from God. "I am in the world but not of it." This is the entire key.

An Illustration

Imagine there is a tall window, infinite in height, consisting of an infinite number of horizontal slats running top to bottom. Apart from the very highest slat which is a pure transparency — unconditioned, entirely clean and pure — each slat from top to bottom contains more and denser imagery (like a stained glass window). At the very bottom, the slat is completely dense, black with no light or life or color or 'space' in it whatsoever. No light can get through it. Each successive slat down from the top contains more imagery, more density, and less transparency, less light. So the second slat has a minuscule, hardly visible image on it somewhere, a tiny, very faint concept. As light shines through that very faint image, experience — the world — now contains a very slight hint of something other than pure sunlight.

Now imagine, each degree (slat) down contains another little wisp of a concept. The third slat has more concept, more imagery, but still very, very faint, hardly noticeable at all. Nevertheless, the world of that pane of glass has within it that conceptual embodiment.

Now let's travel all the way down to what we call 'our' (the human) degree of conceptual experience, where the entire experience is conceptual. Everything of our experience, until we awaken, is conceptual, conditional, finite, everything seeming to be outside of our sense of being. Even the body is an outer sense of body, something it seems as if we have little control over, some aspects of it more controllable, some less; a world which has, as its very nature, both good and bad experiences — all of this is the 'pairs of opposites' of the human, worldly experience. And then we travel infinitely below 'our' level, where there is ever denser conceptual experience, until it becomes one complete density, one blackness.

But can an image, a form of its own self, be good or bad, healthy or unhealthy, rich or poor, happy or unhappy? Of course not — no more than the puppet of its own self can be, or the wave or sunbeam of their own selves can be.

The Inherent Innocence of Experience

Realize: before belief, all conceptual experience is God, good, oneness simply experienced conceptually and as multiplicity — the "many members". All of experience and everything experience contains is *of its own self* — before belief, before thought, before judgment — good, innocent and perfect: God and nothing but God, simply experienced conceptually. It is like the experience of a stained glass window. Sunlight shines through the stained glass forming light-images of whatever is painted on the window. The image, the form, has no life or power, quality or condition of its own self. Its entire 'body', its 'life' is the body, the life of light pouring through the window. The light *is the form, is the body* of the image. There is no other form or body, no other substance, no other power, no other presence about the image or form.

In this way, the entirety of the world — the conceptual experience — is nothing of its own self and is pure, innocent, and impotent, of good, God, alone. No matter what being, form, activity, place or condition is witnessed, it of its own self has no life, no power, no substance, no presence, no principle or law to uphold it. It is God and nothing but God (because there is nothing but God). It is simply a conceptual experience of God but the conceptual experience has not changed God. God is the only! Therefore the conceptual experience can only be, and is, one hundred percent God and nothing less. God shines through the conceptual mind producing conceptual experience, and because God is unconditioned and unconditional, mind is equally unconditioned and unconditional (because mind is God); therefore, all the formation of mind (this world) is unconditioned and unconditionally of God.

Nothing of negativity, disease, injury, poverty, starvation, sadness, loneliness, injustice, cruelty, atrocity exists *but belief makes it appear to be so.* Experience without belief simply *is*, that *is* being God alone. "The earth is the Lord's, and the fullness thereof . . . the earth is full of the goodness of God."

Belief and False Experience

Then we introduce belief — a false idea or conviction — *about* God, *about* truth, *about* that which we are observing. In believing that any he, she or it of experience is something different from God or other than God or devoid of God, experience instantaneously becomes false.

Instantaneously, the nature of experience is infused with belief, and because belief is experience, experience is now filled with the forms of belief rather than truth. All believed form is false, unreal, with no law or principle to uphold it. Nevertheless, as long as belief infuses experience, that false experience has to be suffered to be so. The only way of freedom from it is the lifting into, and being, spiritual being. Spirit *is* freedom.

Belief thinks. Therefore, experience is filled with the thought of the believer, the personal sense. Belief and thought *are* aspects of personal sense alone. Belief and thought *are themselves* the pairs of opposites experienced, *are themselves* the good and bad of experience — while all the time, experience is *actually* pure, good and innocent, God alone.

Belief believes that every he, she and it is an entity of its own self. It believes every person is a being and body unto its own self, a life, mind, ability, nature and expression of his or her own self. Belief believes in amounts, opposites and variability: an abundant or sufficient amount of money versus a small or insufficient amount, an easy life versus difficult, a wonderful, loving and joyful relationship versus an argumentative and struggling relationship, peace and harmony versus war and discord. Because thought itself is the pairs of opposites (no thought is without an opposite), suddenly the innocence, freedom and joy of experience is imbued with the good and bad of belief.

Spiritual Consciousness Dispels Belief

When spiritual consciousness arrives on that scene, truth rather than belief is known. Despite the appearance caused by and witnessed by collective belief, spiritual consciousness knows that only God is. It knows that the form being presented as collective belief is actually and only God. It knows that the form of belief is nothing of its own self. It has no power, no law, no principle to uphold it in the presence of truth — just as the shadow has no power, no law, no principle to uphold it in the presence of light. In the presence of spiritual consciousness all false form is dispelled to reveal truthful form — the true form always actually present, the 'image and likeness' of God as form.

Belief is having an illusory experience, a misperception, a false conviction of that which truly is, and that is God alone, truth alone, spirit alone. When spiritual consciousness arrives on the scene, all falsity is dispelled and dissolved, revealing truthful mind, body and world. Spiritual consciousness is empty of the belief in matter, therefore all forms of so-called matter respond and react in the only way they can — as truthful, unconditioned form. Spiritual consciousness does not think of matter, is not interested in matter of its own self, does not judge by appearance, does not believe that which seems to be but knows and 'judges' righteously, that *only God is, despite all and every appearance.*

The mind that isn't thinking of matter, isn't judging matter, and because there is no material judgment but only, or mostly, spiritual awareness, experience is filled with truthful (spiritual) form. "The earth is full of the goodness of God." When consciousness is spiritual, experience is spiritual, of only good, abundance, love, harmony and peace.

SATISFIED WITH GOD ALONE

Form Contains No Error, Belief Is the Error

Form contains no error, no disease, no discord, no lack, no limitation. *Belief is* error, *belief is* disease, *belief is* discord, lack and limitation. Only belief — false belief — the belief in form being an entity in and of its own self leaves *experience* to be that of the form being believed.

But even as the believed, discordant form is experienced, the true, whole and free form is the only actual form present. In other words, belief does not change God-form into believed form *in actuality*, but in *sense* alone. The experience of believed form is *sense* alone, never reality, never an entity which we now need to be rid of. We have a believed *sense* of that which is forever belief-less, perfect, whole, abundant and harmonious. Simply bring the presence of spiritual consciousness to the scene and you observe erroneous form dissolve to reveal its truth — its reality, its God-ness.

Judge not; do not judge, believe, hold opinion about. Withdraw belief, and let pure truth reveal that, actually, there is no misbelief or false experience; there is only truth and truthful form at any and every level of consciousness. In the presence of spiritual consciousness, the veil or cloud of false belief-form dissolves to reveal the truthful, harmonious and whole form.

No Actual Error

Nothing contains error, nothing is of error; therefore there is no error to heal, correct, pacify or prosper.

Think. If only God is, which is true, and God is good alone which is also true, and if God is infinite and omnipresent, which He-She is, how can anything anywhere contain or be of error? It cannot, and indeed does not. The belief that error does exist, and then the effort to heal it, is itself the failure of the world to be free of all discord and disharmony. There is no error. Only God is, and God already is absolutely everything everywhere of infinity and omnipresence because "there is none else". It is *this* consciousness that dispels apparent error, exposing error as nothing of its own self, revealing the truth of all form.

This world and every being and thing of it is heaven. If this were not true, then a Jesus, a Buddha and every illumined consciousness could never have existed here. Truthful being cannot also be untruthful being, existing in an untruthful world. You cannot have, or be, God 'and' matter — God and error. Spiritual being cannot exist in a world of matter, but only in a world of spirit — just as light cannot exist in a world of darkness but only in a world of light. It is because darkness is not an entity but just a *lack of light* that light effortlessly dispels dark, making it light. In this way, realize that the world is not erroneous, but the very presence and freedom of God itself — "in earth as it is in heaven"; that only false belief makes it appear to be erroneous; and that the appearing error is instantly dispelled by truthful consciousness.

It is because the world is not erroneous that the great spiritual lights walk and live here just as you and I do. 'Here' is the only place there is: omnipresence, heaven, holy ground. Knowing the *truth* of earth — the truth of form — is the secret of healing erroneous belief, thereby freeing form to be experienced as its truth — perfect, whole, boundless, effortless, purposeful, happy and free being, body, place, circumstance and condition.

If Form Were Erroneous, It Would Be Invisible to Spiritual Consciousness

Think. If the world were error — if form were erroneous — a being in truthful consciousness would not experience it, nor be able to. A 'human' being rising in consciousness would witness objective form disappearing. But this does not happen. It is not what happened to Gautama, it is not what happened to Jesus nor any of the other great seers and prophets of the ages, and it is not what happens today. Rather, the *false sense* of form believed by collective being — material consciousness — is 'healed' by spiritual consciousness, to reveal truthful form.

Form is never healed because it never needs to be. It is forever whole and complete, divine spiritual form, incapable of being anything different, less, or other than the very presence, substance and quality of God itself. *Sense* is healed, never form. False *sense* is lifted, illumined, dissolved to *reveal* that which has eternally been truthful of form in all its wholeness and completeness.

SATISFIED WITH GOD ALONE

In the World But Not of It

The world does not disappear to spiritual consciousness. "I am in the world" — I am experiencing the same degree of awareness, 'this world' of form, just as you are. I see and interact with the world's people, things, amounts and places just as you do. I hear and speak, I smell and touch, I see and taste just as you do. However, I am not 'of' the world.

I know that form in and of its own self is nothing. I know that all this universe of form, from the largest sun to the atom and the subatomic particle, is simply mind-formation, without power, substance or presence of its own self. I know that all — without exception — is God; therefore all without exception is *of* God. Therefore, all without exception is incorporeal, infinite, omnipresent, omniscient, omnipotent, and eternal — and besides these qualities "there is none else".

No Judgment, Opinion, Concept

It is *because* form of its own self is nothing that I do not judge it, have an opinion about it or a concept of it. If I do, I am believing a false sense about it, and because belief is experience, I will have to live with the experience of that false sense for as long as I continue to hold onto it. When I release the false sense, I have released God; therefore God-formation is free to be the 'image and likeness' of God, truth.

My consciousness is belief-less, opinion-less, judgment-less. I am in God awareness — truth awareness — twenty-four hours a day. That does not mean I am unable to interact with people and the world, unable to work, unable to fulfill my duties and responsibilities, but it does mean that I am empty of idea, belief, opinion, judgment which leaves my consciousness free and clear to witness God-form rather than falsely-sensed form.

You see, God and world are not two different places or states or conditions. Only God is, only oneness is. So staying in God awareness is simply staying in the *truth* of this very experience here and now, rather than staying in an untruth about it. That's why it's simple. The very form I am observing — the very he, she, it, amount, activity or place — is God, for there is none but God. "If you see me, you see the father who sent [is] me." "The earth is full of the goodness of God." "The earth is the

Lord's, and the fullness thereof."

The only thing that ever presents itself to you is God. Realize that (the truth!) and then it becomes ever easier and more natural to live in constant truth awareness, not judging, not having an opinion about or a concept about the worldly form no matter what collective belief suggests it is or is not.

The Most Important Clarity

This is perhaps the most important re-clarification given the world since both Buddha and Jesus first discovered, taught and demonstrated it. The world has misunderstood the word 'maya' or 'illusion' or 'form' or the term 'this world'. It has believed that the world is error, that form is erroneous — something 'other than' God. It has believed that materiality is not truth, that the human being is not spiritual being and that the physical body is not spirit, that the good things of life are purely materialistic and nothing to do with God. *Nothing could be farther from the truth.*

Catch the fact that if this world were actually illusion — a nothingness, a lie, a complete untruth — a healed person, thing or condition would disappear from wordly experience. Material consciousness would not be able to see it, or 'have' it. But remember, we are told, "I am ever with you, and all that I have is yours." It would be of no use if "all that I have is yours" were not visible and tangible to every day experience. No, all that God is is tangibly yours and tangibly every person's because all that God is and has is all that you are — 'you' meaning your entire, all-inclusive universal experience — "earth as it is in heaven [truth]".

This world and its beings, things, places and conditions are God, and only God, because God is the only. Nothing — absolutely nothing — is anything but God. Again, let us hear a thousand times, or ten thousand if we need to — the only thing that ever presents itself to you is God, whether what is presenting itself to you is a single thought, a whole string of thoughts, ideas, people, things, amounts, sights, colors, fragrances, activity, your work or business, your family, your home and neighborhood, your state, country, world or universe. *All is God* because nothing — absolutely *nothing* — exists but God, truth, spirit.

Keep in mind, it is only because darkness is not an entity — is without substance, law or principle to uphold it — that darkness is nothing but a *lack of light*, that when light touches it, it disappears. If darkness were an entity, light touching it would not cause it to disappear but to become illumined — just as light touching our homes illumines the home, filling it with light and heat.

This is exactly what happens to falsely sensed form. The form is not *nothing* but *is truthful form*, indeed an entity — the one truthful entity itself: God, spirit, truth. Only false *sense* presents us with a false *experience* of it. When the light of truth shines on it, when its truth is known, it is filled with that light — truthful consciousness, God consciousness — and quickly sheds its false 'clothing' to reveal its truthful form — harmonious, whole, abundant, joyous and free.

It is still seen as mind-form — "worldly' form — because mind-form is and always has been truthful no matter what misbelief believes about it. Therefore, as the light of truth touches it, it immediately responds and reacts, shedding the false sense that clouded it, now free to be witnessed truthfully. In a nutshell, there is the entire secret of healing.

4

Omnipresence: The Multiverse

❧

There are infinite degrees of awareness. What we call 'our' degree, our 'human' life, 'our' world, 'our' universe, is one degree among an infinite number of degrees — one of the "many mansions in my father's house".

Right here where we are, infinite lives are living. Infinite worlds, infinite universes are right here. Science is now calling what has been believed to be the 'universe' the 'multiverse'. In and as this very place where we live, this very earth and universe, multiverses exist, multi-earths exist, omnipresence exists. Do you assume that we are the only degree of awareness in omnipresence? Of course not. There are infinite degrees, and each and every one of those infinite degrees in its purity is God experienced in degree, therefore of good alone.

Each degree of awareness, as long as belief does not enter the scene, is innocent, impotent and truthful — the spiritual kingdom experienced as that particular degree of awareness.

No matter how 'high' or 'low' we each are in awareness, no matter what degree of conscious awareness we're living, which of the multi-universes we're currently being and experiencing, it is only false belief that plagues us as false experience. Diseased or discordant being, body or world is nothing but *a false belief about truthful being, body and world* 'outpicturing' itself, or 'outforming' or 'out-presenting' itself as false experience. Always remember, if form, in its purity, were not true at *any and every degree* of awareness, it would be impossible for ill form, starving form, poor form, unhappy form, insecure form or warring form to be 'healed'. Truth cannot be evident unless truth is already present. Do you see that?

Spiritual healings are witnessed because truth — *principle* — is being revealed. The truth, the principle of God is good, wholeness, completeness, happiness, joy, love, life, oneness and harmony *alone*. It is the truth, the principle, that is revealed by so-called 'healing' consciousness. When belief is withdrawn from the scene, and God consciousness brought to it, the good that is truth is revealed.

Truth consciousness reveals truthful form. Only truth is, only truth exists; therefore only truthful form exists. There is no 'other' or 'outer' power that can change truth and truthful form into untruth and untruthful form. Only God is power and presence; therefore only God is form. As long as belief is not introduced, the pure presence and principle of God alone — truth alone, oneness alone — exists in all its glory, fullness, completeness and perfection, and is perfectly visible and tangible for all to see. When belief is introduced, or re-introduced, form again warps or becomes ill or discordant or lacking in experience.

This is why Jesus warned every person he healed, "Go and sin no more, lest a worse thing come about thee". Go, enjoy your new-found truth, your freedom, certainly! But make sure you stay in truthful awareness. Do not fall back into untruthful awareness, for a worse thing may come about you. The moment we fall into believing form to be something of its own self — the moment we have forgotten or ignored that God is all — we instantaneously thrust our experience into the pairs of opposites. Now we are exposed to the experience of both good and bad, and the bad becomes ever more severe and painful every time we lift, then fall back. The dark gets darker and the cold gets colder.

But as soon as belief is withdrawn, truth is witnessed sitting right there. It always is and it always was. But it requires *truth consciousness* to experience truthful form — truthful being, body and world.

Truth Is Principle

Two + 2 = 3 is not 'healed' to become 4 — something it was not before the 'healer' came along. Two + 2 *is* 4. It forever has been and forever will be. You can go anywhere in infinity and there you will discover 2 + 2 = 4. It is the invariable principle of mathematics. Nothing belief does to the principle changes that principle one iota, making 2+2 actually 3, or actually 7, or making 14 + 14 = 3 actually, as an actual entity, a reality — even a temporary reality. Twenty-eight is forever the truth of 14 + 14; four is forever the truth of 2 + 2, just as perfect being, mind, body and world is forever the truth of you, and all being.

You are, and your world is, one hundred percent spiritual, whole and complete, in perfect order, balance, peace and harmony, and perfectly visible and tangible as wordly form to the consciousness that knows its truth. The truth of you and your world is sitting here all the time as your pure, complete and whole conceptual experience, your God-ness experienced objectively (worldly). That does not make it error. The only error, the only mis-identity or false experience (diseased or discordant experience) is *false belief* about form, about the world. False belief thrusts experience into that of error, that of pain, that of suffering.

"If You See Me, You See the Father Who Sent [Is] Me"

Jesus said, "If you see me, you see the Father who sent me," meaning, who *is* me, *is* all, *is* the one almighty principle that is truth, forever embodied as experience.

Your seeing is conceptual, objective, material simply because mind at this level of awareness is conceptual, objective, material — of three dimensions and five senses. You appear to be a human being with a mental mind, a physical body existing in a material world of things, amounts, places and conditions. But listen to Jesus: if you see form, what you are *actually* seeing is God, spirit, truth. Even though you experience (sense) truth as form, as concept, as object — finitely and locally — the experience (sense) does not make it so. Sense never is reality, but just a *sense of* reality. Sensed experience does not make the mind mental, the body physical, or the world material. Sense is sense, not reality. Reality is God, and because only God is, only God form is. There's the deepest secret of this world — the secret that releases and frees it of all pain and suffering.

When you see me as God, as infinity, as spirit, when you do not judge me, when you do not paste on me your opinion, your idea, your judgment about who and what I am, what I have and what I do not have, then you know me as truth. You know me as spiritual being, just as you are and all are spiritual being.

I am the infinity of being; I am omnipresence appearing conceptually, locally, finitely, seemingly separate and apart and different from you. So what? What *appears to be* doesn't make any difference to truth. I am infinity appearing finite, but that doesn't *make me finite*. I am spirit appearing to be physical. The physical appearance, or experience, is simply a density of awareness, a physical *sense* of spirit, and does not *make it so*. There is no actual mental mind, no actual physical body, no actual matter. All there is is God. God is God, God is mind, and God is form.

Only God is. God is infinite and omnipresent, without exception. If only we would take this literally, the whole world would heal in twenty-four hours. There would be no false belief remaining, and because false belief is false form experienced, all false form — all untruthful form and condition — would dissolve and disappear to reveal truthful form alone.

Withdraw Opinion

Withdraw belief and opinion, and all thought about it, and you have pure God being, living in a pure spiritual experience — mind, body, world and universe. That spiritual being, mind, body, world and universe — inclusive of everything in and of it — is omnipresence itself: good alone, love, life, joy, harmony, peace alone, with nothing of truth lacking, nothing separate or apart, nothing different or less.

Introduce belief, and you have false, misperceived experience, filled with both good and bad, and all of it. This so-called 'human' experience is not real. Only truth is real, only principle is real. Only principle actually is. Only God is, and only God is presence. The only presence is God. There is not human or worldly presence. The human and worldly experience is just the *sense* of God we are entertaining at this level of awareness — this particular "mansion in my father's house". When sense is realized to be nothing *but sense* — when belief is withdrawn — the miracle of God becomes perfectly and naturally visible as all form. The light of truth pours through the mind, now unconditioned by false belief, and truth becomes tangible rather than ethereal. Healthy, wealthy, whole, harmonious and peaceful form emerges into tangibility as the mist of false believe is dispelled.

When I touch your shoulder, I am touching God, because there is nothing but God. I am having a conceptual experience of God — yes — just as you do, and just as Jesus, Buddha, Isaiah, Moses, Nanak, Lao Tzu and Rumi did and do. I experience the conceptual degree of awareness I am being.

My degree of awareness does not 'change' God into that degree. It does not make that degree real. I am not touching a physical body, finiteness, locality; I am not experiencing you as a certain number of years old, a certain character or nature. I am experiencing only one thing: the quality, the nature, the infinity, the omnipresence, the eternality that is God itself, because only God is.

The conceptual experience, in its truth and purity, unblemished by belief, is spiritual, divine, graceful, innocent, impotent and perfectly beautiful. It is truthful being, body and world. If it were not, Jesus could not have existed in it; Buddha could not have existed in it. This world and its entire population of 'hims, hers and its' is heaven experienced objectively as three dimensions and five senses. It is only belief that forms discordant experience.

All Being Is God Being

All being and body is God being and body. You are God; that is all you are. The form I recognize to be you — as long as I am not attached to the belief about you: your name, nature, character and life condition — is the perfectly visible truth of being, the one wholeness and divinity of being, not physical being but spiritual being, living in the universe of spirit with spiritual family, spiritual home, spiritual abundance, and spiritual purpose and expression, all one, all omnipresent, all eternal and always fulfilled.

Ye Are Gods

Do you catch this? Do you catch your truthful identity? Do you catch that you are a god with, certainly, a lower case 'g', yet with all that God is and has? "I am ever with you, and all that I have is yours."

The Master points out, "Is it not written in your law, I said, ye are gods?" The law Jesus is referring to is found in Psalm 82:6 — "You are gods; you are all sons [the presence, the expression, the being] of the most high."

Jesus knew his truthful identity and the truthful identity of all. He knew that his being, his mind, body and world was God because God is the *only*. "I and the father are one." Therefore what God is, I am. Indeed, I am and have all that God is and has, yet I of my own self am nothing." You are god, I am god, all is god. There is nothing wrong with this being, mind and body appearing as you, and there is nothing wrong or erroneous with your entire world. The only error is in believing you and your world to be something other than God. Imbue experience with belief and you can experience nothing but the forms of that belief. If I imbue my experience with 'my' belief, 'my' idea, 'my' opinion, then I instantaneously thrust my experience into the pairs of opposites which include the pain and suffering of disease, disharmony, lack and limitation. One moment of experience is good, the next is bad, and sometimes both good and bad are happening at the same moment. We all know it.

5

A Revelation

❦

December 2012, a friend told me how he's seen other students struggle with the idea of the 'nature of error'. We have unwittingly been given a term which suggests that all worldly (objective) experience is error. But this is untrue. The world and everything in it and of it is pure and true spiritual presence and, *if untainted by belief*, is experienced as the pure and spiritual God-form it is, the "image and likeness" of God itself. God — oneness — is simply experienced objectively 'through' the three dimensional and five-sensed mind.

Realize that 'the nature of error' needs to be termed 'the nature of experience'. Without belief, the nature of experience is true; with belief the nature of experience is untrue — misperceived. It is now simple to understand that experience can be either truthfully perceived or misperceived, and that misperception presents us with the experience — not reality — of error. That misperception, that error *is itself* the experience of both good and bad. Error, therefore the pairs of opposites, is false sense only, never reality, even temporary reality.

In false sense, we have an erroneous, unstable, unreliable, variable, limited, lacking experience of life, requiring constant and vigilant effort, skill, persuasion, and struggle to survive. This is where the survival instinct originates — the inherent need to learn how to survive in a world believed to be, therefore witnessed to be, both hospitable and hostile.

But actually, only truthful being and world exists. God is the only truth and reality of life, the only substance, the only body, the only amount, the only world and universe, *and the only consciousness.*

Can Misperception Change or Harm Truth?

Now tell me, can misperception actually harm you? Can misperception change what is true? Can 2 + 2 = 3 actually harm 4, or you? Let us understand this. If you are operating with the belief that 2 + 2 = 3 you may well be harmed *in experience.* You may even bankrupt yourself if you keep charging only $3 when the true price is $4. But is the truth — '4' — ever harmed? Of course not. Is there something of negative or lacking or discordant principle acting upon you that is causing harm to you? Or are you just harming yourself in experience by misperceiving what is true?

There is only one principle, one law, one truth and that is God — oneness, goodness, completeness, wholeness, joy, harmony, infinity, omnipresence, omnipotence, omniscience and eternity. That is the one and only principle, the one and only truth. There is only one truth, law, principle and practice of mind, body, world and relationship. If we live a degree of misperception, no principle, no law, no truth upholds our experience. It is for this reason that experience is temporal, variable, unstable, unreliable, of both good and bad — of collective consciousness. Experience is the form of belief alone, and infinite degrees of belief.

Consciousness Is Experience

Remember consciousness is experience; therefore, if we're operating in belief, then there is a pseudo-principle in operation. It is not real principle, but is a pseudo-law, a pseudo-presence or activity without law or principle to uphold that misperception.

So the very moment we withdraw the misperception in the realization that actually only the one principle — fully embodied, fully manifest, fully demonstrated, visible and tangible is — then that withdrawing alone, in the realization of *is*, reveals the truthful, one principle as whole and perfect body. It appears as healed body or condition. It often appears as a miracle healing. In front of your eyes, untruthful form or condition is witnessed as truthful — there is the whole and perfect body; perfect amount; safe, secure and fulfilling home; loving relationship; peace and harmony. It stands solid and permanent. Yet all that has healed is awareness — misperception has healed, and truthful perception, truthful experience has been revealed. Truth was always there. The disease or discord was nothing but diseased or discordant perception, belief which has absolutely no truth, law or principle to uphold it or maintain it in experience. That is why the very moment belief is withdrawn and truthful consciousness brought to the scene, untruth dissolves to reveal the truth that has always been there.

Belief Is the Pairs of Opposites

Belief *is* the pseudo-presence, 'power' and 'form' of illness, disease, disharmony, lack, limitation, a temporal span of life lasting from a few hours, days, weeks, months or years — even one hundred years. Only belief is and has pairs of opposites, including the one set of the pairs, the bad, we wish we didn't have to live with (and we do not!).

Belief itself *is* the experience of aging, decrepitude, tiredness, weakness, lack of vitality, illness, disease and finally death — only belief. There is no truth, no law, no principle upholding these false experiences, these misperceived experiences.

All the while we are experiencing these misperceived activities, amounts, conditions, there is the one truthful form and presence *being* your body and every part, function and organ of it, *being* your relationship, *being* your home, *being* your family, your neighborhood, your world. Where we watch or experience war — a war between the cells of the body, between family members, neighbors or colleagues, a war between companies or governments, or a war between countries — there is no actual war. Truth does not, nor can it, war among itself. There is no truth, no principle behind the activity of war. Because truth is not at war with itself, and because truth is the only real presence, no war is actually taking place in the same way as 2 + 2 = 3 is not actually taking place. The war or the '3' is taking place only as false belief, and because belief is experience, war or '3' seems to be real in experience. Yet it is absolutely unreal and can be proven as such the moment true and consistent spiritual consciousness is brought to it.

Walking Side-by-Side with Gautama or Jesus

If you walked side-by-side with Gautama or Jesus or Moses, could you see everyone and everything of the earth — just as you do today? Could you touch them, feast with them, work and laugh with them, interact and transact with them? Yes, of course, just as the masters themselves did and do today.

This proves that the world and all its beings, things, and places are true — simply objective mind-forms of the one: God. Only false belief about them makes them false to experience. Do you think there was something untruthful about the embodiment of Jesus or Gautama or Moses, Isaiah, John, Paul, Shankara? Each of these beings had the very same worldly experience we are having, yet each was not *of it* of its own self. This was their secret, and ours today.

Each was continually tempted by appearing misperception and each had to work consistently to stay lifted in truthful awareness. Read the temptations of all of the masters. Read the three temptations of Jesus. Read the struggles each of the masters had, until they each finally lifted completely above belief. They each had and lived in the same mind degree we do — the same "mansion in my father's house". They experienced the world with and through three dimensions and five senses, they interacted with the world as we do, but they were not *of it*. They *knew* that all is God, and that God appears as the objective universe through the objective mind, but never changed, never different, never devoid of or lacking all that God is and has. There exists no power in the whole universe that could cause such a change, difference or lack.

A Revelation

Healing is Revealing of Truth

Healing is the revealing of the truth that forever exists. You cannot make what appears to be an ill, injured, starving, poor or dying form into a whole, vital and fulfilled form if truthful form were not truth in the first place — anymore than '3' can be healed to reveal '4' if 2 + 2 = 4 were not true in the first place. You cannot heal error into more error. You could not witness finiteness or lack become boundlessness and abundance if finiteness were real. Only infinity is real and that is why infinity is witnessed by spiritual consciousness where finiteness or lack seems to be.

Form is not finite just because it seems to be. Only infinity is; therefore all form is infinite. The body is not physical just because it seems to be. Only spirit is; therefore only spiritual body is. "I am in the world" — I experience form and physicality just as you do — but "I am not of it." I know that what appears as finite, physical, of matter, *isn't*. I know that *only God is*, and I live consciously *as* only God consciousness.

The Sun, the Patch of Light, the Stained Glass Window

What appears as a patch of sunlight on the wall is not actually a patch but the whole of the sun. If we didn't know better, we'd believe the patch of light to be separate and apart from the sun, a small body of light and warmth in and of its own self. We'd believe it was and had a life of its own and was nothing to do with the sun. But we know better, we know it is an experience of the sun itself, therefore of the nature and quality of the sun alone. The patch of light is simply a finite, locally-sensed experience of that which is the whole of the sun.

When we know that, we do not believe the patch. We do not judge it, or have an opinion about it. We do not hold a false sense about it. We do not expect anything from the patch of its own self. We do not ask *it* to give us more light, and more heat. We turn to the sun — we turn to the truth of the light — for more light and heat.

In this way, we turn to God for truth and its formation. We turn within and come to that place where God is felt happening within. *There* the truth of everything of experience is fully evident, visible and tangible.

As we rise in awareness, there is less and less objective belief, and more and more wholeness, more and more oneness, tangibly experienced as the world and all its formation. No degree of awareness nor any of its formation is inherently erroneous, wrong, of its own self. We do not say the sun is in error as it shines through the stained-glass window, appearing as colored form. We do not believe the stained glass window is error, nor its form or color is error. We simply and freely behold the window, the form and the color as an innocent experience.

The World Experience

Now become aware of your world, without belief, without opinion. Take into mind people or things or conditions you are familiar with, but now observe them as the pure form they are — pure spirit, pure God, the incorporeal not the corporeal. Do not attempt to 'do' something or 'see' something happen to what you're observing. Simply be aware *spiritually — incorporeally* — rather than humanly or materially. Observe, or be aware, 'before' judgment, 'before' opinion, 'before' knowledge.

You can never know what any 'he, she or it' is or is not — either a good 'he, she or it' or bad — so don't try. Worse, don't believe you do know. "Your thoughts are not my thoughts, and your ways are not my ways." Your knowledge is not God's, so never assume you know what truth is, or how it should look. Never assume you know what the solution — the healing — should look like. You will *never* be right, and will only witness it when it witnesses itself for you — just as you can only witness the sunset when it witnesses itself for you.

Observe Both Good and Bad as Nothing Actual

Bring to mind a dozen 'hims, hers, its or conditions' and now be aware of them innocently — without idea, opinion, judgment. Release God. Release the world for the truth it is. Simply and gently and without attachment *observe, behold, witness.* Become a beholder rather than a thinker. Accept all form, all experience as simply *is*. It simply *is*. There is nothing good or bad about it. It just *is*. In this way, we do not condition mind or thought; therefore form is free to be witnessed truthfully.

Observe your world, or imagine it, but without opinion, without judgment. Belief wants to say how good or how terrible it is: Oh, that's wonderful, beautiful, or that's terrible. Look at that suffering, look at that pain. Look at the cause of the effect we're experiencing. This is all of belief only. It is like observing 2 + 2 = 3 and saying, Well, this is terrible. Look at the pain and the suffering caused by 2+2 = 3.

Again, let us be reminded that *at that level of experience* it most certainly is painful, and probably costly. Let us never misunderstand or be insensitive to a person's discordant 'reality'. We know the truth, but that doesn't entitle us to go about preaching to those in pain and suffering. Never say to a person, Oh, don't worry, only God is. Just ignore the problem and keep your mind on God. No, no, no! Keep truth to yourself. The only value we are to anyone and to our world is in the actual demonstrating or evidencing or revealing of truth where untruth seemed to be. That is our only value, and until we've achieved that degree of God awareness we must be quiet and secretive and get on with lifting our *own* awareness clear into truth. "By their fruits ye shall know them."

Discord Is 'Real' to the Person Experiencing It

At the level of experience that beholds pain, suffering, lack or limitation — whatever the discord may be — it is real. Whatever degree of awareness we are being is 'reality' to us. Spiritual consciousness has only spiritual reality and is able to see — perfectly tangibly and visibly — the non-reality of 'lesser' levels of awareness. Material 'reality' is completely non-real to spiritual consciousness, just as a non-mathematician's belief about trigonometry is completely unreal to Pythagoras. As spiritual consciousness, we have spiritual discernment which tells us of the non-reality of both material discord and suffering *and* material good and happiness. The whole stable of the pairs of opposites is entirely devoid of truth. We know that what is collectively believed to be has no principle, no law, no truth upholding it. It is misperceived experience only, never reality, never truth, nor able to witness truth. Nothing but God is, and nothing but God is presenting itself to and as experience. Therefore we have no opinion, no judgment about the pairs of opposites in and of their own selves. "Neither do I condemn you."

SATISFIED WITH GOD ALONE

Do Not Wish for Anything from the Pairs of Opposites

Bring to mind something of pain, something of suffering, something of hardship either in your own experience or another's, or the world's. Look at it without judgment. Do not wish anything for it of its own self. Do not desire it to be anything different, to be healed, to be pacified or prospered. Judging, wishing, desiring will prevent your realizing that the pain or suffering or hardship of its own self is nothing. You think it is a 'something' that needs helping, healing or pacifying. Just observe it. Do not judge it, do not desire anything for it, or from it. Do not think you know what's happening. You never know what's happening. The closest you can get is the realization that only God is, that only God is presenting itself to you as that form or condition — *not in or as the way it appears to be* but as *is* alone, God alone.

The One Principle and Presence

The one principle and presence of truthful form is right there. The collective misperception of God — appearing as disease, discord or lack — is not an entity, is nothing of its own self. Only God is, and God is always omnipresent. So there cannot be, and is not, any real discord, disease or lack of anything good, whole and complete whatsoever. Only the one principle is, the one truth is – the one truthful mind, body, and world.

Now bring to awareness someone or something beautiful, harmonious, happy, successful, fulfilled. Observe the form but again with no belief, no judgment, no opinion. Do not be happier or more relaxed about this 'good' form than you were about the 'bad' form of discord or lack or pain or suffering. Again, it just *is* — a picture or image presenting itself to you. But you know, *the only thing that ever presents itself to you is God.* Therefore the form is nothing of its own self. He or she who is happy, in love, healthy, intelligent and successful is nothing of his or her own self. Therefore do not feel happy or relieved about the seeming form presenting itself to you. It just *is;* it's just an image, a concept which, of its own self, has neither good or bad in it, no substance whatsoever of its own.

You see that both good and bad appearing form is nothing of its own self. Therefore, they require no thought, no effort. They just *are.* They are just 'happening' in experience but you do not attach to them, you do not take ownership of them and then try to 'do' something about them or for them. You leave them alone and get on with staying in God awareness, the awareness of incorporeality being all.

It is just the same as keeping your awareness on the principle of mathematics. Mathematics *is*. The sum 2 + 2 = 3, or 1.5, or 6 or 5 or 9, doesn't matter because it isn't truth. There is no principle upholding the discordant picture or experience. The discordant number might be presenting itself to you at the moment, but it of its own self is nothing. Only mathematics *is*, only the one principle *is*. In this way — the moment you observe either good or bad experience yet keep your mind, your attention and your interest on God alone — you remain relaxed and rested, and effortless and spacious. Your awareness is then in the right place, and you begin to *feel God happening within*. That feeling is God form experienced — truthful form experienced.

Ignore What Belief Tells You

Ignore what belief tells you about experience. You have just one interest, and that is *feeling God happening within*. The Master told us, "I am about my Father's business." Yes, I am only interested in getting on with the father's business, the business of staying in truthful awareness — spiritual consciousness — and being still and empty and receptive enough to *feel God happening as my being* in the realization that God is always fully embodied, fully manifest and demonstrated, fully visible and tangible.

The feeling happening within *is* the visibility and tangibility, *is* the demonstrated and fully manifest truthful form, *is* the actual, tangible, visible, manifest embodiment of God as form — the image and likeness of God witnessed through mind.

Our faculty of objective awareness is mostly, to begin with, slow. The experienced truthful form — God felt happening within — often takes some minutes or hours or a day or two to become completely tangible three-dimensionally. Never doubt though, even in the slowness of it appearing clearly, that truth has been witnessed as soon as God has been felt happening within. Even one second of feeling God happening within is the full and truthful, revealed "image and likeness" form. It's done. No more truth can, or has to, happen.

Remember that God is indivisible, always whole. You do not experience a little portion now and then if you wait in silence ten minutes longer, experience a larger portion. God is indivisible and omnipresent and fully tangible and visible, fully real and forever fully available — in fact, forever seeking expression as and through you just as sunlight is forever seeking expression through the windows of your house. The whole is the only, so the very second you begin to *feel* God welling up within — the experience of truth welling up within — you *have* the whole of truthful form.

Awareness Can Be Slow for a Short While

But awareness is slow to begin with. Therefore you may not yet see (experience) the whole and healthy form — the healing. Know this and do not be concerned. Stay centered within as much and as often as possible, feeling the presence of truth happening. Then one fine moment there the healing is, perfectly and beautifully evident for all to witness. But the full healing, the revelation, the actual experience of truthful form *has come through as tangible experience* the very second you feel truth welling up within.

As long as you do not waver in truth awareness — false belief to truth, false belief to truth — continually re-believing the discordant-appearing form to be something of its own self, and believing that 'nothing is happening', then the truth and wholeness of form is quickly evidenced.

I hear this all the time from students: *I feel peace regularly but my world is not changing.* You see, the problem exists right there. They are still believing a world 'out there' as being something of its own self. They are waiting for something to happen 'out there'. They don't yet understand that the observed form — any observed form — of its own self is nothing. Only God is, only oneness is, and God has been fully experienced the very second truth is felt welling up within. As long as that is known; and as long as it is known that that is the very presence, the very truth of experience *itself*, despite appearance; and as long as we stay within, experience fulfillment within (as long as we are satisfied with God alone, satisfied with the experience of truth welling up within *alone*, knowing it itself as the revealed truth of being, revealed truth of world and all form), then ... then ... very soon truth is witnessed as the healing, and wholeness and harmony is restored.

But if we carry on like a yo-yo, to and fro, to and fro, first hoping on truth, then still believing the discord, assuming that nothing is happening, that the illness or disease has not yet healed, the war or disagreement has not yet pacified, the needed abundance, the needed supply has not yet arrived, then we are completely lost in the belief of two worlds (two states of consciousness). Actually, we believe untruth more than we believe truth, and that is the best way ever devised to slow down, or veil altogether, the visibility of truth from experience.

God Experience is Natural

There we have the nature of experience — the nature of formation. Do you catch it? Do you see how it entirely changes everything of experience? When you catch it, the unwitting mistake of believing form to be something of its own self is gone. You are free in God experience.

When you feel this — and it may take a few minutes or hours or days to fully grasp what has been given in this chapter — but when you feel it, you can do nothing but feel relaxed, safe, secure. You can do nothing but feel love and protection, all-ness in this very experience because you are now not applying belief to the world. You've withdrawn all opinion, all judgment. You realize that every thing, every person, every activity, every amount and condition is actually the goodness and wholeness of God-form itself. You now know, deeply and certainly, that only God is.

You do not need to have a blazing, mystical experience as you lift into truthful awareness. Not at all. You may, but you may not. It doesn't make any difference whether you do or do not. All nameable experience is simply effect, not reality. Never seek a named or nameable experience. Seek only God *for God.*

SATISFIED WITH GOD ALONE

I Experience What You Experience

For the most part I experience exactly what you experience objectively. The only difference is that I do not believe it. I am not of it. I am no longer threatened by it or fearful of it. Nothing of it is threatening because I know nothing of it is real.

The sum 2 + 2 = 3 cannot threaten you the very moment you know that it is just false perception, and know that math itself is the only reality. The '3' has no power, no substance, nothing of it that can harm you. It is nothing but false sense, as we've said throughout; sense is powerless, substanceless, harmless. So an error cannot harm you; the misperception cannot harm you. How could it? It is nothing of its own self. Only belief is appearing as a discordant form, so as belief is withdrawn where does a threatening form exist? Nothing of error can touch you, and if it wanders into your awareness — as it does regularly, just as it did in the Master's experience — your consciousness of truth quickly dissolves its untruthful appearance to reveal truth.

Where is disease the moment belief in its being a form and activity of its own self is withdrawn? False belief is all disease is — the belief in a lack of God in actual experience. But belief does not make disease real, even temporarily. Only God is real, and so when God is realized, disease is witnessed dissolving and health is revealed.

Where is starvation when false belief is withdrawn? How can starvation possibly be a real condition? How can anyone in our entire consciousness starve when we know that, actually and literally, only God is, and God is fulfillment, oneness, wholeness always fully embodied? All being, all condition, all place is nothing but the presence of oneness, wholeness and fulfillment. Therefore, how can a single person starve? It is impossible in truthful consciousness. How can a person be injured? How can a person be lonely? It is impossible in truthful consciousness. You cannot starve, you cannot be injured, and you cannot be lonely when the only presence is omnipresence, wholeness, oneness, fulfillment.

How can you be separate from anything of God, good, when you realize that God — even as formation — is omnipresence and all form is God-form? The finite, objectified experience of omnipresence doesn't make omnipresence separate, apart, lacking some of itself. It makes all form omnipresent form, complete form, *truth form*. Truth form is all there is — infinite, omnipresent and eternal, invariable and unchange-able, in-separable from the whole, *being* what every 'he, she and it' *is* and *has*.

As you now allow this to well up within and start living you, you'll feel all threats from the world disappear in a second. You'll feel palpable, universal peace, safety and protection, and you will witness it as all the forms of your experience.

6

Put Away Your Sword

꙰

Can you begin to see why we never need do battle with a problem, in fact, why we *must* not? If we do, we sustain it. We only do battle with that which we believe to be real, a real entity, something we want to or need to be rid of. But now you know: a problem is not God, therefore is not real. It is false sense, not reality. If we 'make it real' by believing it, then battling to be rid of it, we only 'cement' it further into experience.

Rather we withdraw belief, attention and interest in it in the realization that actually only God is, only the one principle is, which means only life is, only love is, only infinity is, only omnipresence, only eternity is. Life does not 'become' healthy or healed form by or through spiritual realization any more than mathematics 'becomes' 4 from a discordant 3 through mathematical realization. Two + 2 = 3 does not 'become' 2 + 2 = 4 through the realization of mathematics. It is already and eternally 4.

We simply *awaken* to the truth of the 4 that's forever been there. Our *awareness* rises. False belief — misunderstanding, misperception — turns to truthful awareness just as dark turns to light as the sun rises. Mathematics hasn't changed, *our awareness has changed.* Awareness has lifted from false or misperceived into true. We have *become aware* of the one principle, the one truthful form of 4.

At and as that lifted state of awareness, the eternal, finished, complete and whole form of 4 is clearly visible — fully manifest and demonstrated already — standing right there as it always has been for our tangible and practical and only possible true experience.

False Belief Is Tangible in Experience

Because whatever is believed is experienced — because 'consciousness *is experience'* — false belief is tangibly experienced. What is believed is the form of experience, either collectively or individually, and it appears to us to be completely real. We can see it, touch it, examine it, and because belief exists in, actually *as,* the kingdom of opposites, we can always eventually discover its opposite.

There seems to be a cause for illness or disease and, indeed, in the kingdom of opposites, there is. We can always eventually detect it and then solve it. The entire medical profession and pharmaceutical industry have made substantial careers out of doing just this. Good heavens, it is a wonderful activity that saves millions of people *at the human, material level of existence* from pain and suffering, and even death. Likewise, there seems to be a cause for lack and then a multitude of financial consequences as the effect of that cause; there seems to be a cause for war and all its consequences. The pairs-of-opposites world is full to bursting with professions and industries that have created solutions for practically every problem an individual, family or organization can experience.

Belief *itself is* the pairs of opposites, continually latching onto one or other of the pairs and pointing to *it* as being either the cause or the effect, the problem or the solution, the disharmony or the harmony. It doesn't realize it is latching onto the forms of its own false perception and calling them reality — the 'real world' I hear from beginner students all the time.

If you observe me 'materially' or 'humanly', I seem to be a life of my own self, separate from your life and all other life. So, in that misperception, it seems as if something negative or fatal could happen to my life while your life is untouched or vice versa. This sense of 'reality' is nothing but misperception.

You may observe a person and see he has lack of money. Collective (material) belief says, That person has a lack of money but I have plenty. This is misperception. First of all, God is incorporeal not corporeal, therefore does not contain 'a person' nor 'money'. God contains only itself. Second, God is omnipresent not locally present or personally present, therefore does not have a 'local place' where a 'personal person' can experience a 'personal and local lack'. Third, God is one, and one alone, therefore does not contain pairs of opposites. So the entire belief in the person and his condition of lack is erroneous. That is the error, and has nothing to do with the true person and the true condition, which is all God, all one and omnipresent, therefore whole, complete, and harmonious.

The Pairs of Opposites Witnessed

It is the *belief* that the person is someone of *his own self*, experiencing lack which is something of *its own self*, that outforms itself as the appearing and seemingly very real problem requiring its opposite — in this case more money — to solve it or heal it. Right here is the reason the problem exists in experience. Right here are the pairs of opposites witnessed, the good and bad, the sense of separation from God, the belief that individual life is separate from and different from God alone, therefore separate and different from 'each other' and each other's circumstances and conditions. Your set of circumstances is different from mine because you are not me and I am not you.

You can have good health while I can be sick, you can be wealthy while I can be poor, you can be enjoying a loving and fulfilling relationship while I can be enduring a bad or no relationship, or you can own a car while I have only a bicycle. On and on we can believe in variable possibility or variable reality, therefore observe what appears to material consciousness to be separation, multiplicity, difference, opposites, degrees and entire lifespans occupied by trying to manage them, overcome them, and satisfy them. The majority of human beings sadly achieve nothing much more than managing the pairs of opposites simply to survive the experience.

Withdraw Belief, Then Discordant Form Dissolves

Do you see the importance of withdrawing belief, and living in and as the strength of spirit, the strength of truth, the maintained spiritual consciousness? Do you see the necessity of constantly turning away from that which appears to be — completely and utterly, no matter how suggestive, even threatening, it seems to be, or how painful it is on the material level of experience — even when it makes itself almost impossible to ignore?

The one requirement is the turning away from the appearance, the sensed form of discord, ignoring it as the nothing-of-its-own-self it is, thereby breaking the back of the believed suggestion that *is itself* the discordant or misperceived, illusory form. It is broken by the ignoring of it and by 'strong' spiritual realization, strong spiritual presence (consciousness), just as light dispels dark by 'strong light presence'. Light is fully present, unwavering, 'tenacious' — a real entity. *That* is why its presence dispels the dark which is a non-entity.

Can you imagine light wavering in its uncertainty about dark — its false belief that dark is an actual entity, real (rather than nothing but a lack of light), and therefore being weak or inconsistent in *being light?* The dark would never be dispelled in the presence of such weak or inconsistent, uncertain light. This is just how weak our spiritual presence is if we hang onto the belief in form being an entity in and of its own self, and are, therefore, fearful of it, convinced it needs correcting or harmonizing or healing or prospering. We simply cannot witness truthful form — healthy, wealthy, harmonious and peaceful form — without a strong, consistent, living *spiritual* consciousness.

Conscious God Awareness

It must be realized that *all* form of the pairs of opposites (the material consciousness, material belief) — both the good and the bad of it — *in and of its own self is nothing*, and is nothing but a lack of *conscious God aware-*

ness, conscious God presence in the same way as dark is nothing but a lack of light. Form of its own self has no principle to uphold it or sustain it, no law, no substance, no body. It is not an entity, but a *lack* of entity. Only God is entity. Form is of belief alone, and at the level of belief that is believing it, it seems to have, and indeed acts as if it has, power of its own self. It seems to act upon us, either in a positive or negative way. It often seems to have power over us, leaving us temporarily or permanently powerless over 'it'. But it takes a believer for belief to operate in experience. Remove the believer — your or my false sense — and all the belief in the universe can't touch you, can't operate for or against you, can't have power over you, cannot hinder you anymore than all the dark in the universe can hinder the sun, cannot affect the sun, cannot have either good or bad power over it, cannot dominate it. "Rise, take up thy bed, and walk."

Both 'Pairs' Are Belief Believed

Both of the 'pairs' are the same thing — belief believed. *It takes a believer to experience belief.* Belief of its own self has absolutely no power unless a believer accepts it. If a believer arrives in the midst of belief, then — wham! — the believer falls under the spell of belief. Equally, the whole universe experienced by material consciousness can be (is) the formation of belief (all belief, all consciousness is formation), yet the one individual who does not believe belief remains untouched by it.

It is because believed form has no substance, body, entity, law or principle upholding it that it varies, is unreliable and inconsistent. The good of today can change to the bad of tomorrow, or even the next minute, and equally the bad of this minute can change to good the next minute or the next day. All such experience is one hundred percent of belief — false sense.

Truth Is Invariable and Eternal

Truth is invariable. Anything that varies, or can do, is of the pairs of opposites — belief. In this realization, Solomon told us, "I want neither riches nor poverty". I do not want anything I can name, either the good or the bad of it. I do not wish for a solution to the problem because that would only be replacing a 'bad' of the pair with a 'good' of the pair — neither of which are God, truth.

I want only God, only truth, only the true "image and likeness". I want the principle revealed, nothing else, nothing less, nothing different. When I have that, I have permanent good. And so I withdraw belief, attention and interest from the entire scene, the entire picture, the entire formation as it appears to be to my senses. I stop being a believer. Instantaneously as I stop being a believer and have, therefore, ceased giving the scene, the problem, my attention and interest, my desire and effort, it no longer has power over me. In releasing what seems to be, I have released its apparent reality. It's like turning off the projector light. Instantaneously, the images on the movie screen are powerless, substanceless and 'dispelled'.

Remember, we went throughout your world looking at something of lack, limitation, pain or suffering, even tragedy, and we heard that its experience just *is*. It is nothing to believe, nothing to have opinion about, judgment about, nothing to attach to or to believe is 'yours' any more than a cloud passing by is yours. It just *is*, and so all material form and activity, both good and bad, just *is*. It's just a picture. But it's something we've believed to be real, and named and entertained to be real. Therefore, it *is real to us* as long as we carry on believing it to be.

Just a Picture

Anything we can name is just a picture, a substance-less form, a false sense of that which truly is: God. The false sense of form just *is*. It isn't something to be concerned about, to do something about, or take ownership of. It's just happening as a harmless form floating through consciousness, but it never is anything of its own self. It never has power, life, amount, body — of either good or bad nature or ability — no real, truthful, God presence or power at all. It is imagery only, a puff of nothingness. Just like on the cinema screen, there is nothing there but image, whether of good or of bad.

It is for this reason that we withdraw all belief about it, of both bad and good, poverty and riches, ill-health and health, remembering that if we can name health or riches or peace or love, then that name is just as much misperception as its opposite. "If you can name it, it isn't it." Realize that anything we can name has an opposite, therefore is of belief, of opinion, idea and judgment which *is itself* the pairs of opposites. Realize this, and then stop thinking in the 'pairs-of-opposites' way. By withdrawing this type of thought activity — just letting the form be, remaining non-attached, knowing it has no power of its own self — we begin to be empty and spacious, a transparency of consciousness, and it is the transparency of consciousness, empty of false belief, that witnesses truthful experience.

Remember, 2 + 2 = 3 has no actual power. The moment you realize that, and forget about it (release it as being just the *is* it is), and sit still and silent in truth, then soon you will witness truth emerge as tangible experience.

Truth Does Not Dispel Mind

God *is* mind *is* form. God is truth, mind is truth (one of the "many mansions in my father's house") and the formation of mind (the universe and everything in and of it) is truth, spirit, God. We are having a material *sense* of that which is one hundred percent spirit and spiritual, but that *sense does not make it make it real in and of its own self.*

When the truth of 2 + 2 is revealed as 4 not 3 — when 2 + 2 is 'healed' of 3 — numbers do not disappear, nor does mathematics as a whole disappear. Only the false *sense* disappears to be revealed as the *truthful* experience of that particular form or place or condition or body or amount. Everything of 'this world' is of this level of awareness we call 'human', this particular "mansion in my father's house". Without belief, it is heaven, perfectly visible, tangible and real, just as 2 + 2 devoid of false belief is the 'heaven' of 4, perfectly visible, tangible and real.

The form is still very present and recognizable, but now experienced truthfully. In spiritual consciousness spiritual form becomes visible and real as what is sensed as 'material, physical' form. We are having, at this level of awareness, a material *sense* of spirit — a corporeal *sense* of the incorporeal — but that *sense alone*, devoid of belief, is truthful, spiritual, good, of God. It is the "image and likeness" of God. It is the same sense Jesus had, Gautama had, and all spiritual being has at this level of consciousness, the 'this world' level. It is not being *of it*, not believing it of its own self, but forever being *of God* that is the key to healing, freedom and harmony. I am in the world — you see me, hear me, touch me just as you do everyone and every thing else, and as they do you. But "I am not *of* the world".

God Is Good, Mind Is Good, Form Is Good

Always realize, God is good, mind is good, and mind formation is good because *all* is God; therefore all is *of* God, good. Only belief in its being something other than or different from God, something possessing its own life, power and quality is false belief which presents itself as false form — diseased, discordant, limited and lacking form or its opposite, good belief-form — all of it unreal, temporal and unreliable, often volatile. Therefore, withdraw all belief, attention, opinion and judgment and live day in and day out in God-only consciousness. "I live and move and have my being in God, and God lives and moves and has its being in and as me, my world and everything everywhere of it."

Belief-form just *is*. It just floats by as a cloud floats by, but never is it 'yours' or 'mine'. It just *is*. It's just *happening*, but not 'to' you or 'in' you or 'for' you or 'against' you. We can't deny its presence. *Something* is present. Just as $2 + 2 = 3$, or $7 + 7 = 17$ is undeniably *something*.

Never Deny Experience

Never deny presence. Never call it 'appearance'. Students have unfortunately adopted the bad habit of replacing the word 'evil' or 'disease' or 'lack' or 'pain' with the word *appearance*, thereby making a new false entity of something that never was an entity in the first place.

Today, everyone's trying to be rid of their 'appearances' instead of their diseases, lacks and limitations, and having the same difficulty in doing so as when they called them by name alone. I receive such requests every day, "I have an appearance of flu or cancer or a broken bone, please help." In other words, please heal me of the flu or cancer or broken bone appearance. It's funny, they still call the problem by name even though they believe the word 'appearance' added to it makes the problem less real.

Do not deny the experience of a problem but *do* recognize the *truth* of all experience, and the untruth — the nothingness — of all pairs-of-opposites form, both harmonious and discordant. "The only thing that ever presents itself to you is God." Therefore, do not resist or be fearful of a false experience of God; just know it for what it is, in and of its own self — nothingness, false sense only — and then rest in God consciousness alone. Soon, and with a little patience, the light of truth fills your awareness and truthful form and condition emerges into clear and natural visibility just as mist dispelled by the dawn reveals a clear and beautiful morning.

Nothing Belief Does Changes God

All experience — without exception — is God because there is nothing but God. Experience in and of the pairs of opposites is always *actually* real experience, simply *misperceived.* It is not the presence or form of its own self; it is the *misperception* that is error. The 'he, the she, the it, the amount, the place, the condition, the circumstance' is always *actually* real — the truth, the one principle, the one true presence, the spiritual, perfect and eternal form. Nothing the mind can do or fail to do disturbs it, alters it, warps it, lessens it, brings any kind of actual error or falsity to it. There is no false reality. There is no false mathematics, no false aerodynamics. There is only the one mathematics, the one aerodynamics. If we experience a discord in mathematics or aerodynamics, it is we having a false sense of *it*, not it being an actual falsity. Our false awareness fails our experience; it itself (truth) is never failing.

If we misunderstand what aerodynamics is, our airplanes can't take off, or if they manage to lift off the ground a little, they keep crashing back to ground. If we misunderstand or haven't yet sufficiently awakened to the principle of mathematics, we will keep getting our math wrong. That is our experience of discord but is nothing to do with mathematics itself, which is forever at one with itself, in harmony and completeness with and as itself.

And so we withdraw belief and rest in truth, listening, attentive, receptive. You have nothing to do but withdraw belief and rest in truth because what's actually present seeks you. Truth is forever seeking 'outlet' as and though you, your consciousness, and is able to do so in a tangible and perfectly visible way when you know the truth, and then rest in stillness, silence — attentive and receptive to *truth felt happening within.*

There Is No False Reality

There is no false reality — there is only one reality. There is false perception, yes; false sense, yes. But misperception — false sense — does not create false reality. False sense is not an entity but forever just sense. It simply presents the believer with a false *sense of* that which is real: God, truth. Stop accepting false sense, and all falsely-sensed form is dispelled.

Misperception cannot harm you or your experience the very moment you know its nothingness. I watched this proven with disease. When I woke up to the nothingness of disease (in and of its own self), I discovered that it could not touch me. Practically overnight it had no power over me, and no power left for itself. It withered and died by itself just as dark withers and dies in the presence of light.

All the power that seemed to be operating harmfully and perhaps fatally as cancer was dispelled spontaneously with the realization of its nothingness, and the awareness that all presence, all experience, no matter what belief believes *about it, is God. The only thing that ever presents itself to you is God.* Pain continued for a while; the experience continued for a while, but all the 'power' of it, all the progression of it, couldn't do anything (was made impotent) from the very moment I realized that literally only God is, therefore disease of its own self is literally substanceless, powerless, entity-less. Even the pain — I've shared it in classes with you — could not continue in the presence of spiritual awareness, my turning within and realizing:

Spirit fills all space within me. Spirit is the only principle happening as this being called me.

There is no other principle. There is no false being, therefore no false being happening as the being I am; there is no false principle operating anywhere in infinity. There is God alone, spirit alone, God-principle and God-law alone.

SATISFIED WITH GOD ALONE

How can there be false principle? There can be a false sense of principle, a misperceived belief about the one principle, and because all belief is form, false form will be discordant or diseased experience. That is what pain is; that is what ill or diseased or lacking or limited experience is. But from the very moment you truly know the truth of God and the nature of experience, you find yourself resting in stillness and peace ever more each day — attentive to truth, silent and receptive to God felt happening within — and discover yourself free of misperception, therefore free of the false forms of experience.

The moment you've reached that point of realization, then nothing of misperception — which is the entire gamut of the pairs of opposites including all human suffering and human struggle — remains. The whole world *of itself* has gone even though you are very much still in it. Remember that. We still observe homeless people, people needing to beg for bread, people in wheelchairs, people sick and diseased in hospitals, people poor and people hungry, people sad and people lonely. Jesus saw all these things — always remember this. If he hadn't, he would have had no one to heal. But the people came. He recognized the people, recognized the false forms just as we do, but . . . but . . . he was not *of* them. He wasn't of belief. He was and is of God alone as all.

Take No Thought

Take no thought, the master consciousness says. Withdraw belief. Take no thought for your experience in or of or for its own self; take no thought for even one breath of it. It is imagery only, form alone, and of itself, before belief and before the thoughts we have about belief, it is nothing but perfect imagery, perfect experience, perfect existence, the "image and likeness" of God, the presence of the whole of God. So take no thought, withdraw the mind, and then you are instantaneously safe. Rest in *is*, and you begin to feel the safety, the protection, the nothing-to-fear-in-the-world *truth* of being and experience. Lift into no thought, no judgment, being in the experience but not of it. Don't think about it, don't judge it, don't believe.

Remember now, the only thing ever presenting itself to you is God. It doesn't matter that it is appearing as finite, objectified, limited, separate, what we call human, what we call this world. It doesn't matter; the entirety of form is innocent in its purity, its truth. The only he, the only she, the only it, the only condition, the only circumstance, the only presence, the only form, the only object, the only activity ever presenting itself to you is the one presence itself, the one truth itself: God — love itself, life itself, omnipresent good itself, infinity itself, the fully manifest presence of God witnessed conceptually. Good, good!

What a beautiful experience, a miraculous truth! Here, right here, is heaven. "As in heaven so on earth."

I Am I

Begin to observe the same world you're familiar with but now without thought, without judgment, without opinion. Imagine it is the first time you're seeing this world, so you have no idea what anyone or anything is. You simply *observe* without idea, without desire, without effort in the realization that all is God. Even though witnessed objectively, you know that all you are observing is God, heaven, paradise. Awareness operates but with idea withdrawn, so that if you asked any 'him, her, it, condition, place, or amount' what it was, it would tell you *God. I am I, God.* If you asked anyone or anything in the world who you are, it would say *God. You are I, God.*

No matter what you observed, whether of good or bad, suppose it turned to you and asked, What am I? You would say, *God. You are I, God, for there is nothing but God.* Imagine four thousand hungry people in front you, asking, What am I? And imagine yourself being able to say, *You are God and nothing but God*, knowing with absolute conviction and strength of living spiritual awareness that because all is God, there is no lack or dissatisfaction, no hunger, nothing of fulfillment separate or apart from any being or any place. Omnipresence makes such an idea impossible.

I have witnessed impending floods, violent storms and tsunamis lose their power in less than sixty minutes the moment spiritual consciousness was brought to the scene. When you realize the absolute non-power and presence of an apparent threat — no matter what the threat is — and the absolute and literal *one power and presence of God*, it is enough to be still and silent and transparent "in the eye of the storm" and witness even the most aggressive 'threat' become impotent and dissipate into nothingness. Why? Because — literally and tangibly — the only presence is God, and God is love, grace, intelligence, harmony, peace; not aggression, violence and destruction.

What seems to be a destructive act of nature, is an activity of disturbed awareness. Because all awareness is formation — consciousness is always embodied (there is no unembodied consciousness) — disturbed awareness is witnessed as disturbed experience. Fear, stress, frustration, anger on one side of the pairs, and love, peace, harmony and grace on the other side — all states of being are embodied because *all* is consciousness. Whatever individual and collective consciousness is being *is* the form and activity of experience.

Consciousness Is 'Innocent'

All is consciousness, and consciousness itself is innocent, pure, the divinity of being. Belief taints the experience of pure consciousness — pure being — like dye taints water. Belief, idea, opinion, judgment and their thoughts are the 'dye' of the pairs of opposites, the misperception of experience we call 'humanity, this world, materiality'.

Thinking *about* experience — that is misperception; having a thought *about* a him, her, it or condition — that's the problem. Remember what we heard: as soon as you have one thought, there is the personal self, there is the sense of separation, there are the pairs of opposites. And the more agitated being is, the more of experience is agitated. There is a pressure that builds up and suddenly — bang — we experience what we call a natural disaster, or what we call an individual, family, neighborhood, town or country disaster of disease or financial collapse or relationship collapse. How it looks doesn't make a difference; it is all the same thing —the agitation of misperception, false identity, false belief.

When Presented with Discord . . .

When we are presented with the image of discord or impending destruction, whether it be in the 'body' or in the 'world', we immediately realize that whatever its given name or nature, it is *actually* a false suggestion — false belief — happening in and as the one body of awareness.

Belief is convinced that the discord is 'here' or 'there', happening 'in' or 'to' a particular 'organ' or 'function' or 'part' of the physical body, or 'in' or 'to' a particular 'place' of the world. Belief looks out at itself and points to its form 'out there' and says, 'there's the problem' and 'there's the cause'. But nothing exists 'out there' of its own self. 'Out there' is nothing but a three-dimensional image of what's happening 'in here'. Spiritual discernment tells us that all 'outer' discord, disease or destruction is the discord of false awareness — the false belief that experience consists of multiple powers, some good and some bad.

What do we do when presented with such discord or threat? We have no judgment, no idea, no opinion about it. "Judge not according to the appearance, but judge righteous judgment. . . Neither do I condemn you." Judging a form, having an idea about what it is, and having an opinion about the consequence is condemnation. But the Master said, "I do not condemn you". Fear is condemnation. We condemn that which we fear by judging it to be bad, threatening, inharmonious. But all is God; therefore we wrongly judge, wrongly fear, wrongly condemn. All opinion is nothing but that — opinion. Opinion is never reality. Only God is reality. While false belief is engrossed with itself, what is truly present is God-form — perfect, beautiful and eternal as all being, body and world. The one true presence and principle exists fully at every point of infinity simultaneously, as all body of experience, no matter what belief mistakenly judges it to be.

Withdraw Belief

And so we withdraw belief, opinion and thought from both the storm and the calm, both the poverty and the riches, both the disease and the health or healing. The pairs of opposites are left behind altogether; otherwise all we are doing is attempting to fix or pacify or heal one of the pairs, the bad, with another of the pairs, the good. Where is God in that picture? God is *incorporeal.* Both pairs of opposites are corporeal, therefore nothing of God. It is often believed there is more God in the good of the pairs of opposites than the bad. This is entirely untrue.

There is no God whatsoever in any corporeal form, in any name, in any belief, opinion, idea or thought. "Take no thought for your life. . . My thoughts are not your thoughts."

The opposite of a storm belief is a calm belief. Both are corporeal, just opposite ends of corporeality. God is nowhere to be found in corporeality no matter where we search for Him in it. Believing in corporeality is misperception, and so we must withdraw all belief in form being something of its own self.

We must withdraw our belief, attention, fascination and effort in the corporeal. Then we have God alone. We can never know what God 'looks like' — never, never. Therefore, we cannot desire one form in place of another, one experience versus another. If we do, we are still in the pairs of opposites, still in misperception, still in belief.

Seek God for God Alone

But if we do (and the moment we do) withdraw all belief, all 'thinking about' experience, no matter how it appears to be or what it appears to need, then we make 'room' in awareness for God to be visible. We've uncluttered awareness of false belief. We come within to the "secret place of the most high", the most pure consciousness, the place before thought, the place (consciousness) of God, and we seek *God alone for God alone.*

We do not seek God 'for' anything. We do not seek God for the rectifying, the healing, the pacifying or the prospering of a misperception — of the pairs of opposites. We seek God in the same way we seek aerodynamics. We seek aerodynamics for itself rather than for our airplane. We cannot bring aerodynamics into our airplane, but we certainly can bring our airplane into aerodynamics. We can 'make' our airplane aerodynamic and then we will discover the form of it able to fly, and fly forever.

In the same way, we seek God for God alone. We never attempt to bring God 'into' form to heal or pacify or harmonize or prosper or free it of its own self. We cannot bring or fit the infinite into the finite. The finite does not actually exist of its own self — is not an actual entity — but just a conceptual *form* or *image of* the infinite. But when we seek God for God alone, we quickly discover all form to be God-like — the image and likeness of God and God alone.

"Take No Thought for Your Life"

Seek the kingdom of God. Take no thought, but rather, seek the kingdom of God. How is that done? How do we witness the kingdom of God as actual, formed experience — heaven as it is on earth? Are we to pick up more books, listen to more classes, ponder more truth statements? Well, we may do so for a short while each day, or if something is really disturbing us, we may read or listen and then ponder for an hour or so. This is good and effective as long as we are pondering God for God, never for the 'solution' to the problem. Always remember, the key is to 'lift up' to where God is rather than expecting God to 'come down' to where you are or where the problem is. Lift your awareness up into God consciousness. Seek God for God, spirit for spirit, the incorporeal for the incorporeal. Then you are right on track. As Paul says, God is *for God*, not for misperception, not for 'this world' but for God alone; not ever for conceptual, believed form but for God itself.

Continue pondering truth until you begin to feel the presence 'happening' within. *That — the presence felt happening within — and that alone, is when we have succeeded in our seeking.* We have found the jewel. We have mined for gold — dug and dug and dug — and then found a nugget. Except with God, we have not found a single, solitary nugget but the *whole*. God is omnipresent and indivisible so when we find God, we instantaneously *have* the whole.

We have sought and found only when we *feel the presence happening within*. That feeling of — experiencing of — the 'happening' within *is itself* the experienced world of the fully manifest presence and form of God — the image and likeness in perfect tangibility and visibility in real experience. *This* is the 'real world', no other.

Live There without Falling Back 'out' into Materiality

Now let us see if we can live *there* without falling back into belief, into materiality, into falsely accepting form at its face value, as being something of its own self. You will still observe the formed world; you will still hear news reports, gossip, human conversation, human opinion; you will still observe your body and every other body. But now there is a major difference: you are not *of it*. You know its truth; you know that it of its own self is nothing. You no longer judge it, have an opinion about it, praise its good or condemn its bad. "Neither do I condemn you." You know that only God is real and you now consciously live and move and have your being in God consciousness rather than in material consciousness.

Never condemn what you observe; do not judge it, but consciously realize that what you're observing just *is*. It is neither good nor bad. It's nothing of its own self, just a picture, an image, a form, *not an entity*. In order for it to be good or be bad it would have to be an entity, but only God is entity. Form of its own self possesses no power, no substance, no quality, no law, no principle to uphold it or sustain it any more than the image on the movie screen does. There is no power in form, no power in belief, in opinion, idea or judgment, nor in thought. If God is the only power, which it is, and if God is not thought, which it is not, then how could thought have power? It cannot and does not. Only God is, and only God is power.

Power Is Omnipresent, Never Local, Never Personal

Observe without condemnation. Go within, ponder until you feel the welling up of truth itself, then realize that *that felt-happening within is the one power*. Realize that you now — as you are experiencing the feeling within — *are* and *have* the power that is God. When you are not experiencing the feeling within, you do not have God power — just the same as the light bulb has the power of electricity when it is plugged into the socket but does not when it is unplugged.

Is that power, that experience of God, the image and likeness of God as experience happening in a 'physical' place within? No, even though it may feel as if it is. It is happening as the entirety of your experience — the entirety of consciousness. God is omnipresent, not local, not personal. The power and presence of God is happening as the *omnipresence* of experience, as the *entirety* of your consciousness, equally and simultaneously. Remember, the whole of God is present at every point of itself infinitely and simultaneously — which means the whole of God is present as the entirety of *your consciousness* simultaneously *but only when God is felt happening within*. That experience is the only God experience, truth experience, the only omnipresence. Otherwise experience is filled with thoughts and words *about* God, and those thoughts and words, as we have seen, are nothing, nothing. They are void and empty, nothing but vain repetitions, as the Master pointed out. They forever have no God in them, therefore can offer no God experience.

Thought about the Sunset is Not the Sunset Itself

In *The Giving Self** we heard that if we have never seen a sunset but have read about its beauty, its magnificence, the deep colors and majesty, the grandeur and magic of it; if we've discussed it, attended classes about it, listened to audios about it but *never witnessed the actual sunset*, then we have never *experienced* the sunset. Never. We can study, ponder and discuss it for eternity, but unless we actually *experience* it, then there *is no* experience. Only when we go to the ocean's edge, or up on a hill, or upstairs in our home looking through the window, and experience the *sunset itself*, is the experience real for us.

We experience God in the same way. Only when we actually *feel —* experience — God *happening within* is all of truth now *real and tangible* for us, and spontaneously real. The experience must be one hundred percent happening 'for us' or 'in' or 'to our experience' rather than our making any effort for it whatsoever. When it is happening one hundred percent without effort on your part, then you can know it is God and God alone being experienced. Just as you cannot do anything to make or bring on the experience of the sunset, you equally cannot do anything to make or bring on the God experience.

With the experience of God happening within, you have and are the power, you have and are the very presence of God itself as, and throughout every breath of your consciousness, every grain of it, every place of it. The whole of God is omnipresent and simultaneously being everything everywhere of experience.

*The Giving Self by Paul F. Gorman

SATISFIED WITH GOD ALONE

Stay in God Consciousness

If you stay there, if you do not become disturbed or *re-disturbed* about the continuing images, or new discordant images, then you will witness the storm dispelled and truthful form appearing — harmony, wholeness and peace — the image and likeness of God appearing.

If you jump in and out, to-ing and fro-ing like a yo-yo, attempting to bring God 'down' to harmonize form for its own sake, to bring God into belief to harmonize belief, you will fail. You cannot make truth be untruthful; you cannot make the incorporeal be corporeal, the infinite be finite or omnipresence be local presence. If you attempt such a feat, all you will achieve is a "house [form] built on sand", and you know what happens to that house: "The rain fell, and the floods came, and the winds blew and slammed against that house; and it fell — and great was its fall."

Unwavering in Truth

It is not easy for those experiencing disease or poverty or injustice or homelessness or hate or a sense of worthlessness or depression. It is a hard thing to endure, and many give up. Many people are suffering this hour — many, many people. But if we are to prove truth, and more importantly, if we are to not only prove truth for ourselves but others too, we have to stand strong and *unwavering in truth* despite all pressing appearance to the contrary.

In the 91st Psalm we hear the secret, and that is that we must stay in God consciousness come what may. As we stay in truth, as we now *live* what we've heard today, then as did every illumined consciousness — Jesus included, Buddha included, all the great prophets included — we witness a thousand fall at our left, and ten thousand fall at our right, but no discord coming nigh us. Discord cannot touch us because we are not being a believer. We are being God consciousness — not in or of the intellect but *because we are experiencing and living as God felt happening within.* Whatever and wherever the rain and the flood and the wind, the storm, is in experience — disease, discord, lack or limitation, 'here' or 'there' — it cannot and does not come nigh you.

Put Away Your Sword

The Miracle of God in Practical Experience

There are accounts throughout history of certain individuals among thousands who understand truth — the one truth — and live it (which means they are living with, and from, and as, the experience of God felt happening within) who themselves experience and can demonstrate for others the practical presence of God where good or harmony or safety seems to be very, very lacking.

These individuals *know* and *live* by truth *itself* rather than attempting to do so by word or thought alone. Living by the actual, tangible experience of God within is the only tangible evidence of God, the only actual form, the only tangible truth, the only tangible life, the only tangible safety, protection, abundance, love. You read or hear about these individuals who are never touched by war, by natural disaster, by disease, by contagion, by injustice, by cruelty, by lack. Yet to their left and to their right, thousands *are* affected and thousands do suffer because they do not know truth, let alone live by it.

The thousands believe whatever it is they experience, or the world experiences, to be reality, a something of its own self, an actual entity they have to endure or somehow stop or fix or pacify. They believe and accept a bad power and presence at its face value, are afraid of it, react to it, and then search for another power of good to act for them, to overwhelm or destroy the bad power acting against them. They are completely embroiled in the pairs of opposites, and completely unable to witness God. God remains a frustrating mystery to them.

The 91st Psalm

What the 91st Psalm does not make clear is that as we individually know the truth, and more importantly *live* truth, experience truth living us, experience the welling up living itself as itself as us; as we are able to, without thought, observe through the mind the conceptual world and all its people, all its things, its amounts, as nothing but God, innocent in and of their own selves; as we're able to observe without judgment, without condemnation, without opinion or idea, therefore without fear, without reaction, without effort made for that conceptual experience; as we

99

really do know our neighbor as ourself, as the same one and only one being and presence of being, principle of form, principle of activity and condition; as we really know this and live the experience of it, then we begin to witness less and less 'falling' at our left and at our right.

We begin to witness more and more harmony, love, peace, more and more health and wealth as collective experience not just 'ours'. We begin to witness the literal omnipresence of truth — "good measure, pressed down, shaken together and running over" — all over our land.

We are the window of truth, the window of heaven, the transparency of consciousness filled with truth awareness, forever seeking God alone, seeking omnipresence alone, the incorporeal alone — not 'for' anything we can name, not 'for' anything we desire or think we need (although all desire and sense of need has by now vanished) but for it itself, God for God, the experience of God happening within for its own sake and never for anything 'else'. It is *that* consciousness — not ever a lesser consciousness — that is the truth consciousness that *is*, observed through the mind, the healing of mind, body and world.

Where the Presence of the Lord Is

"Where the presence of the Lord is, there is liberty." Where the presence of spiritual consciousness is, there is the consciousness of the living truth, the *living truth* . . . do you hear that? The *living* truth, which means *God living,* God *being felt — felt happening within* — where that living presence is, is liberty witnessed.

The 'presence' has to be tangibly felt happening, tangibly experienced; otherwise, it is no presence at all in practical experience. Mind must not be used for thinking about believed sense but must be a transparency, simply observing, simply as an avenue or faculty of awareness for that which truly is. It mustn't be a faculty of thought, but a faculty of awareness — that is the consciousness that is transparent and able to *witness* the Lord being liberty of form, the truth of form; the consciousness that witnesses the freedom, the wholeness, the oneness, the harmony, the peace of all of experience, being the good of the whole, the joy of the whole, the love of the whole.

Be silent with this for a few minutes. . .

Nothing to Fear

You see now that form has nothing in it or of it to fear. Of its own self, form has no more power, substance, quality or character than does a rag doll or an image on the movie screen. "You . . . have no power over me except that which is given you from above; for there is no power but of God." When you know this *and live by it*, all form is neutral, innocent and harmless, and only the one power of God is operative as your experience. "The earth is the Lord's [that of the one power and presence alone], and the fullness thereof."

If I put out a breaking news bulletin that warned 10 + 10 has just dropped to 17, would you be fearful of that news? Would you worry about your bank account, your savings, your investments? Would you quickly check your balance? Would you put a stop to an intended investment? What about its opposite? What if it was reported that 10 + 10 has jumped to 26? Would that excite you? Would you rush to invest as many tens as you can? Of course not. You would know the non-truth of such a report and instantly dismiss it. In fact, you'd be able to laugh at it.

Remain Non-Attached and Non-Responsive

In the same way, we lift into and remain so thoroughly in truth, that when disease or poverty or depression or homelessness or hate or war is reported, we look at it with no belief, no condemnation, no judgment, no idea and no fear. We do not invest it with emotion or even response. It is nothing, just an image of belief — false belief. We *know* that it of its own self is nothing because *only God is*. The claim has not changed, nor ever can, change God. The claim is not a false reality, not even a temporary false reality; it's of no reality whatsoever. It need not be embraced, reacted to, dealt with, solved. It is as impotent as is the shadow, or the image on the movie screen.

Everything of name, good or bad, is literally without power and harmless because only God is; therefore the 'named' form is both incorrectly named and perceived; the only thing ever presenting itself is God itself. But you know as well as I do, that until we've lifted to the point of actually realizing this truth, it is often hard not to react and try to 'do' something about an experienced discord. We find ourselves still believing it and fearing it; we find ourselves still tempted to apply mental or physical effort to solve or pacify it. But by doing so — remember — all we do is solidify and prolong that very false belief in experience. The more we entertain false belief, the more it occupies our experience.

Illumined Awareness Exposes Remaining Darkness

Most if not all reading this, have had the experience of a problem worsening when spiritual awareness has been brought to it. As we rise in awareness, our problems often temporarily worsen rather than heal. The reason is we're still attached to the belief, believing it to be some form of entity, some form of reality, albeit false reality. We call it a 'false reality'. We call it an 'appearance'. We've made an entity out of false reality, or appearance. There is no such entity; there is nothing present other than a false form of imagination, opinion, judgment, thought.

We must now lift up to the purity of spiritual consciousness in which no matter exists at all, the consciousness that is able to literally look at anything and everything (just like that report warning of 10 + 10 being 17 or 26) with neutrality:

You of your own self are literally nothing. There is no power, no law, no principle, no presence to sustain you. You are nothing but suggestion, a false image, a false idol. You have no cause to sustain you, no truth, no principle. You are not God. You are of belief alone.

When we've lifted to that height of truthful awareness that is able to dismiss the discord as non-reality, and we can truly say, "Neither do I condemn you. I have no response for you. I have no interest in you. I'm neither fearful of you nor excited about you. Whatever you are, I have nothing for you," then it is we are able to rest and relax in truth itself — feeling the presence happening within, and then quickly witness truthful form emerge where untruthful form seemed to be.

It appears to be the healing of disease, the prospering of lack, the bringing together of love where no love seemed to be, or the pacifying and harmonizing of individual, group or worldy discord. But what it really is, is the revealing of truthful form where a false sense existed, that's all. It is beholding the principle, the eternal, truthful form revealing itself, emerging from the fogginess of misperception (the fogginess of belief) into perfectly clear and wondrous visibility. And all is well.

7

Before Thought, I Am

❦

Immediately let us turn within — withdraw attention, interest, engagement from what seems to be 'outer' to what seems to be 'within' and gently become aware that *only God is*, which means that only *God felt happening within* is. The *felt happening* is the only *is*, so silently and gently ponder *only God is*, right here within.

The kingdom of truth, God, spirit, you, is here within; the world is here within — everything, the body, the world, the universe, infinity and everything of infinity is here within. Its truth, its reality, its limitlessness, its nowness — it is all here within.

Ponder this, and begin to feel it welling up within as an actual *presence felt happening* for a few minutes. . . .

Before Thought, I Am

As you feel spirit happening within, realize *this is truth; this* is my reality. *Before thought* is my reality. This felt reality, felt life happening in or as what we may term 'within' is eternal life happening as itself as you, untouched by whatever belief believes it is observing.

Truth felt happening within is the only embodiment, the only form, amount, substance, character, place, but we've mis-identified; we've believed that outer form — physical, material form — is what we are, what we have and where we live. We think we exist *in* or *as* or *have* a physical body. The physical body is just imagination, just a dense level of awareness, a low degree of illumination. The body is in you; you are not in it.

If You Can Name It

Anything you can name is an aspect of awareness — by definition. If awareness as we know it did not exist, forms as we know them would equally not exist. If you can name more than one thing — oneness itself — then what you are naming is not your truth, not the truth of any person or thing throughout infinity. You are oneness because God is oneness and God is all. You mis-identify as soon as you begin naming appearing forms as being something of their own selves, which you then give 'own- self' names to. Belief, idea, opinion and judgment forever mis-identify that which actually is — God, and God alone — and because belief is experience, that which is believed (therefore mis-identified) is experienced.

Only when you recognize (identify) nothing but God, and only as you live by experiencing God felt happening within, with nothing you want from it — no form, no name, no 'other' — do you *have*, and are you *experiencing* the infinity, the omnipresence and the freedom of your truthful being and world. Because God is forever manifest, forever tangible, visible and demonstrated (always remember, there is no 'unmanifest, intangible, invisible or undemonstrated God), when you have and are experiencing truth, you have and tangibly experience the "image and likeness" of God as mind, body and world — as everything everywhere.

God does not think; only belief thinks. Is *is*, already and eternally. What would God think about? And what for? That which is incorporeal, infinite, omnipresent, omniscient, omnipotent, eternal and already wholly finished and perfect has nothing to think about. Only a personal sense of being that believes its self and its world is *not* incorporeal, infinite, omnipresent, omniscient, omnipotent, eternal and already finished has something to think about.

A thought is belief and takes place within you, not 'outside' of you. I am not having your thought; you are having your thought. The plant, the flower, the house, the dollar and the furniture are not having your thought; you are having all thought that exists about that which you're thinking. But if your thought about everything is not *spiritual*, it is false thought. You are mis-identifying yourself and your experience and unfortunately — because belief or mis-identity *is* experience — your experience is filled with falsely-witnessed, mis-identified form *in sense*, never in reality. God is entirely unaffected and unchanged by false thought; therefore all form is entirely unaffected and unchanged. The perfect spiritual form and wholeness forever exists even while we have false thought about it, and while we carry on day-in and day-out mis-identifying and having opinion and judgment about it.

Truth Exists Fully Manifest and Already Demonstrated

You, every cell and grain of your truth, exist fully manifest and already demonstrated this minute in your consciousness — before thought, before belief, before mis-identity. Therefore, seek it before thought, before your sense of who you are and what your body and world is. Seek before thought, before sense — "Seek the kingdom of God", not the kingdom of 'you'. So in this way, we have to now invert the entire way of being so that we experience reality, not a misperception. By living the inner life, we live who and what we truly are, and what everything everywhere truly is — the infinity, the omnipresence, the eternality, the invariable completeness of being — you, the whole omnipresence of life *being you*, being itself uniquely and individually as the presence you are.

This morning as the sun rose, I looked out of the window and gently observed the morning frost bathed in the early light — a beautiful time of day, still and peaceful, magical, before the world gets busy. As I stood, simply observing, I realized that *I am before* the window and everything of the morning visible through the window. I exist, I am happening before it, yet I am able to look through the transparency of the window and witness a very beautiful objectified experience. But it isn't I; it's an aspect of I happening as experience. I am always I, and am never the experience I am having. Anything happening 'out there', good or bad, does not affect me. It just *is;* it's just happening in experience, but it's not me nor mine.

How Strange It Would Be . . .

Then I thought how strange it would be if I assumed it was me. How strange it would be if I identified with that which I was observing instead of the I that is standing here 'before' and completely detached from the experience. Indeed, how strange that would be! How strange it would be to believe that 'out there' — the objective in and of its own self — is my body, my supply, my love, my relationship, that 'out there' is owned by me. How bizarre that would be! I would watch seasons come and go, people, things and conditions come and go, and believe that I, what I am and what I have was coming and going — my health, my supply, my love, my safety and security — abundant then lacking, strong then weak, present then absent. My state of being would be variable, dependant on objective experience. I would live from the outer to the inner. My expression would be limited by how the outer appeared, how much objective form I had available at any one moment, how much objective opportunity I had today, this month, this year. My freedom would be determined by the state of my objective environment. Would that not be gross mis-identity? Would that not in fact be gross self-imprisonment?

It would be as if mathematics were limited to 10 + 10 = 20 or even one million plus one million equals two million (all I 'am' and 'have' is '20' or even 'two million'), or depressed by 10 + 10 = 14, or excited by 10 + 10 = 25. Can mathematics be made to alter its state of being by what is 'out there', its infinity of being bound by anything of objective expression, by any one set of numbers 'right' or 'wrong', harmonious or discordant, large or small? Can you imagine math being affected by outer-appearing numbers, *whatever they may be?*

Can you or I be affected by any 'outer'-appearing conditions *whatever they may appear to be?* Of course not — anymore than math is affected by correct *or* incorrect numbers, the sun is affected by objective light *or* dark, or aerodynamics is affected by flying *or* grounded airplanes. We peer through the window of awareness simply beholding whatever the scene is and whatever its ingredients — unattached, unaffected and unconcerned, non-reactive and non-involved, effortlessly knowing that *it of its own self* is nothing, and that what is truly present, in a completely tangible and practical way, is God, infinity, omnipresence.

The Truth of Life

This is the truth of life, the truth of being. You are life itself simply witnessed objectively as and 'through' mind. But life never changes, is never lessened, altered, never anything but the fullness of itself — infinite, omnipresent, one. Why is this true? Because *only God is.* This is the one truth, the one principle, there being "none else". Think. If God is one, and God is the only, then God is the one and only presence and experience. There cannot be God (the one and the only, there being none else) and then a 'different' experience. Students have forever believed that experience — this world — is somehow different from God. This is one hundred percent incorrect. Why? Because only God is. Only, only, *only* God is.

Only God exists — literally. All existence (no matter what belief believes it to be or believes are 'different' categories of existence) is God and nothing but God. There is nothing but God, one, one*ness* (which is experience 'happening'). All existence, inclusive of all 'categories' of existence — which include all of experience and 'categories' of experience — is one hundred percent God and *of* God.

We vainly repeat, "Only God is; only God exists in truth"; and then promptly think, "What about me? What about my health, my rent, my mortgage, my relationship, my business, my happiness?" No matter how many times we hear and repeat statements of truth, God is not the *only* in our awareness, therefore not the *only* in our world, until we drop the 'and' *we ourselves are being* (the 'I, me, mine' we are being by believing it, or believing the 'me' I am 'at the moment' — this human, physical, worldly me) and its list of worldly needs and desires.

Before Thought, I Am

Only God Is, and Only God Exists

Only God is and only God *exists*. Only God is and only God is *experience* — inclusive of all forms of experience. If you exist, you are that one existence. If you are having an experience, God is that one experience. You and I may be mis-identifying it, yes! You or I may mistake it for being something of its own self, yes! But that doesn't change the fact, the truth, that it — whatever 'it' is, whatever 'he or she or the place or condition' is — is in fact God, holy ground, whole consciousness, unchanged and *incapable of* change or difference or being any 'other'.

You cannot do anything to or about the fact that God is all, any more than '2' or '100' or '1,000,000' or '7,000,000' can do anything to or about the fact that mathematics is all mathematics is. God is all, the one, the only; therefore you are that, and all is that despite your awareness or lack of it, or none of it. You are that, and you will quickly discover you are the moment you cut out the 'and' in you and in your experience.

Life Does Not Die

When you do what the world calls 'die', you'll discover you haven't died at all. Just as the tree doesn't die when its leaves fall at the end of the season, you do not die when you shed this body-form at the end of its season. You never die. How can life die? God is eternal and God is life; therefore life is eternal — *all life*, without exception, because there is nothing but God; therefore there is nothing but eternal life. If anything is alive, it is forever alive because there is nothing but eternal life. There isn't temporary life. There isn't a short span of human life or animal or plant life, even leaf life. All life — *all, all, all* life — is the only life in existence, that being eternal life.

Can you imagine the tree mis-identifying itself as its leaves alone? If it did, then it certainly would believe that it will die at the end of the season. If we believe we are the body, we believe that we die when the body is shed. But now realize: even if the tree does believe it is the leaves, that belief does not 'make it die' when the leaves fall. Belief never changes reality, and belief does not change the eventual experience of reality — no matter how deeply or how long we've entertained the false belief. At the end of the season, as the leaves fall to the ground, the tree discovers itself just as alive and just as embodied as it ever has been, with a brand new experience of body and in the same world in which it has always had its roots.

Likewise, when you shed this body — this 'leaf' — at the end of its season you discover yourself standing right where you were before the end of the season and before the 'old body' dropped, with a brand new, healthy and vital body (a newly experienced form of the one eternal spiritual embodiment you truthfully are) *despite what you may or may not have believed about body being 'you'*. Truth is unaffected by belief; therefore you are forever unaffected. The moment you drop belief, your immediate experience is unaffected and visibly nothing but truth.

You Are Life, Love, Infinity Itself

You are and have infinity; therefore you are and have the infinity of all form, all experience, all substance, despite what belief may believe and despite what may or may not be observed this minute. As long as you do not identify with that which is believed or observed, but you stay constantly in I, God, spirit, truth, then you are living as truthful identity. Your good is limitless and omnipresent and is witnessed to be all over your land. You *have* your truth, your freedom, your fulfillment because you are *consciously being* truth, freedom and fulfillment as spiritual consciousness, not 'thing' consciousness.

You *have* eternal life because you are *being it* — you are consciously being spirit rather than 'thing' — and when the season comes to drop the old body, rather than passing through the experience unconsciously, you will now be perfectly conscious and alive as you find yourself in exactly the same place and time, but now with the new body (the new 'leaf').

You *are* love, and you cannot lack love as long as you do not identify yourself or your state with that which you observe. You are love itself. Nothing observed can affect that truth — change it, lessen it, delay it or leave love 'unembodied'. There is no such thing as 'unembodied' love because God is love, and there is no such thing as unembodied God. Love does not 'come' to you, love *is* what you *are* and *have;* therefore love cannot be withheld from you. You cannot receive more love or better

love or new love. You can only realize the love that you are and have —
love itself — and then *be more of love.* Then nothing in the universe can
stop the embodiment of love being your objectified experience.

The same is true of prosperity. You are and have infinity. If you believe
wealth is that which you call objective, then you have entirely mis-identified yourself and your wealth, and will have to live with that false identity
and its false form ('both' being one) for just as long as you continue to believe that the 'outer' is what you are and have. But when you wake up to
your truthful identity and start being it — being the omnipresent consciousness of infinity — then an infinity of form is ever at hand.

Do Not Identify with That which You Observe

As long as you do not identify with or as that which you observe, but
stay in truth, then you discover your infinity of experience being 'fed'
by the you — the *I am* — 'before' thought, 'before' form, 'before' experience. *I am the life of the world . . . I am the food . . . the wine . . . the water.* As
long as you realize that God alone is, then God alone is your experience.

Only God is, period. God is life eternal, God is love eternal, God is
abundance eternal — omnipresent and unconditional. But remember,
'only God is' becomes the tangible experience of only-God-is, *only when
God is felt happening within,* and when that *felt happening within* is how you
live, what you live on and by, what you rely on. Now you have the tactile
and visible — actual — experience of being life eternal, being love eternal,
being abundance eternal, being freedom and fulfillment eternal. Now
your body of truth — your truthful identity inclusive of all experience
— is perfectly visible, real and practical.

You Are Spiritual Being

You are a spiritual being living in a spiritual experience (world). God
is spirit and truth. God is not matter. God is not mentality, physicality,
materiality. God is not cause or effect, time or space. God is not objective
or objectified. God is not corporeal, and God is all; therefore nothing is
corporeal . God is incorporeal — spirit and spiritual. You are a spiritual

being living as a spiritual universe, a spiritual experience.

You may believe that you 'and' experience are two separate things but you'd be mistaken. There is no 'and', there is only one, oneness, omnipresence. You 'and' experience are actually you *being experience* just as the sun is being the experience of itself. The sun does not witness light and heat, it *is* light and heat. There isn't the sun 'and' light and heat. There isn't you 'and' experience, 'and' body, 'and' thing, amount or activity. There is just you — the I of you, consciousness, spirit, omnipresence being the you you are. There is no 'other' type of being — of you!

You are the very incorporeality, oneness, infinity, omnipresence and eternity of being itself, experience itself — but *God* life, *God* experience, heaven as earth — with absolutely no limit to you, no human or material effort required by you, nothing to 'gain' or 'achieve' or 'restore' because all is already whole and perfect, infinite, omnipresent and eternal. Your one requirement and one effort is to rise in conscious awareness of truthful identity, to spiritualize awareness.

All is Spirit

All is spirit. It is the spiritualizing of awareness that 'makes' the spiritual kingdom real and visible as experience. Material awareness cannot see the divine harmony, peace and wholeness that exists all around it. Here and now, your entire being, body and worldly experience — no matter where you go, what you do, or whom you do it for — is full of, and is itself the presence and form of the "goodness of God".

Sense lifts or transforms or rises* from material (false sense) to spiritual (truthful being). Nothing 'actual' changes. God already is. God does not change, only *awareness* changes — spiritualizes. The world doesn't change. A person doesn't heal, lack is not supplied, and war is not pacified. This is the effect spiritual consciousness *seems to have on discordant material experience.* But actually, truth emerges into tangibility as spiritual consciousness witnesses the harmony and completeness of itself.

Earth is already and forever has been heaven — "as in heaven so on earth" — and as soon as awareness becomes heavenly (spiritual), heaven

---

* See *Rise in Consciousness*, page 9

becomes perfectly and naturally visible as whole and harmonious experience — earth.

Inverse Awareness of Being

We have to invert our awareness and activity of being. We must realize that everything we observe is not *of its own self* truth. Form of its own self has no truth in it or about it whatsoever. Form — earth, experience — is not an entity in or of its own self anymore than a patch of light on the wall is its own entity. This is why we cannot 'bring truth to form'.

Yes, spiritual consciousness *seems* to do just that. Indeed, where spiritual consciousness is, all form harmonizes, pacifies, becomes whole and complete, free and fulfilled. "Where the presence of the Lord is, there is liberty." But if we wish to be the consciousness that witnesses the miracle of truth, we must first know the truth of the miracle and the 'how' of it. When we know the truth, and then be it — be spiritual consciousness with no materiality in it whatsoever — then material sense is dispelled to reveal spiritual reality, the harmony and wholeness of being inclusive of all experience. "Know the truth, and that very truth will set you free."

Being spiritual consciousness is like being the sun. Where the sun is, dark is dispelled. Where spiritual consciousness is, material sense is dispelled, and because sense is experience, the material/believed discord is dissolved, and spiritual sense emerges as or 'looking like' — being — harmonious experience. Nothing has changed but awareness. The lifted — spiritualized — awareness witnesses itself as earthly (experienced) harmony and wholeness.

Strong in Spiritual Awareness

Stay strong in spiritual consciousness, despite the way form appears to look or act at this moment. The way form or condition appears to be is not what it truthfully is — *this minute* not what it truthfully is. What appears to be ill or lacking or discordant in any way, is not *actually*. Appearance is a lie. Everything — everything(!) — is God, therefore whole and harmonious. Material awareness — the awareness that believes appearance to be something of its own self — cannot see truthful form. Only spirit sees itself; only spiritual consciousness sees spiritually whole and harmonious form — the "image and likeness" of God, truth.

Stay *consciously one* with God, consciously *as* God consciousness, consciously *being* God consciousness, rather than material consciousness. Be *consciously* aware of God as all, rather than form as all, and in this way you remain 'connected' with truth, and truth then becomes evermore visible and real to you and as your experience.

We cannot evidence truth *in* or *for* that which we observe. It's impossible. All we can do is lift into the consciousness that is already and forever the *truth* of all, just like lifting into the truth, the realization, of 2 + 2 = 4 from the untruth of '3'. It is utterly impossible to bring truth to '3' — to fit '4' into '3' to make it a truthful 2 + 2. No matter how much we may attempt it, there is no truth in 2 + 2 = 3 and there never will be. 'Four' is the truth of 2 + 2, and until we lift to it itself, we won't 'have 4'.

The only truth is God, and the only actualized God there is, is God felt happening within — the activity of God felt happening in and as being — deep within in the secret place 'before' thought, 'before' form, 'before' the world. There is no other demonstrable truth. God felt happening within is infinity, is omnipresence, is the demonstration, is the miracle. That is it. That itself is the infinity, omnipresence and harmony of all form. That itself is your perfect, divine, eternal, never-changing mind, body and world. There is no other mind, no other body and no other world; there is no other form, substance, amount, place, condition, activity. We have mis-identified what being and world is and because of that mis-identification, we have been attempting to bring spirit to bear to, or as, or for, that which is observed — form in and of its own self — and in so doing, we've completely missed the truth.

Come Within to the Secret Place

Close your eyes to appearance, and come within now, to the secret place of the most high, the most tangibly manifest and visible truth. Bring attention to the deep within-ness where you feel a peace and stillness, a rest, a 'something' happening — some kind of presence happening

within. Bring your attention to that happening. Don't think; don't analyze it or attempt to understand it.

You are not required to think about truth or understand truth. You
were never required to make such effort. Rather you have been told to
simply and effortlessly be still . . . rest . . . relax . . . let and behold. The
23rd Psalm is full of the instruction to rest, relax, let:

The Lord is my shepherd; I shall not want.
He makes me to lie down in green pastures: he leads me
beside the still waters.

He restores my soul: he leads me in the paths of righteousness
for his name's sake.

Yea, though I walk through the valley of the shadow of death,
I will fear no evil: for thou art with me; thy rod and thy staff
they comfort me.

Thou preparest a table before me in the presence of mine enemies:
thou anointest my head with oil; my cup runneth over.

Surely goodness and mercy shall follow me all the days of my life:
and I will dwell in the house of the Lord for ever.

Rest and relax in the secret place within — deep within 'before'
thought, 'before' the world of form. Withdraw from the world, and lie
down in the green pastures and still waters of truth. Rest, bathe, let go.
In this rested, relaxed and open state — without effort, without understanding, without even bringing to mind a single truth statement — let
truth restore your soul (your awareness). Let truth dawn in awareness
and fill you with light, just as the dawn fills the earth with light. You cannot bring God to awareness anymore than you can bring light to the
world. Only the sun itself brings light to the world, and only God itself
illumines awareness.

The *feeling* of truth happening within — the *feeling* of peace and rest,
warmth and comfort and safety, the *feeling* of release of the burden of
false belief and falsely-sensed form — is your awareness being illumined,
restored and set free. As awareness is restored, all form is restored because awareness *is* form. Whatever degree of awareness you are or I am
being, *is* the form of itself witnessed.

SATISFIED WITH GOD ALONE

Realize now and forever, the 'happening' — the presence you *feel happening* in your rest and relaxedness, in your deep withinness — *is itself* your truth experienced. It *is itself* the demonstration you've searched for. There isn't any other type or form of demonstration, embodiment, experience. Yes, it appears as if the inner experience is different from the outer, but this is one hundred percent untrue. We simply have a material *sense* of spirit, a formed sense of omnipresence, oneness, God. But always *all is God* and God alone.

Truth Felt Happening Is Truth Embodied

Truth *felt happening* is truth embodied — the formation of truth. There is no other form. Only God is. Anything that 'is' is God, therefore God felt happening *is* the only form — not form 'produced, healed, prospered or pacified' but the very *is* of God-form itself, the very image and likeness of God, the already-and-forever presence of truthful form. "God felt happening within *is,* and is the only *is.*" Remember that, and you will never be confused and will never go wrong again.

Truth felt happening within *is* your body — not only your 'physical' body and every cell, organ and function of it, but all body, all form, all amount, activity, place and all condition of experience (earth).

Truly understand now, truth *felt is* truthful body, truthful form, truthful experience, truthful earth. There is no other body. "I am the Lord, and besides me there is none else." As truthful awareness 'shines through' the mind — which at our degree of awareness is of three dimensions and five senses — it appears as truthful form: physical, material form, the "image and likeness" of God.

Form is not physical or material; it is spirit and spiritual. Spirit is the truthful state — identity — of being which you feel first and then witness 'through' mind as form (earth). You are experiencing truthful (healthy, harmonious, whole and free) body and form *only when you are experiencing God happening within and beholding it as all 'outer' form appearing or transforming.*

The True Body

God is the only; therefore God is the only body. That is why God *consciously experienced* is whole and healthy, 'healed' body consciously experienced. 'Consciously' experienced means 'tangibly' experienced. You only know your true body when you experience its truthful form — which is one hundred percent spirit and spiritual — *felt happening*, not seen, heard, tasted, touched or smelled.

You have believed your body to be physical, of a certain gender, size, weight, color and age. But your truthful body is spirit and is only truly experienced as it is felt happening within, 'before' the three dimensional and five-sensed, dense, 'physical' experience of it.

Now tell me, does that felt experience have gender, size, weight, color or age? Does it have density? Can you injure it? Can you injure the feeling happening within? Can it succumb to contagion? Can it be ill? Can it be diseased? No, and because this is your only actual body, realize that all so-called 'other' bodily experience is simply belief and thought about the belief, therefore unreal. Your physical sense of body literally, tangibly, is not real. Only God is, which makes God the only reality. Know this, and live it, and then you discover that your body is safe, protected, vital and purposeful. You discover that it literally is life alone, eternal, never dying. In this way, you finally discover and identify with truthful being and truthful body.

No Need To Be Afraid of Truth

It is often assumed that when our attention is or our hold is released from the 'outer,' that we may lose what is dear or valuable to us. Many students believe they have to give up so much of what they love and still enjoy of 'this world'. This is often the resistance to truth. We want truth to transform some departments of our lives, like our health or our finances, as long it doesn't change others like our relationship or our family. God, give me health and a sufficiency of money but leave my relationship, my family and my hobby alone.

We are unwilling or hesitant to invert our identity, and live by truth alone. Perhaps we assume we have to forego some of the enjoyments of life, perhaps live in some kind of poverty or enjoyment denial. This is utterly untrue! Who ever told you that, other than orthodoxy? Listen to Jesus: "I am come that they [all] may have life, and have it more abundantly."

Every person and thing you love is true, and by realizing truth you discover more, not less, of that which you love — that which is your truth. Only untruth falls away, and who does not want to be rid of their untruth? Untruth is that which you do not love, that which is frustrating, stressful, limiting, unfulfilling. That which you truly love and are truly fulfilled by is true experience. The only 'result' of your now lifting into and living by truth is your *greater* joy and fulfillment of these people and things, and a never-ceasing experience of more truthful people and conditions coming into your life. "My own shall come to me."

Mis-Identity Is the Only Problem

Mis-identity is the root of the only problem man has ever had. *Merriam-Webster Dictionary* describes "mis-identity" as "lost consciousness of one's own identity".

Because we have mis-identified the forms of experience as being entities in and of their own selves, we have sought more, better and healed form *for* more, better and healed form. Our attention, desire and effort start with form, continue with form, and stop at form. But that is like seeking more, better or healed calculations without attaining a greater realization of math. If that were the case we could say, "Where is math in our effort to improve incorrect calculations in and of and for their own selves?" And we can say, "Where is God in our effort to improve or heal form in and of and for its own self?" And we'd have to answer, "Nowhere".

It is not that wanting or needing an improved or healed life is wrong in any way. It is not. It is good. It is a natural, inherent impulse. But in seeking better form *as and for its own self*, we seek amiss. "You ask, and receive not, because you ask amiss." "Seek not for the things of life, but seek the kingdom of God, and all these things [truthful forms] shall be added unto you [your experience]. Fear not, little flock, for it is your Father's good pleasure to give you the kingdom."

The moment we stop seeking more of the good of that which we observe, and seek more conscious awareness of that which it truly is — God, then "all these things" (all the truth and good of form) emerge into beautiful, bountiful and eternal visibility where discord or disease seemed to be.

To seek truthful identity, to "seek the kingdom of God", is to seek *God felt happening within,* and to realize that to seek *that experience* and *that experience alone* is to seek correctly, truthfully. God is not objective, but incorporeality, infinity and omnipresence itself. This is what we feel happening within us (within our sense of being) when we seek God for God alone — the inner for the inner alone, never the outer for itself alone.

That is truth, the incorporeal, the infinite, the omnipresent, not the forms we observe, not that which we can name, but *incorporeality, infinity, and omnipresence* all of which we cannot objectify and name. "If you can name it, it isn't it." We must let go of false identity, not only of 'ourselves' but everything of the world. "Seek not the things of the world" for they are false sense of that which truly is; they are finite, limited, temporal and often discordant sense-forms; they of their own selves are not what you are, nor what you have; they are not what they appear to be. All is God, all is incorporeality, all is infinity, all is omnipresence and it is experienced by being *felt.* God felt happening within is the truthful body, the truthful love, wealth, peace and relationship — the relationship, the love, the wealth, the peace of *oneness,* of wholeness, of God, of spirit and truth actually experienced as the *feeling of peace or wholeness happening within.* There it is, and nothing less than this is truth demonstrated.

My talents, my skill, my purpose and success, my wealth, my strength, my beauty, my fulfillment of being — all of these aspects of experience have been mis-identified. If you want to find your truth — boundless, unconditional and requiring no 'human' effort — then turn within to *what* it is, and *where* it is. Truth is forever fully manifest and demonstrated within your consciousness. It lives as the life you are, here and now, perfectly whole and visible, unhindered, infinite and omnipresent, twenty-four hours a day; *but you've gone off somewhere in false sense* believing that form is what you are, therefore believing that to improve life you need to improve form. No! Come back home. Come *here, within* and feel your truth happening; feel God happening individually and utterly uniquely as you and the entirety of your world. Realize that God — the felt happening — is fully manifested and fully demonstrated as your being and world (experience). But hear that — *God is,* not what is perceived, but *God is* that truth.

SATISFIED WITH GOD ALONE

Yes, we still have objective experience, but no effort, no thought has to be taken for it of its own self because *it is nothing of its own self.* "I am in the world but not of it." God is, and that means *only God felt happening within* is. There it is. There's the embodiment, there's the quality and the condition, the life, the love, the amount — all infinite, all unconditional, all effortless.

Effortlessly Witnessing God as Experience

God, and God objectively experienced, is free. It is the free experience of oneness, truth 'happening', one being and its experience tangibly manifest, one presence visibly witnessed: omnipresence freely evident.

The gift of life — the life "more abundant" — is free. God seeks you. You never need 'persuade' or manipulate your thoughts, or even align or atune them, for the God experience. Thoughts are not God. Only God itself is God, and because God already is, the God experience is free. "It is the Father's good pleasure to give you the kingdom." *Give you*, not make you work for, struggle for, earn.

God experienced — felt happening within — is effortless, is it not? It is as effortless as experiencing the sunrise or sunset, as effortless as experiencing wet water. *You* don't achieve it. *It itself* is the experience 'for you'; God itself is the God experience 'for you'. You don't have to pray for it, meditate for it, chant for it, go to a holy place for it, earn it, struggle for it or wait for it. In fact, the very opposite of these is all you have ever been required to do — rest, be open, and simply receive.

God is, and God already is. If you know this truth, then turn to 'where' it is — within, 'before' thought; then God which already and forever is your truth, fully manifest and demonstrated, emerges as your experience just as the sunrise, the sunset or wet water emerges as your experience when, and as spontaneously as, *you make yourself available to it.*

Truth is not found in outer conditions. Truth can never be brought to outer conditions. There is no outer, and there equally is no actual inner. There is only God, and God is *omnipresence:* not local or outer or inner presence. It is for this reason that you cannot have a holy concept, a holy perception, an actual holy place or form. Only *omnipresence itself* is holy place and form, and perfectly visibly so. God felt happening within is the only true prayer, the only true silence, the only true expression, the only true form, the only true word. "In the beginning was the word, and the word was with God, and the word was God."

Only God Can

Who's expressing? Who's happening? Who's experiencing and who's the experience? You? No, God. Why? Only God is; therefore only God can. Did you hear that? *Only God can . . .* Now you fill in the blank: only God can be body; only God can be love, relationship; only God can be home; only God can be peace and joy; only God can be wealth, achievement and success.

Only God is. Therefore, only God can be, and what is God? Incorporeality, infinity, omnipresence — nothing of belief and nothing of thought, but 'before' belief and thought. God is only evident as you and your life when God is your living awareness, and when you live by and rely on the feeling of God happening within. Only when you are feeling truth happening within do you *have* God, do you *have* truth, and the full, instantaneous embodiment of truth as your experience.

Travel throughout your consciousness a million miles up, down, left or right, or come right here and rest one inch from you, or closer than one inch, and there you find God being the entirety of your being and experience. Your consciousness is spontaneously "full of the goodness of God" (and visibly so — when and only when) you keep your awareness morning, noon and night on God as the only, *and* by the degree that you live by and rely on the *feeling* of God happening within.

If You 'Unplug' from God

If you take yourself away from God in awareness, if you unplug yourself and wander back into belief, you equally spontaneously cut yourself off from being able to witness truth. Yes, the fruits live for a little while in your experience, but you're devoid of the life and presence of truth itself. You're unplugged, and you know as well as I do how short is the life of a fruit plucked from the branch of its life. You live on yesterday's manna for a little while; but as soon as you unplug yourself, you quickly discover your mind, body and world depleted of the goodness, effortlessness and and freedom of truthful life. Your energy, your vitality, your intelligence, your wisdom, your supply, your business, your love and relationship all deplete just as the fruit plucked from the branch depletes.

All of experience in one way or another begins to deplete, becoming variable, less consistent, unreliable, limited and lacking, ill, weak and 'old' — all for one reason only: You have taken your conscious awareness away from God as all, and from the *felt happening of God within*. You are living a prodigal life — tempted again by belief; entangled in believing form to be something of its own self worth striving for, worth getting more of and better of, or worth saving and protecting. In so doing you thrust yourself into such finiteness of experience, such limitation and struggle of experience, that it is . . . well, it's indescribably hard to watch and even harder, of course, to experience.

The Earth Is One and Full of God

If only you will truly and deeply trust that the being you are, and the earth you experience (every grain, place and condition of it), is one, and full of God, you would be free of all discord inside of a week. God already is — we must never forget this. This is why the God experience is "quick, sharp and powerful" the moment we 'enable' it by knowing the truth, maintaining the conscious awareness of truth, and living by and relying on its felt happening.

Truth is tangibly and visibly evident when it is being felt within. Truth is omnipresence; therefore, as you feel truth happening, you instantaneously *have* omnipresent truth. If only you will realize that truth is spirit, not object; God, not matter; incorporeality, not corporeality, then you will cease looking for or believing you need *forms* of truth. Paradoxically, as you give up believing in, and seeking form in and of its own self, knowing and seeking and being *satisfied with God alone*, it is *then* you have all good form in experience. "He that loseth his life for my sake shall find it."

When we realize that the felt happening within is literally, tangibly, the living, visible truth of body — all body not just the personal, 'physical' sense of body — why would we not wish to live that body; experience the treasure, abundance and vitality of that body ever more of each twenty-four hours? Why? It doesn't make sense not to the moment we've realized the way of its experience.

As we live the experience, we observe the freedom, vitality, intelligence, wholeness, beauty, perfection and purpose of all in life. We watch the physical sense rising and illuminating to be the truthful sense — the spiritual, the Godly, the truth itself. Our being now exists 'before' belief and thought, here within, before the 'outer' forms of experience. We are free and blissful in truth. We behold that freedom and bliss feed, and become visible as, the forms of our world.

Experience no longer includes thought. We are not feeding thought. Mind is now used truthfully as a beholder, not a doer — a faculty of awareness and service, not a faculty of creation. We simply observe without effort, witness without desire. We know that that which is observed in and of its own self is nothing, and even as its form, is just an infinitesimal, objective sense of the boundless infinity and omnipresence that it truly is. We observe without thought, without judgment, opinion, idea, belief. "Judge not according to the appearance, but judge righteous judgment."

We realize that all form is actually, despite its appearance, the very presence, substance, character, nature and quality that is God. We observe as and through the perfectly beautiful and truthful avenue of awareness we call mind — the unconditioned mind, the "window of heaven" — and we realize that if mind were not true, we could not have it. Mind is indeed "one of the many mansions [degrees of awareness] in my Father's house". Until now it has been mis-identified. We have believed mind to be us and ours, and we've looked through it at a world believed to be separate, out there, and different from us — a world certainly without an affinity for our needs. We have identified with form, with the objectified, observed experience.

If we will stop that and now use the mind as its divine and purposeful faculty of awareness, simply observing the innocence and impotence of form, we will easily find ourselves in continual God awareness, and easily feel God happening within many, many times throughout each day and night. Then, without thought, without effort, we behold our mind, body and world filled indeed with the oneness and good of God.

We are now as Malachi says, "the window of heaven" — the consciousness of God, without thought, just a transparency and vacuum of being, where truth alone resides. We are the truthful being — spiritual being — existing in and as spiritual fulfillment, before belief and before thought. Fully manifest truth shines through the thought-devoid mind, revealing truthful body, truthful relationship, truthful amount, truthful activity, truthful home, neighborhood, truthful world, peace, harmony, joy, union, and love as irrepressible form.

If we re-introduce belief and thought, we instantaneously thrust ourselves back into mis-identity, back into the pairs of opposites and now have to live it to be this way until we shake ourselves free again.

The Infinity and Omnipresence of Being

Realize now and for evermore that the being you are and the world you have is the infinity and omnipresence of being and world, the fullness of God being all. "The earth is the Lord's, and the fullness thereof." You are that: you have infinity and eternity of life, love, resource, object, amount, condition, activity and relationship.

Why — as the infinity and omnipresence of being — would you mis-identify and choose to live a fractional, limited, unreliable and often painful life of pairs of opposites? Why would you choose finiteness over infinity? Why would you choose local, limited supply and resource over omnipresence? Why would you settle for an unhappy relationship when you are love itself and will always have the objectified forms of love if you just know your truth and let it live you, instead of your attempting to live a life separate and apart?

It makes no sense whatsoever. It would be as if Warren Buffet lost conscious awareness of his billionaire status and resorted to scratching and begging for his next meal, or struggled to earn sufficient dollars to pay his monthly bills. If he fell into a state of mis-identity, he could well believe he needs money to feed his family and pay his bills. But in his truthful identity, even materially, such an act would not make sense. In truth, no material act makes sense. Only God is; therefore only living as and by, and being *satisfied with God alone* is sensible.

You have to invert your way of being. We have to live from within out. The kingdom is within so you turn within, and *there* you are in truthful being. *There* you ponder truth — the truth that only God is, o*nly God is*. If you, from this hour, make truth your way of life, you *are* the freedom of all experience. You *are* and *have* the freedom, the infinity, the omnipresence of all of truth and truth's resources. I am, and have, truth when I *feel* God happening within. I am desire-less, effort-less, yet vital and purposeful because I am now *being the living experience of truth happening as the being I am.*

8

Rooted In Truth

❦

Wherever you look, there is the center of yourself. What you observe as experience is your degree of truth awareness, the degree of you that is devoted to truth felt happening within, versus the degree of material awareness and belief still happening in you.

The more you feel and live truth happening within, the less you believe and think about form as anything of its own self, and the more neutral you are with and among that which you observe, the more of God you witness — the more of the fruits of true life, true love, true peace and harmony, true beauty and bounty you witness as experience.

You do not do anything to help experience any more than the vineyard does anything to help its branches, buds, blossoms and fruit. It *witnesses* the fruitage. It witnesses the abundance of experience, the truthful forms of experience, as it stays rooted in the ground.

Think about what would happen to the vine if it kept jumping out of the ground as we jump out of God awareness, if it only stayed in the ground as intermittently as we stay in God. Would you expect a healthy, strong and vibrant vine? Would you expect leaves, buds, flowers and fruit to fill the branches of the vine? Of course not, yet we are surprised that the goodness of God does not fill our experience even though we devote little time to 'staying in God'.

Remember, 'staying in God' does not mean thinking about God, keeping our minds on God, or even meditating on God *alone*. God is not mind, God is not thought, nor *in* a thought, nor can God be brought 'through' a thought. God is God, and God alone — pure one and oneness, pure incorporeality and none else, 'before' mind, 'before' belief, 'before' thought. Yes, it is important, very important, to employ our thinking in the pondering of God, to meditate on God, and to do so morning, noon and night. But all that 'keeping our minds on God' is not God itself anymore than keeping our minds on the sunset is the sunset itself. What keeping our minds on God does is keep us in the 'place' of God, consciously on 'holy ground' (in God awareness) so that we are ever ready and receptive for the actual God experience *itself* — like the sponge is ever ready to soak in water.

The secret meaning of 'staying in God' is staying in the actual experience of God — staying in *God felt happening within*. The Master gives us the secret: "As you abide in me, and I abide in you."

"As you abide in me . . ." is *our* thinking about, pondering, meditating on God from morning to night, and night to morning as being the *only*. *Only God is* is what we ponder and meditate on day and night.

". . . and I abide in you . . ." is *experiencing God happening within* — actually *felt happening within* or *as* our being.

Experiencing God is not a mental feat. It is not achieved by taking thought anymore than the sunset is achieved by taking thought. It is the opposite of taking thought; it is being empty of the personal sense of self, open and receptive to that which *is:* God itself. It is *witnessing* that which is, not trying to 'make' it happen. "Not by might, nor by power, but by *my spirit*, says the Lord." God is already the whole of itself happening as the presence of being. Your presence is God, not 'you', and because it is God, it is the whole of God. "I of my own self am nothing," yet because the self I truly am is the only self there is, God, I am and have the whole of that which God is. "Son, I am ever with you, and all that I have is yours."

Be still, and know that your truthful being and world is already God and all that God is and has. You never have to make effort to have and to fully experience that which already is. Therefore rest, relax and let God be felt happening as the very presence of you. Realize that God actualized is God *felt happening*. There is no other God, just as there is no sunset other than the sunset you *witness happening*.

I Abide in You

"I abide in you." The beautiful statement of the Master in John15 means nothing until you *feel* "I abiding" within, and live by *it itself* alone. Then the fruitage of life is rich just as it is for the vine that stays rooted in the earth. As it abides in earth, it has only to be still and witness abundant buds, leaves, flowers and fruit fill its every branch. "Every branch that beareth fruit, he purgeth it, that it may bring forth more fruit. . . Herein is my Father glorified, that ye bear much fruit."

If the vine stayed in earth as little as we stay in truth, it would struggle, wither, live and eventually die in the poverty of little or no fulfillment. "If a man abide not in me, he is cast forth as a branch, and is withered; and men gather them, and cast them into the fire, and they are burned."

How Much Do You Abide in God?

How much of each twenty-four hours do you think the average truth students abide in the truth they're studying? How much do they study and think about God versus actually experiencing God itself — actually feeling the activity of God within? I can tell you, it's a pitifully tiny amount of the average student's day. God is kept in the mind, in knowledge and thought, but not actually experienced. And then we turn to God and ask, Where are you? Where's the health, the love, the wealth and the happiness you promised me? Where is it?

We even ask, Where is my understanding? I need greater spiritual understanding. How can I get it? This is like the vine, its roots out of the earth, dangling in mid-air, asking, Where is the life, the vitality, the talent and the rich fruitage truth has promised me? The promise of truth never changes, and its fruits are infallible. But if we do not stay rooted in truth, how can truth live us, and show forth as our fruit and its purpose? It's very simple, really, isn't it?

Understanding and Wisdom

You see now that the only true understanding is understanding *felt happening within.* True understanding has nothing to do with intellectual understanding. The intellect cannot grasp or understand God. "My ways are not your ways, and my thoughts are not your thoughts."

You may not have realized, until now, that the feeling of truth welling up within — the experience of God happening — is *itself* understanding and wisdom. It is the only true understanding and the only true wisdom. This is the highest meaning of the Master's instruction: "You must know the truth, and that very truth will set you free." You must know — be familiar with — God consciously (felt) happening as your being. You must live as and by the actual God experience, and that very God experience will set you free.

Solomon knew this truth and it made him the wisest and the most successful, wealthiest and sought-after man of his time. His great wisdom and fame is admired and spoken of still today. "Give me neither poverty nor riches [I seek not the things of sense], but give me wisdom and understanding [give me God itself as tangible experience]." Solomon devoted himself day and night to "abiding in me" and many hours in silence experiencing "I abiding in you". The result? "God gave Solomon wisdom and understanding exceeding much, and largeness of heart, even as the sand that is on the sea shore. . . And king Solomon passed all the kings of the earth in riches and wisdom. . . And all the kings of the earth sought the presence of Solomon, to hear his wisdom, that God had put in his heart."

Solomon knew that there is no 'unembodied' God, no 'unembodied' wisdom or understanding. He knew that when he lived by the God experience itself — forever seeking God *for the God experience alone,* God's wisdom and understanding *for itself alone,* never for a reason, never for an objective or quantifiable, witness-able *form* of God — he would forever have an infinity and omnipresence of the good *forms* of earth (experience) wherever he went and as whatever he set about to do.

God is one and omnipresent, not two. God does not 'become' — through some process of changing incorporeality into corporeality, spirit into matter — good forms of materiality. No, only God is; and God experienced within, then observed through mind, is forever the "image and likeness" of itself as form. Solomon knew this, and therefore sought only God for God itself, knowing that the "image and likeness" forms would then be ever more bountiful and infinitely present the more God was experienced each day, and the more the experience was what he lived by and relied on one hundred percent. There is Solomon's secret, and there is ours too.

When All Studying and Contemplating Is Said and Done

When all is said and done — when we've done all our truth learning, all our contemplating; when we've taken in all the truth statements that speak to us, pondered them, contemplated their meaning, their truth — and we look out and see our branches of life still lacking fruit, we finally arrive at a great and life-changing place of realization: we must "know [actually experience] the truth . . . let me abide in you [be experienced in you]". When I abide in you . . . that very truth [that very felt happening, felt experience] will set you free . . . *is itself* your freedom and all the good, healthy and abundant forms of it. Nothing else is your freedom actually experienced, nothing less, nothing different, nothing 'other', nothing of the mind, nothing of belief, nothing of thought, nothing of effort.

You know as well as I do that you can study truth for an entire lifetime. You can contemplate truth for a lifetime and feel relieved and encouraged by it. You can intellectually understand, even intellectually feel the truth of truth, and be quite satisfied by your knowledge. But has all this study and contemplation actually *evidenced* one form of spiritual good in your life? Is your body healthy and vital because spirit abides in it twenty-four hours a day, and *is* the life and animation of it? "I live, yet not I, Christ lives my life." Is your wealth, your success that of spirit being it, rather than matter and material effort being it? "The silver is mine [me], and the gold is mine [me], says the Lord." Is love itself the body, activity and fruits of your relationship? "God [God itself] is love. If you have [all the attributes and things of the world] but have not love, you have nothing." Is your mind, body and world peaceful, happy, fulfilled? "My peace [God, peace itself] I [God itself] give unto you [which you feel happening within you], not as the world gives, give I unto you."

Know the Truth; Know Thyself

Know the truth. Get to know it. Get to know truthful identity. Get to know that only the deep withinness where truth is *felt* happening can be called knowing the truth. In the same way, we only know the sunset when we *experience* the actual sunset. Now we know it. All the reading about it, discussing it, pondering it, was wonderful and satisfying as far as it went. But it didn't, nor can it ever give us the actual experience of the sunset. Only when we're standing there, right out there in front of the sunset actually happening, can we say we know the sunset.

In this way, get to know the truth. Only when we feel truth happening, when we are experiencing the happening deep within, can we ever say, or finally say, we know the truth. Then indeed, that very truth, *that very truth* — no other, no other version, nothing less, nothing of the intellect, nothing of belief and nothing of thought — *that very truth itself felt happening* sets you free: *is* your freedom and all the form of it, *is* your completeness and all the form of it, *is* your perfection and protection and all the form of it.

"Know thyself", said Plato. Well, we never know our true selves until we're feeling the one being, the one truth happening within. Feeling (experiencing) truthful being and world happening is the greatest and most vivid, most alive sense of being we can ever experience. We experience the one universal self — the one infinitude itself, the all-inclusive infinitude of being and universe itself — happening right here as our very being. Indeed, know the truth, know thyself. In so doing, you witness the truth you are experiencing as the one formation — the image and likeness, heaven as earth (experience).

Know thyself. Identify only with thyself — God, spirit, truth felt happening within. If this moment — any moment — you are not feeling truth happening within, then you are not this moment experiencing your true self. You are not "know[ing] thyself", nor experiencing, being and having the infinity and omnipresence, the wisdom and understanding of truth. You're unplugged, disconnected in experience, and are withering. Life is now of the pairs of opposites and will be, at least partially, in some areas, a struggle. Certain aspects of life wither and die, go wrong, if not this minute, then next; if not this hour, then next; if not this day or week or month or year, then next.

The withering and dying is unfortunately inescapable because the truth of life — life itself — has been disconnected from and ignored. The vine has been taken from the earth and is no longer connected with (no longer one with and as) its life, substance, intelligence, wisdom and the infinity of its finished kingdom of expression.

The withering and dying is inescapable because the only life that is being the life of the formed experience, the conceptual experience, is life itself, and life itself can only be experienced by the feeling of it happening within. That's the fuel, the juice, the substance and the form. That's the life and the form of life, that's the abundance and the form of abundance, that's the harmony and wholeness and the form of harmony and wholeness because God is one. God itself 'and' the 'image and likeness' of God as form are one — omnipresence itself as all being and all experience, fully manifest and forever demonstrated — not two, not different, not requiring mental manipulation to experience.

No 'Unmanifest' God

Always remember, there is no unmanifest or unembodied God. The belief that there could be an unmanifest or unembodied God is myth, not fact — mainly believed and taught by orthodoxy.

Think. How can God or any part or aspect of God be 'unmanifest' while others are manifest when God is one, oneness, omnipresence and infinity? How can *one* have 'other' parts or aspects of itself? How can oneness, which is omnipresence and infinity, have anything other than oneness, omnipresence and infinity to it? No, God is one, infinite and omnipresent, having only itself in it and of it. That one and only is then logically, and indeed truthfully, the one and only manifestation, visibility, tangibility and demonstration (experience).

Go Beyond Believed Truth

It is time to go beyond believed truth to true truth — the one truth. No belief is true, only truth itself is true, and quickly proves itself as you let *it itself* be your knowledge and your wisdom.

"Prove me now herewith if I will not open you the windows of heaven [the windows of knowledge and wisdom fully manifested as the abundant fruits of form], and pour you out blessings, that you shall not have room to receive them", says Malachi of truth. Truth is infinite. When you seek it itself *for* it itself and for no earthly reason, it very quickly proves its infinity of all, so abundantly, quickly and consistently that indeed — "you shall not have room to receive it".

Do not listen to, believe and blindly accept any truth teacher or teaching — including Paul F. Gorman and the Miracle Self! — but rather let the teaching prove itself. God is your truth, so go directly to God for truth and proof of truth. Yes, absorb the teaching you can see full well is truth by the fruits on the branches of the teacher's life (if you don't see fruits on a teacher's branches, don't study with that teacher). "By their fruits ye shall know them." Absorb good teachings day in and day out. Study and meditate with masters as consistently as you can — certainly, certainly. But your own proof — your own experience of God and the fruit thereof — is the only way you actually know and witness truth.

Feeling God Happening Is *God Formed*

Once you feel God happening within, you have experienced God formed as the harmony and wholeness of experience. The 'healing' has been experienced and is instantaneously perfectly tangible, real and visible. Belief says, "Oh, no. That is not form, that is not manifestation, that is not the demonstration or the healing. Manifestation is something tangible that I can see, hear, taste, touch, smell, or think about — the 'state' or 'thing' or 'condition' or 'amount' I need to heal or correct the problem". So belief — still mis-identifying truth and believing that health or harmony has not yet 'appeared' — waits for what it believes is still to take place, and *that* is why belief cannot see truth.

Only truth sees truth. Only God sees God. Only God sees God

form, God presence — all of these statements being true *because only God is*. Belief, which is material consciousness, cannot see truthful form because truthful form is visible only to truthful consciousness.

Belief Mis-identifies and Misinterprets

The only substance, the only life, the only form, the only body, the only amount, the only love, the only relationship, the only place, the only home, is truth felt happening within — truth experienced. And because God is infinite, omnipresent and indivisible, as it (God) is being experienced, one *has* the whole of God, the whole of truth, fully manifest and tangibly embodied.

But belief mis-identifies, therefore misinterprets. For instance, belief's interpretation of home is a three dimensional, five-sensed form of matter, and different matter (materials), a physical design and size, existing at a certain time in life and occupying a certain place and amount of space as that place. But God is spirit — incorporeal, infinite, omnipresent and eternal — without matter (especially different types of matter), without dimension, without sense, without time and without space.

So where does this leave belief and its false interpretation of home? Nowhere. It is pure untruth, with no God in its interpretation whatsoever. If you wish to experience true home, realize that it is God. Therefore to tangibly experience truthful home, you must tangibly experience God. God does not 'produce' home and God does not 'manifest' or 'demonstrate' a material home, and that's before we even realize that God, being omnipresent and impersonal, not locally and personally (preferentially) present, does not evidence home (or anything at all) for a personal self.

Come Home to Truth Now

Come home to truth now. Truth is not different from you, it *is* you — your very you in your same world, except the infinity and omnipresence and eternity of you and your world! Live within, live truthful identity, realizing that mind and its formation — earth and beyond (universe)

— is one of the "many mansions in my father's house", simply being, therefore presenting, a three-dimensional and five-sense experience of oneness. The infinite variety of form that mind presents is nothing of its own self, but the one form beheld as many — the one presence and the one power beheld as many. As long as you know that form of its own self is nothing, and as long as you know that only God is — without exception and despite appearance — then you learn to "abide in me and let me abide in you" ever more each day and night, and you equally discover truth's fruits filling and fulfilling your every branch of life.

You discover that by living in and by the feeling of God's presence — God felt happening within — you indeed are staying rooted in God, spirit and truth, and in that way discovering your ever-expanding and multiplying truth of being, world, purpose, resource and fulfillment.

Then as you look through the belief-devoid and thought-devoid mind, you are like the vine looking out through its transparency of being and witnessing the rich fruits of truth free to fill its experience. The fruits of truth are your individual and unique fruits of fulfillment in every category of fulfilled experience — health, vitality, beauty and youth of the body, loving relationship and family, satisfying companionship, safe and beautiful home, fulfilling purpose and expression, harmony and peace of experience — all in forms unique to you, just as the vine's fruitage is unique to it. And like the vine, you never need take thought but simply behold the good and fulfillments of experience 'coming' on their own. "It is the Father's good pleasure to give you the kingdom."

By the degree that we ever more devote ourselves to feeling truth happening within, filling us and spilling into and as our whole universe, and as we realize that that felt happening is our only truthful being, and only truthful everything of experience, by that degree can we now look out without belief and without thought and witness the abundant harmony, wholeness and fruit of God's (truth's) life. "I am come that you may have life, and have life more abundantly — the earth is the Lord's, and the fullness thereof."

SATISFIED WITH GOD ALONE

I Am Come

"I am come." Do you see this now? "I am come." I am now 'come' into your awareness, tangibly felt, tangibly happening in and as your consciousness; I am now your truthful identity evidenced. You are now *consciously aware* of this *I* that I am 'happening', being your presence, your identity. Now — as you *remain* in me and I in you — you witness truthful life and the more abundant fruits of it, with "twelve baskets full left over".

We are not speaking of belief's idea of an abundantly truthful life. Belief has only the faculty of material discernment — its idea of 'good' is objective, conceptual, temporary, material good, existing at a certain time in a certain place, and occupying a certain amount of space. We are speaking of the more abundantly fulfilled *spiritual* being — filled with *spiritual* awareness, *spiritual* life, *spiritual* body, *spiritual* family, *spiritual* home, *spiritual* wealth, *spiritual* love and relationship (the *relationship of oneness* . . . ah, let this be seeded in your awareness; it is the answer to life's every problem), *spiritual* activity, *spiritual* talent, *spiritual* business, *spiritual* customer, client, student, friend, *spiritual* intelligence and wisdom, *spiritual* safety and security, *spiritual* happiness, joy and freedom.

Here is the entire secret of the more abundant life — the awakened life, the spiritual life — that for which we've eternally searched: When it is truly realized that being and experience (earth, universe) is *spiritual* not material, then all we ever seek is greater spiritual fulfillment — greater or more illumined or magnified spiritual awareness filling us, overflowing and bursting forth from us. We seek for spirit to so completely fill our conscious senses that wherever we are and whatever we observe as the objective mind experience, it is filled and overflowing with living spiritual awareness, not matter.

The objective in and of and for its own self is unreal to us now. Only spirit is, and we know it. What appears to be, is not what *is*. Only God is, only spirit is. Our focus until now has been on, and believed to be, what appears as formation — the objective, the named, the forms of life in and of their own selves. But we are waking up. Spirit is filling our senses and because sense is experience, spirit is being revealed as our truthful spiritual world — harmonious, whole and free. Like the aperture of a camera opening to allow in more light, our awareness is opening and being flooded with the light of truth. We are becoming aware of our entire being — mind, body and earth — illumined and visible as spirit, its truth. We are becoming aware of our perfectly tangible and visible reality, the image and likeness of the spiritual consciousness *we are now filled with and being* experienced as all formation (as earth and universe) — the oneness and omnipresence of being *being its experience.*

That truthful experience — spiritual experience — is evermore revealed as being full of good: good and permanent health, wealth, love, happiness, home, family; and purposeful, expressive talent whether it be 'named' menial or something that changes the world. It doesn't make any difference whether we are a housewife or husband, a kitchen assistant, a gardener or a truck driver, or whether we discover a talent bursting through us as a musician, a painter, a sculptor, a city planner, a home or office or bridge builder, a computer innovator or a peace emissary. However it appears to be as each individual's talent and expression, we know it and express it as God-being — God expressing in and as experience, serving our world and the people populating it, whether 'our world' consists of just our family or neighborhood, or thousands or millions of people. All these 'quantities' and 'measures' are of the mind alone and not of God. God is one and omnipresent, and we know it; we live it *as and for God alone.*

As we seek and are satisfied with God alone, our health, relationship, home, money, success, business and world is filled *with* God, is itself the formation of God, the image and likeness of oneness, harmony and wholeness, the life more abundant, more fulfilling, more harmonious, peaceful, true and in union. We experience this truth as and through the belief and thought-devoid mind. We are beholders of truth as earth — "heaven as in earth". Through the emptiness, spaciousness, stillness and receptivity of being, we behold the earth (formation as the image and likeness) as God's, "and the fullness thereof".

Wherever You Place Your Awareness, There I Am

And so realize, wherever you place your awareness, there *I am.* You are forever and only observing the very center of you, your state of awareness — whatever that state is. It is actually the omnipresence of *I itself, God itself,* the experience of which is all a matter of and activity of *aware-*

ness. So the only question we ever need ask of ourselves is what is happening as our awareness, our sense of consciousness?

Where is your awareness — on and in and being spirit as all, or on and in and being matter as all? What proportion of your hourly awareness is spiritual versus material? And most importantly, what degree of your awareness is filled with spirit felt happening within, feeding your senses, lifting, freeing and expressing as you? How much are you hanging onto material sense, believing it to be an entity of its own self, judging it, desiring better and more of it, making effort for it, finding yourself still satisfied with its attainment and disappointed at its lack or failure?

You and I of our own selves have nothing truthful to offer the world — nothing — anymore than the vine pulled out of the earth has anything of its truth to offer the world. Listen to the Master, "I of mine own self am nothing . . . for without me [my abiding in you, my being the very life, expression and world of you] ye can do nothing". The Master makes it clear: we are nothing and we have nothing if we are not "abid[ing] in *me* and *I* in you", if we are 'out of God'. "If a man abide not in me, he is cast forth as a branch, and is withered; and men gather them, and cast them into the fire, and they are burned."

But we are awakening to truth. Our awareness is constantly on God as all, filled with the living awareness of the presence and goodness of God as the only. *And we devote ever more of our every twenty-four hours to stopping, being still and open and receptive, feeling I, God happening within.* Now we are and have everything to offer the world — in fact, limitless and omnipresent resource at our very fingertips at every moment to 'feed' every apparent need. "He that abideth in me, and I in him, the same bringeth forth much fruit . . . Herein is my Father glorified, that ye bear much fruit."

The Selfish Self

Devoid of constant conscious awareness of God being all, and devoid of God actually felt living within to the point of *being* the being and world we are, everything about us — our belief, judgment, idea, desire, effort and satisfaction — is an existence of self without truth. Jesus calls it the *selfish self.* It wants for itself, it makes effort for itself, it is satisfied by the degree it has attained the world's goods and secured them for itself and its immediate family. It is satisfied as long as its body is healthy, its finances are stable, its home is fulfilling, safe and secure, its neighborhood is nice, and its prospects are firm. When the selfish self is itself satisfied, it can look over the fence at its neighbor and see dissatisfaction, lack, suffering or pain and still feel personally satisfied: Thank God, I'm okay, even though my neighbor is not and many, many more in my world are not. The selfish self hasn't taken literally — or hasn't yet heard — that our neighbor is God because there is none else, that we ourselves are also God, and therefore, that we must treat our neighbor as ourselves: as God, the one being, the one presence, the one truth. "Thou shalt love the Lord thy God with all thy heart, and with all thy soul, and with all thy strength, and with all thy mind; and thy neighbour as thyself."

Those of a slighty more awakened awareness begin to devote at least a portion of their time to helping, comforting and supplying others. There are many beautifully caring and giving people in the world, some devoting their entire lives to charitable causes at home or overseas. It's a beautiful thing. Yet, these devoted souls are still firmly operating in the realm of belief — helping those who need to be saved from the bad pairs of opposites plaguing them and supplying them with the good. *At its own level* it is a wonderful and tangible devotion — perhaps the highest form of existence in the pairs of opposites, devoting their lives not to themselves and their own alone, but to all.

But when an individual awakens to truth, he awakens to *God as all* — not God 'in' persons or God 'in' earth, but God *as* all being and experience — the *whole* of being and the *whole* of experience. He awakens to the one omnipresence of being and experience, forever whole, complete, and perfect. Omnipresence has no 'in' versus 'out'. Omnipresence *is,* and is omnipresent at every point of infinity at the same time. This awakened realization is itself the miracle of health, supply, harmony and peace as all.

The awakened soul does care very much about others *except in a truthful way.* Our care and devotion is to God *for God alone,* for God revealed as reality — heaven as earth — then witnessed as the image-and-likeness formation emerging through the foggy sense of collective material sense. All intelligence, wisdom, life, wealth, food, home, safety, protection and freedom we find ourselves ever more able to 'give' is that which we realize is already and forever the truth of all being, place and condition. In spiritual consciousness, we are the very being of spiritual fulfillment witnessed as the abundant, unstoppable and indestructible forms (the image and likeness of the truth we feel happening as and through us) witnessed as the abundant forms of good we discover filling and overflowing the branches of our life.

The One Substance and Form; The True Purpose of Being

The only substance and form we have for our world, the only intelligence and wisdom, the only truth we *have* to give our world, is the truth felt happening within. No truth felt happening within is unembodied, devoid of the form of itself as experience. None of God *realized* (felt) is unembodied, unmanifest, undemonstrated or invisible. The more we feel truth actually happening as our being and the more we live and rely on that experienced truth alone, the more forms of good we discover we *have*, not only for ourselves (our 'own' lives are very quickly satisfied when we live by, and rely on, God alone) but for our world. This is the only true purpose of being — to ceaselessly give and serve of our spiritual substance and its formation that we discover filling our branches. "A fruit tree does not consume its own fruit."

God already *is* all being and everything everywhere of the world and universe (experience). "The earth is the Lord's, and the fullness thereof." Remember, *only God is*, and so as quickly as we start living by and as *only God is*, is as quickly as truth is witnessed experientially. Our living by God *actually experienced*, and our total reliance on nothing but the actual God experience, reveal the God-experienced world — the heavenly world, the world "as it is in heaven" before belief and thought disguise the truth of experience.

Indeed, the revealing of truth is "quick and sharp and powerful" because truth is the only actual presence, the only actual form and reality and the only actual visibility and tangibility. Only God is; therefore, only God itself is visibility and tangibility. Can you hear that? If so, your entire life is to change and change rapidly. And so we witness that one and only truth quickly visible and tangible as our reality, and the reality of those who come to us for clear vision. It is as if our spiritual consciousness dispels the fog of material awareness, not only for ourselves but for those who come to us for it to be dispelled.

It is perfectly visible and real — the good, the bountiful, the true, the invariable and unconditional formation of God as experience. And so you see that the only love is love felt happening within, the only intelligence, and joy and laughter, humor, beauty and bounty is truth felt happening within.

Truthful Business

The only time we're truthful in practice, business or teaching is when we practice, sell or teach only that which we find our branches full of as we *rely on, and are satisfied with, God alone,* literally and tangibly *being* everything we are and everything we have. We *are* nothing and we *have* nothing of truth, if we attempt to be something or offer something of our own selves and by our own effort.

We do not offer a practice or run a business or give a teaching for *worldly* gain, recognition and satisfaction. That would be like the sun seeking and being satisfied with patches of light on the wall. The sun is satisfied with *being* itself alone *and then — because it is satisfied with itself alone* — witnesses as many patches of light on as many walls as it wishes to witness. We do not seek or make effort for worldly money, human recognition or industry awards. We do not work for money or other of the world's gain and profit; we work for the *giving* of the talent we find ourselves with, the fruits, the serving of people and the giving to people, organizations and the world, knowing that all being and all world is God and nothing else or different or less.

We *be* and *serve* and *give* and *share as* the presence and being of God, *to* and *for* God. We do not operate in, or with, or for matter. It may seem as if we do, but we know better. We know the truth of that which appears to be. We have awakened to our *spiritual* identity and the *spiritual* identity of all being and world. There is nothing but spirit, and we know it now; therefore our fulfillment of being is ever-expanding spiritual awareness, and our fulfillment of activity is ever-expanding spiritual giving, serving and sharing — inclusive of the abundant formations of God as mind — God pouring 'through' our spiritual (matter-free) consciousness as its image and likeness formation.

SATISFIED WITH GOD ALONE

Listen to that. The only time we are truthful in activity of any sort is when we recognize that every being in our world is the very presence of God herself-himself, and when we realize that they are in our world so that we can serve God, serve truth, bless, give, share; not take, not gain, not persuade people to buy the particular worldly items or service or treatment we have to offer, and to pay us for those items with their hard-earned worldly money, leaving them that amount depleted of their wealth. No. Release all as God, and let God be.

You find your experience full of the good and plenty of God — infinity and omnipresence as its image and likeness as form — as long as you seek nothing but God for God, and as long as you are satisfied with God alone. Truly and deeply think about what this means. Take it deep into meditation day in and day out, and then you quickly discover that "[When] his delight is in the law of the Lord; and in his law doth he meditate day and night . . . he shall be like a tree planted by the rivers of water, that bringeth forth his fruit in his season; his leaf also shall not wither; and whatsoever he doeth shall prosper".

Get on with *being spiritual being, being the omnipresence of spiritual being* — thoroughly and all-inclusively — giving, serving and sharing of your talent and all the forms of fruit filling your branches. Then you never again need be concerned about 'success' and plentiful 'prosperity' because "the silver is mine, and the gold is mine, says the Lord". As you get on with being 'me, the Lord consciousness' which is forever giving and serving of itself, you find yourself with all that God — infinity and omnipresence — is and has at your disposal.

The Divine Appointment

Every meeting with another is a divine meeting. Nothing at any time is coincidence, but is God witnessed — omniscience and omnipresence witnessed as experience. There are no 'accidental' meetings in omniscience, nor anyone or anything but divinity in omnipresence. When you meet another, it is a divine appointment, whether you simply pass on the street or meet for what belief describes as a 'reason'. "The only thing that ever presents itself to you is God."

The only reason for meeting another is the one spiritual reason, and that is always to know the truth of the 'other' and to give, serve and share *of* truth if and as applicable to the moment. As we live by and rely on the actual God experience day and night, we find ourselves with plenty of fruit for the world. Indeed the daily hours devoted to stillness and silence in which we feel God actually happening within are abundantly fruitful. The more we know that our purpose and the fruit filling our life is for giving, not for self-consuming, the more and more fruit we discover ourselves with. It is the constant giving, purging, flowing forth of all we have that reveals ever more. "Give, and it shall be given unto you; good measure, pressed down, and shaken together, and running over, shall men [the world] give into you."

Give of Your Particular Talent and Fruit

Whatever your talent is, give of it, and whatever fruits are populating your branches, give of them. Start here and now, no matter if belief believes you have little or no talent yet to give, or little or no fruit yet to offer. That belief is false — one hundred percent false. You are and have infinity, and the omnipresence of it, this very minute. Do not believe appearance. "Judge not by the appearance." The truth is that you are and have the whole of visible, tangible and perfectly real infinity and an omnipresence of it *this minute*.

No longer look or believe materially; look and believe only spiritually. Look with your incorporeal faculties — your truthful faculties — no longer with your corporeal *sense* of faculty, which is 'dark' and unable to see that which *is*. As you look incorporeally, you see the universe of incorporeal infinity and omnipresence as one with you ("I and the Father are one") — as the very you you are ("I am that I am") — forever at hand, forever tangibly available at your fingertips, with which to freely and ceaselessly give to, serve and 'feed' the world.

Whatever we have to serve with, whatever our practice is, our teaching is, our product, service or treatment is, our vineyard consists of, our storehouses consist of — *serve of it*. It doesn't make any difference what it looks like; this is just mind imagery. What it really is, is God, the infinity and omnipresence of all that God is — the earth, the formation of experience, filled with the goodness of God, the holy ground we stand on (the consciousness we are).

I give to you all that I have this hour, this day, this meeting with you. This is our way of being. We constantly ask, how can I give? How can I serve? We recognize every person, place and thing as God, as Buddha, as Christ. We constantly ask of ourselves, how can I serve this person, this group, this day, not what can get from you or from it. *How can I give, serve, share?*

The More We Live Truthfully, The More Forms of Truth We Have

It is easy to realize that the 'more' the sun shines, the more light fills the earth. In this way, the more we live as truthful, spiritual being — our business being the Father's business ("I am about my Father's business"), the constant living from within-out by the feeling of the presence happening — the more we *have* of the fruits, the forms, of truth with which to give and serve.

The more being and its form expand — which are one and the same thing: the expansion of spiritual awareness, the ever greater spiritualizing of awareness and activity — the more of heaven is visible and functioning as earth (or *visibly functioning* as earth). The more of truth we *be*, and the more we *give*, the ever more we *have*. We could say the more the vineyard knows its truth, stays rooted in that truth, and lets *truth itself be* its every expression and satisfaction, the more 'success, fruitage and fulfillment of purpose' it experiences. All we have to do is look out at the breathtaking acres of the wine regions of Italy or France or Napa, California, every branch of every vine abundant with foliage and fruit, to witness what happens when being is rooted in truth, transparent, a nothingness of its own self — the presence of God unhindered by belief and thought — beholding the free and bountiful flow of fulfillment of form, always with "twelve baskets full left over".

We behold objectified abundance filling our branches of form — the forms of individual life and each aspect of life. We know the abundance is for giving, not for self-consumption, just like the vineyard. The fruitage I witness filling my life is not 'my' fruit; it is God's fruit for God's purpose as the fulfillment of formation — that of feeding the world. "I am the light of the world; I am the life, the food, the wine, the water." As I stay rooted in truth, I indeed discover that the truthful identity I *am*, literally *is* and *has* infinity and the omnipresence of infinity. And because being *is* experience — the awareness *I am being* is the experience *I witness happening as me* — I find the forms of infinity and omnipresence ever at hand, real and practical as forms of love, intelligence, wisdom, health, supply, idea, service, solution, harmony, and fulfillment of purpose. A new reality has emerged and it is as if the old, false reality never really existed at all.

All these forms of good and fulfillment are the "things added unto you", to paraphrase the Master. But this experience is only yours and mine as we empty ourselves of belief and as we take no thought for our sense of life. We have to know and then live truthful identity, and that truthful identity is God alone *for God alone* — incorporeal being *for incorporeal satisfaction alone; God for God satisfaction alone. Then* the *forms* of truthful being we are being, living and are completely satisfied with, become ever more richly evident, filling our life.

The One Truth

There is one actualized truth of you, and that is God happening as you. Only the mind fragments oneness into millions or billions — the "many members". Belief believes the many members *themselves* to be real. It believes these forms of objectified self and world to be what self *is* and *has*. No. Truth is one and is the one truth — your one truth, and mine. Therefore, you are one, and that one is God — infinity, omnipresence and eternality. The only actualized evidence of self, the only actually demonstrated and evident form of self, is self experienced, felt happening within. No other experience of self is truth. No other.

Here within, where truth is felt happening, is my only truthful being, my only truthful body, my only truthful everything-of-life, and the infinity and omnipresence of it, inclusive of the infinity and omnipresence of the formation of it.

I now release the idea of this body needing my thought, my attention, of this physically-sensed body being my truth of body. I release the idea that I am responsible for it and its health, its supply, its purpose and its fulfillment.

SATISFIED WITH GOD ALONE

I release the idea that dollars are my wealth. I let go of the idea that 'outer' people and conditions are my opportunity and my supply.

I give up the idea that my spouse or partner, my son and my daughter, is my family. God is my family and because God is one, onness itself is my family.

I release the idea that the world of matter is, of its own self, real or truthful. Only God is; therefore only unconditioned God formation is real and truthful.

The truth (including the image and likeness of truth being all form) of body, relationship, family, home, money, talent, expression and its fulfillment is sitting right here, right now, perfectly whole, joyous, free, infinite, omnipresent and eternal. But belief's misperception clouds truthful form from experience. It is as if belief in form, being an entity in and of its own self, throws a veil over the very presence of truth, making what actually is (and is fully manifest and perfectly real and tangible) appear to be somehow discordant, lacking, limited, injured, diseased, disgruntled, unsafe, insecure, uncertain.

But right here and now, as that discordant belief is experienced, the whole and perfect form is present, needing not a single grain more health, supply, love, happiness, joy, purpose or freedom. *Spiritual being has nothing to demonstrate*. It already is whole and fulfilled. It is the whole of spirit existing in and as the spiritual universe, the universe of oneness and omnipresence. Its entire objective purpose of being is to give and share of its infinity, freely and fearlessly, knowing it is and has the whole of infinity and all its good and perfect form, fully and simultaneously existent at every point of itself.

Do you see? With belief and thought removed, *truth* is immediately visible and tangible *because truth is the only actual existence*. With belief and thought removed, there truth is — the truth of the very world with which we are familiar and all its detail.

The True Vine

The one unconditioned (truthful) world *is* the formation of the one unconditioned (truthful) mind. As mind functions free and devoid of false belief, and of false thought about its formations being something of their own selves, then unconditioned, truthful form is experienced.

This is the true vine of which Jesus speaks. "I am the true vine, ye are the branches." *I* — the true or master consciousness, pure God consciousness, the very presence of infinity and omnipresence itself, free of false belief and thought, with nothing in it but God, spirit and truth — *am the true vine. Ye* — the formation of experience — *are the branches.* If you abide in me (truth) and I (truth itself) abide in you (God felt happening within), then the branches of experience are full and fruitful and cannot be anything less. If you do *not* abide in me, and experience me abiding in you, the branches of experience are not only barren, but *cannot be fruitful* anymore than the vine can be fruitful if it is not rooted in earth.

You are the vine, and your 'branches' are the individual aspects of your experience, each aspect another branch. The question is, are you being a truthful or untruthful vine? Being a truthful or untruthful vine is all about the activity of your awareness. Are you constantly *spiritualizing* your awareness, or are you still living in and of and by material awareness?   As you stay rooted in truthful identity ("as you abide in me") and as you live by God felt happening within as your actual lifeblood; supply-blood; love-blood; peace-, harmony- and fulfillment-blood ("and I abide in you"), you are being a truthful vine. Then the result is infallible: "The same bringeth forth much fruit . . . Herein is my Father glorified, that ye bear much fruit." Your branches fill with fruit and an abundance of it, the fruits of formed health, opportunity, money, loving relationship, peace and harmony.

As "you abide in me, and I in you", you simply *behold* — not 'make' or labor or strive for — but *behold* (just like the vine observing the activity of its branches) the activity of your branches filling with the buds, leaves, flowers and fruits of good, purpose and freedom in all forms. You observe as and through the belief- and thought-devoid mind — the true vine — needing nothing and desiring nothing in the awareness that all already *is.* You have discovered the secret of truth: know that only God is, be still and behold the activity of God happening within, that activity then pushing through as objectified experience as the "image and likeness" of the fruits and the good of your branches of life.

And so your attention remains within — not 'out there' — but constantly within or constantly coming back to your withinness, seeking truth happening, seeking the *feeling* of truth happening. As you make this your way of life, your way of health, wealth, family, home, business; as you make it your way of giving, serving, sharing; as you make it your one way of being and purpose of existence ("I am about my Father's business"), and as you daily observe the formations of and through the unconditioned mind, *then* you behold ever more fruit and ever more opportunity to give of it; share of it; supply, help, comfort and fulfill with it.

Those branches are your relationship, your family, you home, your neighborhood, your work, your finances, your opportunity; the substance you are able to give the world, the talent, the wisdom, the life more abundant. "I am come" — I am being experienced — so that the 'vine' you are is full of life, full of love; full of all forms of supply and wholeness, harmony, safety and happiness; the all-inclusive, more abundant experience.

As truth becomes your actual way of life, watch how quickly and continuously your branches are filled with abundant fruit. By the degree that you remain belief-less and thought-less (meaning judgment-less, desire-less, opinion-less, idea-less), by the degree that you remain consciously in God awareness and neutral about that which seems to be, simply observing each day's imagery but remaining unattached and uninterested in it of its own self, you witness good and tangible, purposeful and rewarding fruitage with "twelve baskets full left over".

Imagine the Vine Observing Itself

Can you imagine the vine looking out at its branches — without a single concern, a single desire, a single need — knowing that its very presence and form *is* and *has* the entirety of God, infinity and omnipresence, *being* it and pouring through it as unconditional and infallible fruitage? It knows its true identity. It *is* the life it feels happening. Its life is not the trunk or the branches, its physical form. The trunk and branches, the buds, leaves, blossoms and fruitage filling-full the branches are simply the objectified experience of the infinity and omnipresence that is God as it. "If you see me, you see the Father." "I [my entire being and experience] and the Father are one." Therefore its poverty or its abundance is entirely dependent on that vine knowing the truth, staying rooted in that truth (earth), and then, with no belief and no thought, simply observing the consciously experienced activity of truth pushing through as and into all objectively witnessed good, whether we call that good health or healing, good relationship, peace, business, money, home or world. It doesn't make any difference what belief names it. Forget the 'outer' form and its name. Simply observe God as objectified formation without thought, without judgment, without desire, without effort.

Then watch how quickly your world buds, blossoms and fruits as good and fulfilling forms of experience. Watch how safe and secure your world becomes. Watch how joyous and free, how much opportunity blossoms wherever you are. Watch how the liberty of experience is witnessed, how the body changes, how much new energy and purpose you discover yourself possessing.

The Miracle of Truthful Body

You never again have to take thought for the body the moment you know it to be the presence of God and under God's government. "Your body is the temple of the living God." As you stop taking thought for the body, you discover a miraculous thing taking place: you find yourself naturally making different choices — different food choices, different relaxation choices, different activity choices. The truthful body lives you as you live by God felt happening within. "I live, yet not I, Christ [God, truth, spirit] lives my life." God felt happening lives your life, and you begin to feel the impulse to make a different food choice or activity choice, and you follow it. It is not the impulse of something you 'had better do', but is a feeling of desire to do it. It is your fulfillment, your truthful preference. It is a joy, not a burden.

Never desire anything for the form of body in and of its own self, but realize it as the "temple of the living God" and live it by God felt happening within. Then watch the miracle of body that follows, including the miracle of healing if the body is currently sick or diseased, tired or depleted. There is no such thing as sick, diseased, tired or depleted God, and you'll quickly witness that truth by the degree you live in and by and rely on God felt happening within as the body's life, vitality, beauty and youthfulness.

The Miracle of Truthful Opportunity and Success

Do not desire opportunity; do not desire more success and then run off into the world trying to learn how to achieve that success. Don't do that because everything which you can desire is first of all nothing of its own self, but is also temporal, weak, and will soon wither and crumble.

Anything we can name, any form or quantity, of its own self, is nothing — without law or principle to uphold it, sustain it, make it real and lasting. It of its own self has no substance, no intelligence, no presence and no formation to maintain it and make it true.

If you want to know what true, successful being is; or true, successful practice or business is; true art, true creativity, true expression, true product, service or treatment is; true teaching, true giving, true charity is — whatever it is we individually find ourselves with a talent to do — then withdraw all belief, all desire, all thought, withdraw to your withinness and *live there.* Trust that God felt happening within *is itself* — do you hear that? — *is itself* the infinity, the omnipresence, the almighty one power and abundant form of you and everything of your expression. When and as you continue to daily, even hourly, *feel God happening within* you spontaneously *are being* and *have* the whole kingdom of God as talent, as expression, and as the rich fruits of success. Once you have God as *tangibly felt experience*, you have all. You have the whole embodiment of God — fully visible, tangible, manifest and already demonstrated here and now, infinite, omnipresent and unstoppable. You *have* it; you *have* the whole of heaven.

You watch, then, how you begin to witness fulfillment. And you begin to witness it quickly by the degree that you can stay witnessing without belief, without thought, without desire, without curiosity and without disappointment or frustration, asking, Where is it? Why isn't it here yet? Never do that; never again become entangled in believing that something, anything, of outer appearance is a reality, an entity, an importance in and of its own self. That is judgment; that is belief; that is taking thought all over again. Do not do that.

Instead, peer through, or experience through and as, the thought-devoid mind, the rested, peaceful, spacious, non-thinking mind, the unconditioned mind. Then watch how truthful activity and form blossom — just like the vine witnessing buds suddenly appearing here, there, and everywhere on its branches. Buds push through all over the branches, blossoming into leaves, flowers, color, fragrance, each the expression of joy, happiness, purpose and freedom tangibly happening. Then the fruit pushes through, develops and ripens, and with that ripening comes the harvest time — the giving, the fulfillment of the vine's purpose.

In this way, we too observe our branches of truth, fed by God, felt happening within, blossom and fruit, and as soon as we witness the ripe fruit we begin giving it, serving it, sharing it. We discover, like the vine, that "the bees come uninvited". We watch true health and wealth and love and peace and harmony coming uninvited. We watch customers, clients, patients, friends, neighbors, even strangers, coming uninvited for the experience of the light we are, the love and joy and peace we are, and which we ceaselessly (always silently, secretly, effortlessly, impersonally) radiate.

The Miracle of Multiplication

As we stay rooted in truth, as we live by the actual experience of God felt happening within, as we are satisfied with nothing less each day, and as we ceaselessly give and serve and share of resultant fruits, we witness something miraculous: the *multiplication* of good.

Giving, serving and sharing of our fruits *in truthful consciousness* — the consciousness of oneness, infinity and omnipresence — *is itself* the multiplication of form. Expressing, pouring out, giving without a 'hold' on that being given, but in the awareness of the infinity and omnipresence of all form, *is the revealing* of ever more of infinity. *The giving of the fruit is the multiplication of the fruit.* It is the same one act, one presence, one form, one expression — all infinite and omnipresent, therefore never, not even for a minute, able to run dry or run out. Only our awareness can run dry or run out. But keep awareness *and experience* firmly rooted in truth and there is never a reason to run dry or run out.

SATISFIED WITH GOD ALONE

Three Main Aspects of Being

And so we have three main aspects of being: Firstly, being aware that only God is; secondly, feeling God happening within and knowing the feeling or experience *itself* to be the only true life, substance and form; and thirdly, the giving, serving and sharing of all that we are and have.

God is for giving, not taking. Truth is for giving, not getting.

Truth exists as I, and I exist for that which I can give. Therefore, I live and move and have my being in and as and for God, continually radiating, being and giving of my truth — its color, its fragrance, and its fruits.

I am the true vine. . .

9

Wherever You Are, There God Is

❦

Wherever you are, there God is. Whether belief believes you are in a physical place or in a thought, there God is because there is no place but the one omni-place, "holy ground", God. There is no inner versus outer, no physical versus mental, no world versus heaven. There is *only* God, omnipresence, omniplace, the 'place' where the whole of the infinite exists fully manifest, fully visible and forever fully available as the image and likeness of God, good, fulfillment of being, place and condition as experience — for there is none but God.

"And Jesus said, If those who teach you say to you, 'See, the kingdom is in heaven,' then the birds of the heaven will precede you. If they say to you, 'It is in the sea,' then the fish of the sea will precede you. But the kingdom is within you and it is without you. If you know yourselves, then you will be known and you will know that you are the sons of the living

Father. But if you do not know yourselves, then you are in poverty and you are poverty."

Wherever your awareness is, there is the center of you — there is your state of awareness. And because there is no 'unembodied' awareness, there is the embodiment, the formation, of your state of awareness. We forever observe and experience our own state of awareness. We cannot escape it because consciousness is all; consciousness is what God is, what being and universe is. Consciousness is forever whole, complete, pure, vividly aware of the whole of itself existent at every point of infinity. Consciousness is God, and nothing can lessen or diminish or cloud or personalize God. Nothing of God is hidden or invisible or intangible or unmanifest or undemonstrated, and because God is consciousness and God is all, your consciousness and the consciousness of all, is God consciousness. There is none else. But there are degrees of *awareness* of consciousness, of God being all, of God, spirit being that which *I am* — the "many mansions in my Father's house".

"I Am That I Am"

"I am that I am," but my individual *awareness* of that which I am *is* my formed sense of experience — my tangible, seemingly-real experience — because no awareness is unembodied. You, I and all beings *are* and *have* the whole of God consciousness this minute and eternally. Your consciousness *is* the whole of God — "I and the Father are one. . . I am ever with you, and all that I have is yours". God is omnipresent and indivisible; therefore your consciousness *is* and *has* and is this minute *being* the infinite, omnipresent, indivisible whole of the kingdom, never for a second capable of being less than the whole. But your and my individual *degree of awareness* of the whole of God (spirit being what being is) is what determines the degree of individual God experience.

We never lack God. We lack only God *awareness.* Our mind, body and world — and every breath and grain of it — never lacks God. It *is* God and *only* God. If it lacks any good or freedom of experience whatsoever, it lacks only God *awareness.* The moment we have God awareness, we have God experience. Awareness and experience are one. This is why we must never seek God for anything we believe we need — that which we believe needs healing, harmonizing, prospering or pacifying. We already have the whole of God, and because God is all, all experience is this very minute nothing but God experience — full, harmonious, peaceful, joyous, purposeful and free. If we do not see it, we must simply *lose unawareness.* As we lose unawareness, we see clearly, and seeing clearly is experiencing clearly.

The Omnipresence of Withinness

Withinness is omnipresence, not physical, not local. Withinness is *purity* of awareness — *spiritual consciousness* with no matter in it whatsoever, *oneness* with no 'other' in it whatsoever. When your awareness is pure, omnipresent, one, then you experience that oneness as the image and likeness of itself as formation (the world). God, which is unconditioned and unconditional, is experienced as and through the unconditioned mind as unconditioned form: whole and harmonious body, place and condition.

As you 'turn within' you may have a sense of taking awareness from the 'outer' to the 'inner'. It seems as if there is a physical place called the 'outer' versus another or deeper physical place called the 'inner', a personal and local 'you' with both an 'inner' and 'outer' experience. But no such physical place or places exist. The only 'place' is omnipresence — omni-place. Every 'place' is a place of consciousness, and because consciousness is eternally the whole of itself, omnipresent and indivisible, every place of awareness is in fact, and consists of, the whole of God fully present, manifest and demonstrated — and fully visibly so. "I and the Father are one. . . I will never leave you." I never *can* leave you because I and 'you' are one, not separate, not two, but the one omnipresent and indivisible infinity of pure and whole God consciousness being all. There is none else; therefore I cannot 'be' somewhere 'else' nor experience anything 'different'.

"The place whereon you stand [where your awareness is, wherever that is at any moment] is holy ground [fully manifest and visible God]." Every master tells us that the kingdom of God is within — and you now understand what 'within' means. So although there may seem to be a physical change of awareness from the outer to the inner, actually, wherever awareness is, is the very center and infinity of omnipresence, omniplace. Wherever your awareness is, there is the omnipresence of the 'ingredients of your belief, your sense, your idea, your opinion. But the miracle is that despite your belief, sense, idea and opinion, what truly is there is God and only God. We simply have a low degree of *awareness* of the fact, the truth, that God is all.

Your consciousness is God — God consciousness — God itself, the whole kingdom of God, fully manifest, complete, whole. Because of this truth, you can take or place your awareness anywhere in infinity and *there* God is. What you believe you are aware of, is not what actually is. Only God is; therefore wherever you are — whatever you are being aware of — actually, despite appearance, is God and the whole of God. Tell me, therefore, what could you possibly need or want? What could possibly be in need of healing, improving, pacifying, harmonizing, prospering? Absolutely nothing. Only awareness needs; God already is. The only 'he, she, it, condition or place' you are ever observing, experiencing or thinking about is God, and the whole of God, because there is none else. And because God already is, and is infallibly the whole of itself at every point of infinity at the same time, nothing can or ever could need something 'from' God, or need 'more' of God. All 'he, she, it, condition or place' is already the infinity and omnipresence of God.

And — hear this closely — God is *one*, already fully manifest and demonstrated, forever perfectly visible, tangible, real and therefore wholly practical. Never fall for the belief that God has to be 'demonstrated' or somehow 'made manifest' or — by some clever manipulation of mind or thought — 'changed' or 'brought through' from intangible to tangible, invisible to visible. No! Let's hear it again: God is *the only*, God is *one*, not two. God is not invisible, needing to be made visible by a feat of mind which, if not achieved, leaves one barren of God in practical experience. God is one and wholly visible, wholly tangible, forever manifest and already demonstrated for you.

Free Yourself of Old and Incorrect Teachings and Belief

Again and again and again we have to drum oneness into our awareness so that old and incorrect orthodox and even metaphysical teaching and belief is washed out of us: God is omnipresence, and omnipresence cannot and does not have different departments within it — an invisible versus visible department, an intangible versus tangible department, an unmanifest versus manifest department and a still-to-be demonstrated versus a demonstrated department. Think. How can omnipresence — which is the *whole of God* existent at every point of infinity at the same time, leaving nothing 'else' but the whole, no 'other' left over, no room for a different department or activity, a different form or experience — leave a part of place of itself (you or me) barren of the whole or even a grain of God?

How can that which is the *only*, the *infinite* and the *omnipresent* be barren of itself 'here' or 'there' or at 'this moment' or 'that moment' or until some kind of mind or thought magic is achieved to change absence into presence, invisible into visible, unmanifest into manifest? Such belief is utter nonsense having no truth foundation to it whatsoever, no law or principle to uphold it whatsoever. Unfortunately though, it runs rampant among the majority of truth students. Let us change that this day.

A Divided Consciousness

If we have a divided consciousness — if we believe in an inner versus an outer, an invisible versus a visible, an intangible versus a tangible, an unmanifest versus a manifest, or an undemonstrated versus a demonstrated experience — then no matter how much truth we know and how much of God we are feeling happening within, it will not be, and cannot be *evident* as experience. Remember what we heard Jesus tell us at the beginning of this chapter: "The kingdom is within you and it is without you. If you know yourselves [know the oneness and all-inclusiveness of God as I], then you will be known [all good is known, perfectly and visibly evident] and you will know that you are the sons of the living Father. But if you do not know yourselves [if you believe in two-ness or different departments of being, the unmanifest versus the manifest], then you are in poverty and you are poverty [you are being your own absence of God]."

It is a hard truth to hear, especially when we are in pain and suffering. But also it is the most liberating and quickly freeing truth to hear. The only lack of God (good) *in* actual experience is a lack of God awareness *as* actual experience. When we live with the belief that there is God 'and' us, God 'and' experience, spirit 'and' matter, the incorporeal 'and' the corporeal, then *we ourselves* are being the veil of false sense that disguises the perfectly good and whole mind, body and earth from experience. Only God is, and because God is all, all experience this minute and eternally is God experience, God *being* itself alone, heaven *being* earth, the one presence: omnipresence and none else. But false sense — false belief — *is* false experience. "[If] you are in poverty, you are [being] poverty." We are having a false corporeal or earthly *sense* of that which is one hundred percent incorporeal — a material *sense* of that which is one hundred percent spirit and spiritual — and believing it. "A man's foes shall be they of his own household."

Belief Is *Divided Consciousness*

"Every house divided against itself shall not stand." What is a house divided against itself? Belief — it is *belief* in appearance to be something 'real' in and of its own self. Only *belief* believes in an inner versus an outer, an invisible versus a visible, an intangible versus a tangible, an unmanifest versus a manifest or an undemonstrated versus a demonstrated, and that belief is the divided house. You have an awareness of God 'and' an awareness of something other than God. Belief is unreal, yet always forms its unreality as sensed experience. There's the division — *self division*, the house divided against itself.

This unwitting division in awareness is the entire mistake made by the non-dual and the absolute teachings, and the reason for their inability to heal. They misunderstand Buddha's term "maya" — "illusion" — to mean that there is an inner that is truthful and an outer that has nothing to do with truth. But listen to the words of masters, not believers. Masters throughout history have shown the world, and still do today, that the so-called outer is in fact nothing but the full presence of God, just as the so-called 'inner' is:

Wherever You Are, There God Is

Make the inner the outer, and make the outer
the inner.

Jesus the Christ

The kingdom is within you and it is without you.

Jesus the Christ

There is neither seer nor seeing nor seen.
There is but one reality, changeless, formless
and absolute. How can it be divided?

Shankara

No matter what a deluded man may think he is
perceiving, he is really seeing God and nothing
else but God. He sees mother-of-pearl and imagines
it is silver. He sees God and imagines it is the universe.

Shankara

For the wise all 'things' are wiped away.

Gautama the Buddha

The fact is, there is only one world, there are not
two worlds. People think there are two worlds by
the activity of their own minds [belief]. If they
could get rid of these false judgments and keep
their minds pure with the light of wisdom, then
they would see only one world and that world
bathed in the light of wisdom.

Gautama the Buddha

SATISFIED WITH GOD ALONE

The truth is that *all is one;* there is no inner versus outer, no unmanifest, undemonstrated, invisible or intangible versus manifest, demonstrated, visible and tangible. It is only *belief* — a false sense or concept or idea — that objectified experience (the 'outer') is or can be different from or devoid of God, truth. But belief and everything of belief (thought, opinion, judgment, concept, idea, name) is nothing. It is not an entity.

Only God is; therefore only God is entity. And because belief is not an entity, it offers no resistance to the tangible experience of God as all. This is why healing or transformation of mind, body and condition is spontaneous. If the *recipient* does not resist, spiritual consciousness instantly reveals God as the only truthful mind, body and condition *already present and forever in perfect form.* There is none else; therefore there is nothing standing in the way of, or able to resist or delay, perfectly visible and tangible God experienced as form.

'You' Are Not Involved in Experiencing God

'You' are not involved in experiencing God — the healthy, wealthy, harmonious and peaceful experience. Nothing but God exists, and God *already is,* and God forever *is all.* Matter does not exist; only God exists. Matter is simply a material *sense* we are having of spirit, God. Because matter does not exist, it doesn't need healing; nor can it be either healthy or unhealthy, wealthy or poor, happy or unhappy, harmonious or disharmonious. That which does not exist cannot be anything, either good or bad. Only false sense needs healing, and that 'healing' consists of spiritualizing awareness — lifting from mis-identity as material being to truthful identity as spiritual being.

The belief that you are or I am a separate, personal, material self, living in a material universe — all needing God — is the very mis-identity that clouds and makes God experience discordant. If it could only be truly understood that God *is all,* students would seek only a greater *living awareness* of God for a greater tangible *experience* of God: health, wealth, relationship, reformation, harmony, peace, freedom.

God is all. *God* is experience. *God* is — not the way in which God *appears to be* as observed by belief, but *God itself* is all, inclusive of all experience. God already is the whole of infinity, perfectly and visibly existent at every point of itself at the same time. Nothing is needed but the *conscious awareness* of God as all, which then enables us to feel God happening — that *felt* experience being truthful experience infallibly revealed as form through mind.

Again, think. If God is all, which God is, and the whole of God is omnipresent at each point of infinity at the same time, which God is, then no being, no thing, no amount, no condition or place could ever need 'more' God. All already *is* and *has* all of God.

God cannot be something that God is not. Attempting to get truth to be untruthful for you or for 'him or her or it' has always been, and will always be, a waste of time — just as much a waste of time as attempting to get the sun to be dark, or to shine more over here for 'me' than over there for the rest of the world. God cannot be matter, ever. Matter is false *sense*, not reality — not *any* kind of reality, not even temporary reality. Indeed, belief in matter is temporary unreality.

Get this into your awareness for it is the great key: matter is nothing but a false *sense* of reality, never real reality. Therefore, it does not have, nor ever can have, good *or* bad quality, substance, form, body, activity, amount, character or condition of its own self. Matter is simply a name which has been given to the formation of mind (the universe and all it is and contains) which has been believed to be something in and of its own self. That name and that belief are unfortunate because the only name is God, I, and if only all were identified as God, I, and nothing 'else' or 'different' or 'separate', then there would be nothing other than the *experience* of God, I.

The Master gave two commandments, revealing to us the entire secret of the God experience and the ability to witness the transformation of any and every discordant experience: "Thou shalt have no other Gods before Me" and "Love thy neighbor as thyself". Do you see it? Only God is; therefore do not imagine and then believe and worship something, anything, 'other' than God — God *alone as all* despite its appearing nature, character or amount — because if you do, you will be imagining, believing, and worshipping falsely. And because awareness (imagination, belief, sense) is experience, experience will be false (good and bad). Also, *because* only God is, identify all beings, things, amounts, activities, conditions and places — identify *all*, period — as "thyself", as I, God, spirit.

SATISFIED WITH GOD ALONE

Hear It Well

Hear it well, 'you' — personal sense, belief, thought, even faith — are not involved in experiencing God as all. Yes, not even faith is required. That which *is* (and is the only *is*) does not require faith for its experience. You do not need faith to experience God any more than you need faith to experience gravity, or 2 + 2 = 4. Gravity and 2 + 2 = 4 *is* whether we have faith in it or not. The reason no faith is required is that the *is* of it is principle — just as any and every principle is — and is not changed or distorted or made discordant by either faith or a lack of faith.

This realization is very important. You do not need to 'do' anything or 'stop doing' something for God to be God as the entirety of your experience. You do not have to repair your life, settle your debts, balance your karma, or become a more loving, caring or giving person before every nook and cranny of your life can heal and harmonize, and before you are able to experience God — anymore than you have to before you are able to experience gravity, or 2 + 2 being '4'. In one second, your whole experience is made "whiter than snow" because you forever *are* whiter than snow in God's eyes.

You or I can be *unaware* of God being all (therefore unaware of God, spirit being our true and only identity), just as you or I can be unaware of any principle, and therefore not 'have' its harmony and completeness in our experience. Then we will have to "suffer [the discordant experience] to be so" for as long as we *continue* to be unaware, or for as long as we continue to believe in God 'and' — something 'other' than or 'different' from the pure and whole one principle and presence of God alone.

God Is, and God Is the Only

God *is*, and because God is the *only*, you and your entire universe *is God* — spiritual being experiencing the spiritual universe. "Is it not written in your law, that ye are gods?"

God *is*, and God *already is* before awareness arrives at its experience. Before your foot gets there, gravity already is, and before you do the sum, the answer already is. Before you call, I have answered. Indeed, before you become aware of even the very next second, God already is — that *is* being the perfect, whole, balanced, harmonious and peaceful fulfillment of all being and experience (spiritual being experiencing its spiritual universe) and none else.

Personal self, inclusive of its belief and thought, does not bring truth to bear as experience. It is the *absence* of personal self, belief and thought that *reveals* the whole and harmonious spiritual form ever existent. The personal sense of self (belief and thought) veils or fogs perfect and harmonious, ever-present, whole and boundless form from tangible experience. So the so-called non-dual consciousness is simply the belief that there is an inner truth and an outer nothingness — a *literal* nothingness or void or illusory dream-sense with nothing real to it whosoever. This is one hundred percent untrue.

Despite the way it appears to be, it is God because God is infinite and omnipresent. There cannot be, and indeed is not, something 'outside of' infinity and omnipresence. Yet they who believe in non-duality insist that the three-dimensional experience is nothing. Consequently, the 'outer' does not reveal itself as the 'inner' truth they know. Unfortunately, many discords and even disastrous consequences are experienced because of this "divided house".

Whatever is happening as individual awareness or belief *is* individual experience, just as collective awareness or belief is collective experience. If the believers in non-duality were to remove their false belief about the outer and begin to know it as Buddha and Jesus (and many others) knew it — as being nothing *of its own self*, but actually, despite appearance, to be the one and unchangeable presence of God, simply experienced as mind formation — then they would quickly begin to witness the image and likeness of God visibly present as form.

Because God is, and because God is the all-inclusive *only*, as quickly as false sense (belief) is removed is as quickly as true form is experienced. The veil of false belief is dropped, instantly revealing that which was 'behind' the veil.

All Is One

All is one place — omniplace, omnipresence. Wherever you are, there God is; wherever you place your attention, there God is. When you know this truth and introduce no belief, no thought, about experience being anything of its own self, then experience is 'free' to be the image and likeness of God alone.

But, if you still mis-identify, believing 'I' and 'world' to be separate and different from God, something in and of its own self, then your experience consists of the forms of your overall belief — good and bad, severe and mild, safe and unsafe, and so on. Belief is unquantifiable, infinite in variety and depth, believing different 'facts' about absolutely every different 'him, her and it' throughout the universe. Yet the truth is that wherever you are, and wherever you place your attention, *there the whole of God is*, despite what is believed or disbelieved about it.

The miracle of truth is that you never need deal with or solve the unquantifiable array of belief. You do not have to, one-by-one, correct or dismiss each belief. Belief is false, unreal, not an entity; therefore all that must be done is the dropping of it for the awareness of God being all. That one act consistently lived dissolves all belief. You never need battle that which is unreal, that which is not an entity.

God Is Forever Visible, Manifest and Real

God is, and God infallibly is, and because there is no invisible or unmanifest God, God is forever visible, manifest, real and practical. Therefore, not only is it true that wherever you are, and wherever you place your attention, there God is, but also that there is the fully visible, manifest and practical God.

What you are observing, aware of, or thinking about is actually — despite what you may believe it to be, and despite what it highly suggestively attempts to convince you it is — God and the fullness of God. The whole of infinity and omnipresence is right there, you *being* the whole and *having* the whole. Remember Shankara, "There is neither seer nor seeing nor seen. There is but one reality, changeless, formless and absolute. How can it be divided?" God is one, omnipresent and indivisible, and because God is all, you are that, I am that *and experience is that* — all one, indivisible, infinite and omnipresent, forever *being* the fullness of itself. That fullness is the only place we are (no matter where belief believes we are), the only place we can rest our attention (no matter where belief believes our attention is rested), and the only thought we can have (no matter what belief believes we are thinking).

However — and it's a big 'however' — if you *believe* in separation, division, difference; if you believe there is God 'and'; if you mis-identify yourself and experience as being something other than God — other than one, oneness, infinity, omnipresence; fully manifest, visible, real and practical — then that belief keeps you in the *experience* of belief which is itself the pairs of opposites. In the universe of belief — false identity, false sense, material rather than spiritual awareness — you are left with no alternative than being subject to daily good and bad. Life consists of good as much as it does of bad, with no law or principle to support and protect it and no truthful, permanent solution available to it.

Often, even after years of spiritual awakening, we find ourselves caught in the mire of belief and in great despair. The "armies of the aliens" — the armies of false belief and the very convincing power they seem to have over our bodies or circumstances — appear overwhelming and too big or too urgent to solve. It seems as if nothing can be done to solve the ill-health, lack, limitation, injustice, insecurity, loneliness or fear that plagues us.

The Greatest Mistake Human Belief Has Made

Belief or no belief does not change God one iota. God is *the only* — the only actual presence, the one reality, the one omnipresent, ever-present and true formation (creation). All form, all experience, both good and bad — even the most overwhelming and urgent disease, discord or lack — is nothing of its own self, therefore of no actual power. It is simply belief. The believed activity and form is not what is *actually* present, nor what is *actually* being experienced anymore than the believed '3' or '5' is actually the sum of 2 + 2.

What is truly, actually and tangibly present — the only and most real and perfectly visible form — is God alone, good alone, limitlessness and freedom of all mind, body and world, inclusive of everything everywhere in and of the world *alone*. Nothing has to be done or undone to make truth true. Truth already and forever *is* true — and tangibly so — and nothing can be done to change it, distort it, or make it unavailable, invisible, intangible, unmanifest or undemonstrated in experience. You or I may not be *aware* of God as all we are experiencing, but that is very, very different from God being absent. God is never absent. There cannot be, nor for a minute is there, an absence of infinity and omnipresence, the *only*, the *all*.

There is no place in the whole of infinity, *including right where you stand now*, where truth is not already whole and complete, visible and tangible all around you, fully manifest and forever demonstrated, perfectly real and attainable this minute.

The greatest mistake human belief has made is to suggest that God is different from man, spirit is different from matter, heaven different from earth. If only God is, and God is infinite and omnipresent, where can there be a 'different' state of being or earth (experience)? If God is all, then all is God. There is no exception to this truth. Therefore, you see that even as we experience a discordant or lacking form, what we are really experiencing is God, for there is none but God.

The only thing that can ever present itself to you is God. It is just that we observe God — whole and perfect formation — through a mind filled with the fog of belief. That *fog* is what appears to sense to be lacking, limited, diseased or discordant form. It is never real, and just as the dawn sun burns off the early morning coastal fog to reveal the splendor of the ocean and the beach, so does the dawning of God in awareness burn off the fog of belief to reveal the splendor of whole, healthy, plentiful, happy, free, purposeful and fulfilled being and world.

The Solution

Remove belief in form — *all* form, good *and* bad — as being something of its own self, rest in God alone as all, and *there* the kingdom of truthful form and fulfillment emerges into visibility. Only false sense (belief) fogs or veils or clouds the perfectly beautiful and ever-visible kingdom of truth at any and every degree of awareness *as all*.

We have believed, and unfortunately been widely taught, that we are a human being living in a material world, having human and wordly experience which consists of both good and bad people, powers, places, agendas, activities, amounts and conditions. All the while, the only actual presence is and always has been God being all — the only *actual* being, mind, form, amount, place, condition and activity. Nevertheless, if we are a believer of belief, our belief veils the God experience, presenting us with the belief experience.

Belief and thought (thought is only ever of belief; without belief there is nothing to think about) form a multitude of misperception. One of those misperceptions is the idea that there can be a presence, an experience, called the 'human' and 'this world' experience, *and* a God — two separate, different states or worlds or experiences, one 'here' somehow outside of and different from God itself, the 'other' being God itself. Then we set about praying or thinking about or meditating or pleading to a God separate and outside of us, to come from where He-She-It is, to where we are to heal, pacify, prosper or rescue us from our ills, our dangers, our pain and our suffering.

We ask an 'invisible, intangible, unmanifest and undemonstrated' God to, by some mystical feat, change into visible, tangible, manifest and demonstrated good for us. We even develop belief tricks such as visualization and the 'art of demonstration' to do it ourselves if God hasn't done it for us, or hasn't done it in a suitable amount of time. We eventually discover that no God comes.

"Ye Ask, and Receive Not, Because Ye Ask Amiss"

How can any being, any part of being, or any experience or part of experience need God to heal it or make it harmonious when it already *is* God, and the whole living presence of God, *already* healed and harmonious? All is God; therefore any part of *all* cannot need God. God is infinite and omnipresent; therefore nothing whatsoever can be, nor is, outside of God or lacking in some of omnipresence. Omnipresence cannot lack some of itself; otherwise it would not have been omnipresence in the first place, and nothing can be outside of infinity; otherwise infinity would not have been infinite in the first place.

We've heard this truth over and over, but if, when it comes down to it, we still believe that we are separate from God or different from God, or our experience is, then our belief keeps us imprisoned in the pairs of opposites, and all we can do then is attempt to use the good opposite to rectify the bad. We attempt to replace (and can be somewhat successful in replacing) ill health with good health, insufficient dollars with plentiful dollars, an absence of love with love, immorality with morality, greed with caring and sharing, war with peace.

Every 'he, she and it' of belief has an opposite, and every activity and purpose — *every one*, even the act of getting out of bed in the morning — is driven by the attempt to overcome or replace some form of a bad or lacking or inadequate experience of the pairs of opposites with a good, plentiful, and satisfactory experience. This is a another whole subject which we won't get into here, but think about it deeply and you will come to realize its truth.

'Inner' Peace, 'Outer' Discord

This is why you may have had, or may be having now, the experience of 'inner' peace, yet remaining 'outer' discord or barrenness. I certainly had it for many years. I was feeling peace within, most definitely, but I didn't see that peace on my branches, my tangible experience. I didn't, and never was able to, witness truthful experience until I realized the reason — I still believed that I and experience was something separate and different from God, that God was invisible, intangible, unmanifest and undemonstrated which I somehow had to learn how to make visible, tangible, manifest and demonstrated. What divided and confused awareness!

I thought that truth had to 'appear as', had to 'change' from infinite to finite and omnipresent to locally present, from invisible to visible, from incorporeal to corporeal good. I believed that the mighty power of spirit would change the less mighty power of bad matter into good matter. I believed my body was indeed an entity in and of its own right, especially as it was in pain, and that that entity needed healing. Well, that is like believing dark to be a real entity needing to be 'made light' — a change or healing of the entity. But just as dark is not an entity and is nothing more than a lack of light, bad experience of any category is not an entity and is just a *lack of God awareness.*

As soon as I realized this truth — the one truth — I stopped looking for truth to change, reform, pacify or heal, and began to seek and be satisfied with God for God alone. Then miracles began to take place.

Let's Be Clear

Let us be clear: what we witness as our conceptual world — the life, the activity, the form, the amount, the condition, the place, whether that place is something or somewhere of your body, an organ, a function, or something or somewhere of your home, your business, your neighborhood, an activity, an amount, the outdoors (all or any of it), the mountains, the snow, the rain, the rivers, the oceans and the twinkles on the ocean, the loving couples and the indifferent couples, war, peace, a blade of grass or grain of sand — everything everywhere of the conceptual world (experience), without exception — is *awareness and awareness moving*. God is not aware, and God does not move. Only awareness (our sense) is aware, and only awareness moves. Principle itself is not 'aware', nor does it 'move'. Principle simply *is*. Principle is 'before' awareness and 'before' movement.

The principle of math is not aware of $2 + 2 = 4$, nor does the principle 'do the sum'. I will tell you at another time, in more detail, that no principle has anything of our interpretation in it or of it whosoever. Principle simply and only and forever *is*, and not only does not 'care' whether our interpretation is correct or incorrect, but is unaware of anything about us or our interpretation. Principle is entirely unaffected and unaffect*able* by any person, thing, activity, circumstance or condition.

Principle *is*, and is entirely whole, complete, and satisfied with itself alone because there is nothing 'else' of it, therefore, nothing it requires to 'be' whole and complete. It *is* whole and complete. *Is, is* — this is the key to understanding principle, especially the one supreme principle that is God — the *only*, the *all*.

Principle Is Satisfied with Itself Alone

Principle is satisfied with itself alone. All of 'our' interpretation, and the benefit gained from it, is for 'our' satisfaction and has nothing to do with, nor affects, principle itself. The sum equalling '4' is interpreted as and for our benefit only. The principle of math is whole, complete and satisfied with and as itself alone, whether 'we' do or do not arrive at '4', or whether we have a million or a billion '4s' — or none. In other words, nothing we do or do not do, or fail to do, or do not know we should be doing, affects the wholeness and satisfaction of the principle one second. It affects 'us' and 'our' experience alone.

In the same way, the principle of aerodynamics does not care, nor is affected, if ten million airplanes are flying today, or none. Aerodynamics is satisfied with itself alone, and needs nothing 'else' to 'make' it satisfied. It *is*, and that *is* is its whole truth — fully complete and satisfied. It cannot, nor does it need to, experience 'more' satisfaction through form because it is wholly complete and satisfied already *prior to* any experience of form and without form ever being necessary to complete it.

Form is simply the interpreted *sense* we have of principle, but never the principle itself. The principle is forever and wholly self-satisfied 'before' and utterly independent of sense. Before you call, I have answered. Before mind formation (experience), I am.

If principle were not whole and complete *in* and *as* and *of* and *for* itself alone, the harmonious and whole form of experience would not be possible. Harmonious and whole form is nothing but mind-form — a corporeal *sense* of the one, *incorporeal*, complete and whole principle everywhere and equally present.

Know This Truth of God

As we know this truth of God, the one supreme principle itself, and are in tune with it — which means when we are *being* the consciousness of God as all: God *as* God, *of* God and *for* God alone *as all* — mind is unconditioned, clear and free of the fog of belief. Unconditioned mind *is* unconditioned form — and right here we have the whole way and experience of truth.

The whole and complete (unconditioned) form (the "image and likeness" of God, the one principle) is experienced as and 'through' unconditioned mind as universal formation, and every grain and wisp of it.

10

Awareness Is Experience

❦

Awareness is experience. Without awareness there would be no experience. God does not have experience; God *is*. *Is* has nothing to experience because whatever it could experience already is. Experience is an individual, ever-unfolding discovery — opening or blossoming awareness — of that which already and forever *is*. "The thing that hath been, it is that which shall be; and that which is done is that which shall be done: and there is no new thing under the sun."

The experience of a new minute, and everything that minute consists of, is nothing more than or different from your or my unfolding awareness of that which already *is*. The more we know the *truth* of that which already is — God alone; and the more we are still, silent and receptive, feeling God, *is*, 'happen' as our being; and the more we are satisfied with that experience alone, the more of the wholeness and harmony of *is* do we evidence as our every unfolding minute.

If we were to cease the *movement* — the activity — of awareness (which of course we cannot, but if we were able to), the entire world — every being, every body, every thing, every amount, all activity, without exception — would instantaneously freeze. It would be like stopping the movie. The whole movie would instantaneously freeze because the 'it' of it — its whole form and activity — is one hundred percent awareness moving (unfolding, blossoming, expanding). There was a movie like this some years ago. You might remember it. The main character had the ability to freeze the entire environment, except himself. With everyone and everything frozen in time, he was able to move anywhere he wanted to go and correct all that had been done wrong without anyone seeing him, or knowing what he was doing. Then he unfroze everything, and all carried on as if nothing unusual had happened.

Experience, and every form of it *of its own self,* is nothing. Experience is all awareness 'moving', awareness 'happening' — the degree of awareness (one of the "many mansions in my Father's house") 'happening'.

The Life Experience

The life you experience — the 'human', 'this world' life — is the collective belief of this degree of awareness, infused with your individual and particular set of beliefs (which are equally not 'yours' but particular collective beliefs you happen to have accepted, mostly unknowingly and *all* unwittingly).

All belief, all awareness is formed, so we experience the collective universe, infused with the particular set of beliefs we happen to have picked up along the way. All of it, every grain, is awareness 'happening'. Take awareness away (which is impossible), and there would be nothing of objectified experience. Do you see that? Without awareness, there is the pure principle alone, prior to and without form, without body, without name, without idea — without what we call 'experience'. The entire infinity of pairs of opposites would not exist in awareness because they are awareness *itself* — just a dim or foggy *sense* of awareness (filled with belief) of that which truly is.

The life you experience is awareness, and because awareness is objectified at this level or degree of awakening, it is full to the brim of objects, objectified thinking and objective effort. Some of this objective experience is believed to be inanimate and some animate, but all moves and changes at certain speeds, all has a certain life and life span, all consists of a certain material, color, fragrance, amount, weight, height, breadth, character, nature — the entire pairs of opposites of good and bad experience. But all of it is awareness alone — awareness moving.

The minute we know this, our only question and concern is how to make awareness more truthful. The more truthful awareness is, the more truthful experience is because awareness *is* experience.

Quality and Freedom of Life

Now let's talk about quality and freedom. What is true life, true love, true fulfillment of being? God alone is; therefore true quality, freedom, life, love and fulfillment is — and *is alone* — *God felt happening.*

We do not understand God and we do not ever need to. We never can. "My thoughts are not your thoughts, and my ways are not your ways." We do not know what God quality is, life is, love is, abundance is, infinity is, peace is, harmony is, fulfillment is. What is God? We do not and cannot know. We believe we understand what perceived God is, and what all the qualities and experiences of God, good, are. But we never do, and we are never required to. Only God is, and God *is already* — prior to and utterly independent of the sense of perception — belief, thought and experience. God is, period. Belief is not required, and thought is not required. Not even experience is required. God is, and God is *already* and *forever.*

God itself, as itself, for itself alone is the one real life, love, quality, freedom and fulfillment of being. Being *is God,* not experience. Experience is nothing but an objective sense of being — the one, the only being: God-being, the incorporeal, spiritual, forever-whole, complete and fulfilled being. Being does not require its objectified sense to make it whole, complete and fulfilled. Being already *is* whole, complete and fulfilled and eternally so because the only being is God-being. This is why we do not put truth into the intellect, into belief or into understanding. This is why it is important not to discuss truth, nor try to understand it, but just to experience God. The evidence — the fruitage in all forms — will quickly be your 'understanding' and your 'discussion'. Nothing speaks louder than fruitage. "By their fruits ye shall know them. . . Thy Father which seeth in secret himself shall reward thee openly."

Therefore, without understanding, without words and discussion, without thoughts and without ever seeking form for its own sake, *live* the experience of God happening within. Let God itself be itself, as and for itself, as you. Be still and silent and receptive, and let *God live you* rather than your attempting to live God. Let God happen within and trust that that life and bliss and peace and freedom you feel happening is the all-inclusive experience of your being.

It is not an 'inner' experience which still leaves an 'outer' devoid of God, good. All is one, being experienced, the *omnipresence* of being, God being absolutely all of God as all of being, awareness, experience — not inner versus outer, not 'over there' versus 'over here', not an inner satisfaction and completeness leaving an outer dissatisfaction, lack or discord. No, all is one, and as your awareness of all being one (that being God) rises and ever expands — *spiritualizes* — your experience heals, harmonizes and pacifies in every way. Spiritual awareness *is* spiritual — whole, harmonious and free — experience.

Feeling Is The Truthful Experience

Continuously seek the kingdom — the experience — of God felt happening within, and know that the *feeling* is the entire kingdom of God *experienced truthfully, tangibly, literally.*

Feeling is the truthful experience; the objective sense of the experience comes 'afterwards'. We know this, so we seek ever more of God felt happening. The more of the actually-felt God experience we 'have', the more of it will quickly be evident as the fruitage of every department of life. The objective experience of life, body, vitality, beauty, bounty, love, happiness, and purpose is witnessed happening just as leaves, flowers and fruits are witnessed happening. These objective experiences or 'happenings' have nothing to do with 'us' or our knowledge, effort, or even prayer and meditation. The objective experience is *witnessed*, not made — is simply witnessed as it shines through the unconditioned mind as objective experience.

174

Do you see why we can never 'make' truth happen, but can only *witness* that which *is*, 'happening' as experience? We simply observe the presence and flow of experience, forever knowing its truth, go with its objective appearance, and serve of it. But experience of its own self neither excites nor disturbs us, hinders nor frees us, fulfills us nor leaves us barren. We are the whole and complete principle itself, and principle itself never requires objective forms of itself for its fulfillment, its freedom, its happiness and joy.

If we were the principle of math itself, it would not affect us one iota if we had a million or a billion or a trillion numbers and calculations in our objective sense, or none. We *are* the whole and complete and utterly fulfilled principle *already and eternally*. Objective experience matters not. We *are* and *have* the whole already. Yet, as we know this truth and stay in it, living it and completely satisfied with being it itself — as and for itself alone — knowing that there is no 'more' we could possibly be or have or experience, *then* the objective 'picture' of that whole and satisfied experience is universally full of 'numbers and calculations" — full of health, wealth, love, harmony, peace and freedom.

"He who loses his life for My sake will find it." As you lose your objectively believed life, come home to life itself, and are completely satisfied with that true life itself — for and as itself alone because you now know there is none other — *then* you discover your universe filled with the forms, the image and likeness, of God, good. "[Then] God saw everything that He had made, and [indeed] it was very good."

Go with the Flow

All we are ever doing is going with the flow (not believing, not thinking about and not making effort for that which appears to be), but going with the flow of experience: unattached and non-reactive to it of its own self, witnessing the 'happening' of God, the 'happening' of truth revealing ever greater, more beautiful, more vital and healthy and purposeful, more universally and impersonally abundant and wondrous objective experience as we get on with seeking, and being satisfied with God alone. "Did you not know that I must be about my Father's business?"

In this way, one fine moment of living as and by God felt happening within, we feel the impulse to eat this food instead of that food, take a longer walk or a shorter walk, leave the gym or join the gym, buy new clothes or a new car, start a new business or carry on with the business we're in, make a telephone call, write a letter, buy a book or give a book, buy a bouquet of flowers or give a bouquet of flowers. It doesn't make any difference what the sense or impulse is. Whenever and as quickly as you sense or feel an impulse to do something, do it. Follow the impulse. Don't question it. Do it. Don't hesitate; act on it this minute. Truth is *felt*, and that feeling is the whole and complete truth experienced. Then the objective sense or the impulse comes through to do this or do that. Do it. Know that it is the sense or impulse of the truth that *is*. This is how the wonder of truth is experientially lived and is perfectly real and visible for all to see.

Never question the felt sense, the impulse, the "still, small voice". If you do, you put it right into belief and start intellectualizing: "Oh, I wonder if this is right? Am I hearing truth or belief? Should I do this or not? I know, I'll call my teacher. He or she will know." You are your teacher! Your God-felt-happening-within experience is your teacher, your way and your already-fulfilled experience — the entire and infinitely expanding formation of it. Go with the flow of sense, of impulse and of objectified appearance, always knowing the great secret: *the only thing that can ever present itself to you is God.*

Taught of God

Be taught of God alone, not of belief, not of man, not of experience. Belief and the man who believes belief has no truth to teach, no truth to give, no truthful direction to share, and the reason he hasn't is that he has no truth-fruits hanging on the branches of his life. If he has truth-fruits, you know he has truth itself because the fruits of truth come only by truth itself — just as the fruits of the vine come only by truth itself being the vine and its entire experience.

"Consider the lilies, how they grow: they neither toil nor spin; and yet I say to you, even Solomon in all his glory was not arrayed like one of these. If then God so clothes the grass, which today is in the field and tomorrow is thrown into the oven, how much more will He clothe you,

O you of little faith?"

As you seek, are taught by, and are satisfied with God alone, you begin to feel a whole new surge of life and fulfillment rising in your being and spilling out as the formation and activity of your experience. You begin to feel the impulse to change the way you operate your work, your business or practice; improve the quality, the amount, the time you give to each individual and to each project. You begin to experience the literal oneness of all and lose the false sense of there being God 'and' experience, or God 'and' form.

That which *is* is now being felt with greater sensitivity. Awareness of truth is expanding — all by your living *God felt happening within*. Truthful mind, body and world is not a physical feeling or thing; it is a spiritual feeling and a spiritual thing, and that spiritual feeling is that which is felt happening within as peace, harmony, joy, bliss, a sense of release or freedom from the objective sense of world, both good and bad. It is a release from all that is not, and the experience of all that is. It is a 'floating' or 'greatly-felt presence of spirit' or a 'deep bliss' filling your whole being.

When you are experiencing anything like this, you are and have the whole of God, spirit and truth — the whole of the infinite, the whole of omnipresence and the whole of eternity visibly and tangibly being experienced as your universe.

Experiencing God Felt Happening

Think about that — not too much though! When you are experiencing God felt happening within, you *are* and *have* your eternal mind, body and world. You, your body, your world and everything everywhere in it and of it is exactly the same but now it is known and experienced as the infinity, omnipresence and eternity it truly is.

Seeking, resting in, and being satisfied with the God experience alone 'shines through' the now unconditioned mind as unconditioned form — the "many members" of experience. The infinite variety of form *experienced* is the one presence *appearing to be* many, but always and only one because God is one, not two, and not many.

For instance, money is the same one presence, one form, one amount (God, infinity, omnipresence, eternality) as any other form. When we think about or observe a dollar, when we touch it, give it, transact with it *in and of its own self* — believing its appearance to be all it actually is — we have been duped by collective false sense to believe that all we have is one dollar, or ten, or one hundred or one thousand. We believe we have 'only' the amount that appears to be, therefore only the limited value the appearing dollar amount buys. Even if we have a million dollars, we believe that 'million' to be the amount we have — not more, not less but 'one million'.

Yet, what we truly and literally have — here, now and always — is the tangible and perfectly visible form of infinity and the omnipresence of it. The only form there is, is God, and because God is infinite and omnipresent, then this form we call dollars has to be, and indeed is, infinite and omnipresent — *the* infinite and *the* omnipresence itself, simply observed objectively as form. Form is not 'changed' or 'finitized' God (nothing, *absolutely nothing* can change or finitize God). Form is nothing other than the whole of God omnipresent, because nothing but God is. *Only, only, only God is!*

Anyone can experience true wealth at any time. You do not have to 'make' wealth be true, or 'make' wealth come to you by clever personal or business activity, or 'make' dollars multiply by some 'spiritual magic trick'. There is no such trick. Wealth already is, and because wealth and form are the very same one presence (for there is none else), you forever *have* all the forms of wealth you can ever want or need. In fact, it is impossible to be without the whole of wealth because God is indivisible and inseparable; and because God is you and God is wealth, you are and have all wealth.

Then, if your experience lacks dollars, the question is *why?* And the answer always comes back to false belief. You have believed that dollars are something in and of their own selves — a form different from God, an entity, a reality, a certain amount large or small, a form worth getting as and for its own self. We idolize money, yet we have been told not to make false idols, and the reason is that if we do, we discover ourselves lacking and limited. We have shut the doors of infinity to every form of experience, and now all we have is finiteness, and we will have to live with it for as long as we keep mis-identifying the forms of experience.

If you want to experience the infinity of money, realize that the only wealth is the one wealth itself, God, and then realize that the tangible *experience* of wealth *is the tangible experience of God.* Knowing that wealth is God does not do a single thing to evidence it. Hearing and reading and even contemplating this truth also does nothing to evidence it. Only God itself, which is wealth itself, experienced (felt) happening within evidences wealth as infinite and omnipresent numbers of dollars, sufficient at and as every step.

The Physical Experience is Unreal, the Spiritual is Real

Altogether give up the belief in the physical experience being real. Only God is; therefore only the God experience is real. You can see, therefore, that only the God experience itself is life itself, wealth itself, love itself, peace itself and satisfaction itself. There is no other. It is just that material belief has mis-identified the form as being the reality.

As you now live the true experience, the forms of it increase, expand and multiply. The heavenly treasures fill your every branch of life and are witnessed as the effortless and season-less fruits of health and wealth, loving relationships and happiness, successful endeavor and purpose.

Feel the presence of reality, God, happening within now. Take a few minutes to be still and silent and receptive. Simply be very still and let God be felt happening. Gently bring your attention to the 'happening' of the presence of you. That presence is God, the infinite, the omnipresent. Feel the stillness or peace or a sense of good or release or freedom happening within as you simply rest from the believed physicality of life. It is untrue, and it is untrue this minute. Therefore rest, dear one. Rest, be still, relax and bathe in that which is.

Simply rest here, within. Rest, rest. Bathe in the presence of love, of truth, of bliss — the secret place where all of you (your entire mind, body and universe) is whole and complete, perfect and free, happy and fulfilled in every way.

Now realize, the presence felt happening is not a physical activity. It may appear to be, but because only God is, and because God is consciousness, the presence felt happening is consciousness. As you ever more withdraw attention from the physical sense, and dwell in God — in consciousness itself — you live as and in and for God alone, consciousness alone.

SATISFIED WITH GOD ALONE

Once you know that the physical is unreal and that only God is real, therefore that only the God experience is real experience with all its forms freely 'added' (inclusive, all being one), you become addicted to experiencing God. As you live as and by God felt happening, your life experience becomes ever greater, ever more effortless and impersonal, yet filled with good and plentiful fruits. You discover yourself ever more able to serve, not only your immediate loved ones and family, but your expansive world family with the ceaseless flow of love, life substance and wisdom in all the creative and productive forms you discover filling your branches. You are a fountainhead of life, of love and of supply. "I am the life, the food, the wine and the water."

No Birth, Death, Time, Space or Measure

As you live by, rely on and are satisfied with God felt happening (because you now know the God experience itself, the felt happening itself, is the only reality of experience and all its forms), you quickly come to know that it — your truth and the truth of your entire experience — is timeless and limitless, birthless and deathless, space-less and measure-less.

God experienced happening is infinity happening, omnipresence happening, eternity happening as itself as you and every aspect (experience) of you. There is no beginning or ending to you; there is no time, no space, no amount to you. God is, therefore you are, I am and all is, eternal, infinite and omnipresent. As you come to know this — and you quickly will as you now faithfully live as and by and for truth experienced (felt) happening — you *consciously* live eternally and infinitely. You *consciously* are the presence of omnipresence happening, God happening, truth happening — alive, real, tangible and visible. You *are* the god of your universe, the God consciousness of your experience. And then you behold the greatest miracle taking place wherever you are — "Where the presence of the Lord is, there is liberty".

No longer is anything of experience separate or divided or different. All is God, one, consciousness, infinity, omnipresence, whole and complete despite appearance. Appearance no longer matters; only God matters, and God is forever one, whole and complete, and you know it and live it. You are the very aliveness of it, the very presence-of-the-Lord consciousness as all, being all.

No longer is there an 'inner' versus an 'outer'. The nonsense of false belief has dissolved in your awareness. God is living as your awareness. You are alive and filled with God. God is the one reality, with no other. And because awareness is experience, experience is now filled with the goodness of God.

God Is Never Absent, Lacking, Limited or Unreal

God is omnipresent, forever here, eternally happening as all — as your very being, mine and that of all being, all experience. There is none but God. The whole of God (the whole of infinity, omnipresence and eternity) *is* your consciousness, mine and that of every being. The very life you are alive with, the very consciousness you are conscious with, is God and the whole of God — indivisible, inseparable; one and oneness actually, tangibly and visibly 'happening'; the very presence and manifestation of everything true *itself* — omnipresence, infinity and eternity *itself.*

To paraphrase a pioneer in truth teaching, God is going on inside of you twenty-four hours day, *but are you there?* And when we say 'God' is going on inside of you (as you and every cell and breath of your entire experience), you know that means infinity, omnipresence and eternity is happening as you twenty-four hours a day.

Everything — everything! — of infinity, omnipresence and eternity fully manifest, visible, tangible and already demonstrated for you is that 'going on' of you. Never is the infinity of your truth absent or not happening, and that means never are the actual, real, visible, tangible, manifest and already demonstrated *forms* of your truth absent or not happening. There is no such thing as absent, 'not happening' God — omnipresence. Even slight logic tells us that! *But are you there?* Indeed, we have not been there until the moment we realize what we now realize. *We* have been absent — God is never absent. *We* have been 'not happening' — God is never 'not happening'.

And that means we have not been living our truthful identity — that of God, spirit — which is living as and by and for and being utterly satisfied with God felt happening as the very one substance, life, wealth, love and fulfillment itself, and itself alone.

SATISFIED WITH GOD ALONE

As we continue to, twenty-four hours a day, know that only God is, as we ponder the truth that the only thing ever presenting itself to us is God, then we are loving God (truth) "with all thy heart, and with all thy soul, and with all thy mind, and with all thy strength". Then, every time we turn and rest within — free of belief and thought — there God is *felt* 'happening'. You have conscious awareness of truth happening, and that felt happening is the tangible fulfillment of life — all of life in every one of its ways.

God is happening eternally as you, inclusive of your entirety — 'you' and your 'entire experience' being one and the same one and one*ness*. The peace, the life, the vitality, the wealth, the love and the ever-fruitful expression is all there, fully manifest and demonstrated, forever pouring 'through' and 'out' of your truthful, rested, open and receptive 'withinness'.

Now you know it, live by it, rely on it, and are satisfied with it alone. As a result — just like the vineyard forever one with and as its truth — your life is filled with the abundant fruits of heaven as earth. "In this way is my Father glorified."

11

As In Heaven So On Earth

❦

As we identify with God itself as the only truthful identity, and the God *felt happening* as the only truthful formation of experience — no longer an 'inner' spiritual experience leaving one's 'outer' world devoid of good — we begin, and then ever more expansively, to witness the image and likeness of God as formation. We begin peering at heaven as earth. We observe the presence and 'happening' of truth through the unconditioned mind as the good and wholeness of form (the earth).

Wherever we are, there God is — heaven is, the incorporeal is, the infinite is — and tangibly so because we are *consciously being it* by knowing this truth and living by truth actually *felt happening, felt being, felt as all presence.* This is the great secret — the secret known only to the few saints and seers. This is what every page of every scripture in the world has been trying to impart. We have not had the spiritual discernment to understand but now we do. We know that matter is not real but just mind form. We know that all there is, without exception, is God, that all is incorporeal, all is omnipresence and all is infinity; therefore wherever we are and whatever we observe, we are in the place of, and are observing, 'withinness'.

Now you can peer anywhere; you can be aware of anything anywhere; you can have any person, thing, amount, condition or place in your awareness, and know him, her or it as the presence of the whole of God alone, and feel the great peace of it happening. You are not observing matter; you are not observing a person, a thing, an amount, a condition; you are not experiencing a physical universe. You are being and experiencing spirit and truth, peace and grace, infinity and omnipresence, the kingdom of God, and you feel it.

You live by the testimony of feeling, of spiritual experience felt happening, not by physical or objective testimony. You live by experiencing your truthful identity, your spiritual being and conscious awareness of it, your 'withinness' as all. You have relinquished the mis-identified you, and found the truthful you — spiritual being living in the spiritual universe. You and the universe appear the same. You recognize everyone, everything. But its truth is now known and its freedom is evident. Everywhere you are, there is the very center of you, the very withinness of you — the peace and infinity, the omnipresence and grace, the stillness and wisdom that is God as all, experienced through mind as earth.

Wherever You Are, There Withinness Is

We had a whole class, the Redondo Beach Advanced Class, on exactly this: Wherever you are aware, there is the very center of you, the very center of God, the withinness of awareness. "The kingdom of God is within", the Master revealed — 'within' meaning the *purity* of God consciousness alone, 'before' belief arrives on the scene to create false sense, therefore false experience of truth.

You can now place your awareness anywhere and there experience God. Let us say you are observing a vase of flowers. You have two choices — the spiritual choice or the physical. One is truthful identity, the other untruthful. One will keep you in truth and enable you to witness the miracle of truth, the other will keep your experience shut off from truth.

In spiritual awareness, you know that the consciousness you are being conscious *with*, *as*, and which is *all* — appearing through mind as objectified (in this case as the vase of flowers including all its 'various' and 'different' formations, matter, color and fragrance, the whole 'body' and 'size' you are observing) — is actually, literally and only God, spirit, infinity, omnipresence. You are being the one principle observing itself objectively, like math observing a number or a set of numbers; you are being spiritual being observing its spiritual universe objectively as, at this moment, the vase of flowers.

You know that the objective imagery does not change or lessen or make God different one bit. Nothing has the power to do that because there is nothing else but God, and even if there were something else, which there is not, there is no 'greater' power than God, therefore no power that could change God. The objective form of flowers in a vase is simply an objective sense of God and the whole of God because nothing but God is, and God is forever the same and unchangeable: infinite, omnipresent and indivisible. The vase of flowers is simply one beautiful idea among an infinity of ideas at this level of awareness we call human and earthly — this particular degree of awareness, this particular "mansion in my Father's house".

Non-Attachment

You have no attachment to the vase or the flowers. You wish nothing for them of their own selves because you know they are nothing of their own selves. Why would you wish something for that which is nothing? Yet because you know 'they' are *actually* the very presence of God, all you do is rest and relax in their presence (the presence of God), and by doing so you are keeping the windows of heaven open.

You are satisfied with God alone rather than attempting to be satisfied with the vase of flowers alone. Your satisfaction is 'prior' to the vase of flowers but never excludes them as true God experience because all is one omnipresence of experience, one happening, one place, one form — omni-experience, omni-happening, omni-place, omni-form. You do not 'need' the flowers for your satisfaction anymore than math needs numbers for its satisfaction. Math is already and forever satisfied because it is already and forever whole and complete *as itself alone.* Numbers and calculations are just an objectified imagery of that which is already and eternally whole and complete, and so, as we have heard, math is just as satisfied whether there are a billion numbers and calculations going on in objective sense today, or none.

And we — spiritual being — are just as whole and complete whether there are a billion flowers or persons or dollars or customers or opportunities going on in our objective sense today, or none. Yet, as we live and move and have our being in God, as God, to God, for God and are one hundred percent satisfied with the God experience alone — God felt happening, that felt happening itself alone being our actual, tangible, visible and fully manifest and demonstrated infinity-of-being — then the freedom and grace and bliss and fulfillment of experience unfolds at our every step. Heaven is witnessed as earth. We are *being* the one presence itself, the one awareness, God consciousness itself, being nothing and observing nothing but *itself* objectively.

God Does Not Work 'For Us'

Always remember, we cannot get God to work for us, do something for us, change or heal something for us. We cannot even get awareness to work for us. God *is*, and so when our awareness *is being God awareness*, that *is* the 'work'. The work is done. God awareness itself is the 'work' done, complete and whole, the finished kingdom of God as all, and none else, none but, none different.

Withdraw belief over and over again, ten thousand times a day. Withdraw belief and rest in God. Never desire something magical to happen to form. God consciousness itself *is* the magic already complete and whole. It doesn't need objectified magic to 'make' it whole; it already is whole. It is the living *as* wholeness that makes objective experience whole. Oh, I hope you hear that!

Observe without attachment, without belief, without idea, without desire. Simply observe, similar to how you observe a movie — unattached, non-desirous one way or another. Be neutral about the forms you observe, yet full of God awareness. Observing with neutrality, yet keeping your awareness full of God, is keeping your being within. The kingdom of God is within, so as you do this, you are keeping the kingdom of God 'open' as experience.

Be still. Be very still. Still the physical senses and bring attention 'here', within. Then rest . . . be open . . . be receptive.

As you still the physical senses, you begin to detect the truth, the wholeness and peace of you 'happening'. It is happening twenty-four hours a day, but now you have turned to it, and you begin to feel it. Rest in it, for it is your wholeness, the presence of your truth — the presence of love, fully manifested as your all, your safety, your protection, your wholeness and your freedom this hour, this day and forever.

The feeling you experience 'happening' within IS ITSELF the God experience, and because God is the only, one, all, whole and complete, indivisible and om-nipresent, the God experience you feel happening is your universe of good visibly and tangibly experienced. There is nothing 'more'; therefore there is nothing 'more' you need to experience. The feeling you experience 'happening' within IS all form and an infinity of it. The feeling you experience 'happening' within IS your health, wealth, love, peace, harmony, safety, protection and fulfillment of all your mind, body and world.

The feeling you experience 'happening' within IS the fully visible, tangibly, real, manifest and demonstrated presence and formation of God, spirit, truth.

Is . . . Is . . . Is. . . Be satisfied with Is, knowing that IT ITSELF felt happening within is all.

Hear this and know this well — live it, breathe it, feed on it, rely on it, be satisfied with it, and give it freely each hour to the world: The silence, and God felt happening in the silence, IS ITSELF the presence of the entire visibility of God.

'The silence' is the silence of the physical senses, not sitting in a chair or in the lotus position 'in silence'. It can be this 'formal' silence, of course. But it can equally be the non-attentiveness and non-interest in that which appears, and the living awareness of God 'within' as you go about your everyday activities.

Do not 'divide' and 'separate' even when it comes to 'the silence'. There is no such division or separation in omnipresence. God is om-nipresent; therefore silence is equally omnipresent because God is si-lence and silence is God. You can be silent here, there or anywhere. Silence does not know whether you have your body in a chair or in a supermarket, in the lotus position or the standing, walking or driving position. Silence is the silence of physical attention and interest for spiritual attention and interest, a state in which we are consciously *receptive*, not consciously active; in which we listen, not do; in which we are open to God within, not the world without.

Become used to turning within with your eyes open. There is no need to close your eyes because there is no 'inner' versus 'outer'. "The kingdom of God is within you and without you." The kingdom of God is in the air, in the earth, all around; the kingdom of God *is* the air, *is* the earth, *is* everything everywhere. The kingdom of God is omnipresent! You cannot escape it, nor can it escape you. This minute you are living it, breathing it, feeling it and experiencing its fullness, *but are you aware of it?* This is the key — *awareness*. Be *consciously aware* of the kingdom everywhere and equally fully present, and it is revealed ever more every day.

Retrain the Senses

We have to retrain the senses to be constantly aware of God, oneness everywhere present and as all. We have to be able to be in this world, operate in this world, but not be *of it*. We see, hear, taste, touch, smell and think within these five senses and three dimensions *but are not of them.* We are of God — of the conscious awareness of God, the incorporeal, being the all and the only. The corporeal, physical senses no longer fool us, and belief no longer fools us. That which seems to be no longer fools us. Judgment towards, reaction to and effort for this world is a thing of the past for us. *Only God is.* Therefore, we are constantly about "the Father's business".

We know that only God is; therefore only God fills our conscious awareness. The only 'effort' we make is the effort to stay in God awareness — to live as and by and for *God felt happening within*, and then to serve the world with the particular fruits we find welling up from within us and filling our life. We operate and interact in this world, but without belief and without thought, knowing that every person, thing, amount, condition and place is God, the whole of God, and nothing else or less.

As In Heaven So On Earth

The 'Fragrance' of God

The peace wells up *within awareness*. The peace is eternally present but we have to be or become consciously *aware* of it. Don't be surprised — if you are yet unfamiliar with living by truth — if you do not experience the deep peace this hour, or even today or tomorrow or in a week or two. Do not *try* to experience it. If anything, try *not to*. It is the lack of self-effort, the relinquishing of self or personal effort and the complete resting and relaxing — the abandoning of the personal sense of self — that enables the peace and wholeness of being to be felt and witnessed.

Equally do not be surprised when you feel peace welling up and filling every cell of your being, and then spilling out, filling every cell of your universe. You feel peace or warmth or heat or light or bliss or a release or freedom or spaciousness or limitlessness. Sometimes you are filled with fragrance.

On two or three separate occasions recently as we have been walking, we are suddenly, out of nowhere and with no detectable source, filled with intoxicatingly beautiful fragrance. Belief wants to ask, where is it coming from? We look around and there is no flower or other source from which the fragrance is coming. But it is as tangible — often more tangible — than the fragrance of a bed of flowers, or a whole field of flowers. It is the fragrance of God happening within, detected by the senses which are turned to God (open and receptive to God) rather than to that which appears to be.

Wherever 'You' Are

Wherever you place your awareness, there God is. There isn't another place, another presence, another condition, another experience; *but it is only as we know this truth and are attentive, open and receptive to God as all* that we feel and experience the tangibility that is God and God alone.

When you look 'out' and observe that which appears to be, you are observing 'yourself'. You are forever observing the very center of yourself, and that center is forever whole and complete. This is not true only when you are feeling God happening. God *is*, not only when you and I are feeling it happening, but eternally. The feeling of truth happening is our experience of truth, not God's — just as the experience of flying is our experience, not that of aerodynamics. Aerodynamics forever *is*, and does not care what we do or do not do about experiencing it.

In this way, realize that whether you are or are not feeling God happening within, wherever you place your awareness, there God is. Knowing this truth helps you relax the physical sense and the false idea that you need something or you need to correct or fix or heal something of experience. The only thing you ever need do is know the truth and then rest and relax to the point of feeling God happening. That is the corrected or fixed or healed experience — the experience of *awareness* healed and pacified and made whole.

As long as you know that only God is, and that God is one and all-inclusive without an 'inner' versus an 'outer'; as long as you do not have, or do not allow yourself to have a divided consciousness; then if at this moment you do not feel God happening, it doesn't matter. You soon will feel it as you know this truth, and because of it, start relaxing and resting rather than being concerned and making effort.

The God-Feeling Within Fills Every Branch of Life With Good

God is omnipresence, not local presence, and because God is indivisible, as you feel God happening within, that 'happening' fills every branch of life — in fact *is already* every branch of life, now detected truthfully. The felt happening is not experienced in a 'physical' within, even though belief may believe it is. When you feel God happening, you are experiencing the *omnipresence* of God happening because God — being omnipresence itself, indivisible and inseparable — is incapable of being anything but omnipresence.

It doesn't matter if belief believes you are experiencing God only 'in here' but not 'out there' where you need it. It doesn't matter. God *is* omnipresence, whether you or I feel it or believe it. But as you now start living by the feeling of God happening within, and you know that that feeling is simultaneously felt throughout your universe, which it is, then the fruits of harmony and wholeness are quickly evident on your branches. But you must live by truth, not just dip into it a couple of times a day. That is not *living*; it is dipping, and dipping is no way to *be*. We are *beings* so let us be truth beings.

Then as you live ever more by the actual God experience, you witness your life filling with fruits — the fruits of health and purpose, vitality and ideas and ways of serving, and you immediately begin giving of these fruits. A new dawn springs forth and a new you is born. You live by constant conscious awareness of God as all. Throughout the day and night you seek God for God alone, and you rest and relax and feel God happening. Wherever you place your awareness, there God is and God is felt — the tangible presence of God — because you have withdrawn belief and thought from every place of you, and kept awareness on and in and being God alone.

The Macro Is the Micro

You see, it is a fact (even though belief cannot understand it) that as far as you look out into your infinity, you are only ever observing that which is 'right here'. The macro is the micro — omnipresent at every point of the infinite at the same time. So when you are feeling truth happening within, it is spontaneously happening as the entirety of your universe — every nook and cranny, every grain, every cell, every place at the same time. Therefore in and as and 'out of' the feeling of God happening within, we observe a 'him, her or it' appearing to be 'out there.' As we observe it *in this way* ('out of' God felt happening), then we can be assured that that which we observe *is* — not 'will be' but *is this second* — full of truth, full of life, full of love, full of abundance, full of opportunity, full of freedom, full of purpose, full of harmony, full of peace.

Do you catch that? If we observe with belief and thought, then again *we ourselves* have separated that which actually is — God as all, and fully manifest and visible as all — from our experience of it. We have formed a false experience of the one true experience that is right before us and everywhere about. Now we have God 'and', and we are back in the pairs of opposites where we don't want to be.

An object in your room appears to be an entity of its own, separate and apart from other entities. It has qualities of its own that are not necessarily qualities of other objects. It is made of a certain material; is has a certain size, shape, color, temperature and purpose — all unique to it.

But these seeming qualities are not the truth of the 'object'.

If you can observe the object without belief and without thought, it is just an 'is'. It is not a 'good' or 'bad' object; it is not believed to be of the pairs of opposites which are only imaginary. It just *is*. It is just an image, and if it is a moving image, then so be it; it moves because belief believes that this type of image has movement, but that doesn't change the truth that the image — the experience in and of its own self — is nothing but an 'is'. It of its own self is not an entity because only God is entity. It has no law or principle to make it real. It has no substance, no life, no worth in and of its own self, anymore than a picture on the movie screen has substance or worth. An image it is, and an image it forever will be because *only God is*.

When you know this, and then when you live this moment of experience by feeling God happening within, then you will quickly witness the image of its own self *literally* having no truth or power or life to it whatsoever, and truth revealing itself as the truthful image — and not only the image but the likeness too.

Moment by moment, we live by God felt happening within, not only by the appearance physically observed without. Our entire awareness is filled with truth, and our entire life is filled by and as the actual God experience. Then, by definition, everywhere and everything 'everywhere' *consists of* (is) the presence of truth because nothing *but truth* is living as the being we are being.

Always Remember

Remember, wherever you place your observation (either in thought alone or as physical observation) and whatever its content, it is nothing but the center of you. So the only question you have to ask is, what is 'happening' as the center of me? What am I being as awareness — God or matter? Am I living by the God experience or by belief, thought and effort — mental or physical or both? Am I living in truth or in thought? As long as you are living in truth, and by the actual God experience, you are protected and safe, and as you continue, strong and firm in truth alone, you will soon witness your life blossoming in the most miraculous of ways. You will watch the whole of the earthly experience give its good to you as you give the whole of yourself to God *for* God alone. You will watch as all the "crooked places are made straight" *for you* as you devote yourself to being *for God.* And then, as your life straightens and harmonizes and becomes peaceful near and far, and the fruits of good begin to populate the branches of your life, you freely give of them, serve of them, and share of them.

The Purpose of Being

Why am I alive? Why am I breathing? Why am I here? I am alive and breathing and here to serve you and to give to you. I am not come to be served, but to serve, and to give. . . I am not here for myself — the fruit tree does not consume its own fruit. I am and I have infinity and wherever I am, the omnipresence of infinity is *as* all form and all 'needed' form. The experience of infinity and omnipresence — the very "I" I am, the very presence I am *felt happening — is itself that* which is the life, is the body, is the substance, the amount, the color, the blossom, the fragrance, the fruitage in all forms; is the all that I am which I then observe as and 'through' the objectified sense as my truth-world.

When I know this, my only concern is to stay in God awareness and to live by the actual God experience — feeling presence happening, knowing the feeling as all-inclusive omnipresence, and then witnessing it as the infinite forms of good, the fruitage of objectified sense bursting forth like springtime, here, there and everywhere. I do not do a single thing about witnessing the fruits of experience other than sitting here within, in silence, beholding God happening, and then serving of the fruits I find on my branches.

> *Stand still, and see the salvation [the good] of the Lord,*
> *which he will show to you this day.*
>
> *Wait on the Lord; Be of good courage,*
> *And He shall strengthen your heart;*
> *Wait, I say, on the Lord!*
> *Those who wait on the Lord, They shall inherit the earth.*

Then as soon as the fruits are evident, you immediately start giving of them, knowing that an infinity of good form and ways are now and ever more 'pouring through' your God being. "The earth is the Lord's and the fullness thereof." As long as we are living as and by the felt happening within, we have the "Lord's earth" — we have infinity, omnipresence, omnipotence and omniscience being us and 'working' for us, as our constant, ever at-hand resource of all good in all form. We have the body of Buddha, the body of Christ, the body of spirit and truth, the body of eternal life.

Malachi speaks of this exact thing in his third chapter. The whole of that infinity I am living as actually-felt experience bursts forth, pours through unstoppably until, as Malachi writes, we say, Stop, we can't take it anymore! We can't hold it anymore! We can't give it away fast enough! We can't serve it fast enough! The pouring continues as long as we realize that the earth — individual experience — is the Lord's, and we do not again personalize or finitize experience with belief.

"Prove me now herewith, saith the Lord of hosts, if I will not open you the windows of heaven, and pour you out a blessing, that there shall not be room enough to receive it."

The Experience of God Is the Finished Kingdom

We have to experience the Lord, truth, God happening within, knowing that *it itself* is the *is* of the finished kingdom without anything anywhere of experience left unfinished, and *then* we behold *it itself* feeding the world of experience. "I am the light of the world . . . I am the food, the water, the wine." But if we *wait* for God to be evident materially, if we wait for spirit to appear as matter, then we are expecting truth to be untruthful for us, and we will wait for an eternity.

Even the feeling of God happening within cannot heal our physical body, or prosper our physical business, career or bank account, or enhance our investments, or balance the economy, or bring love between two human beings. God *is* the life, being, prosperity, love, oneness, wholeness, balance and harmony *of itself alone* because there is no 'other'. *God is, God is* — no 'other' is. If we find ourselves waiting for God to appear materially in one form or another, we are living an absolutely divided consciousness. We haven't heard or understood truth at all, and will therefore be unable to witness truth. We will live, probably and yet unfortunately, with the fullest, even most blissful experience of God felt happening within along with hardly a sign 'out there.'

But if you will now live by the feeling of God happening within, rather than by and for the intellectual experience of God; if you will know that only God is — not understand it, but know it — and live the actual experience of it as your all-inclusive being, all-inclusive experience, all-inclusive God, then you will witness branch by branch by branch of your experience filling with the bounty of heaven in the image and likeness of earth.

But if you keep popping in and out of truth, if you keep being truth then untruth, if you keep looking for truth where truth isn't to be found (in and as matter), then you are like a vine pulled out of the earth, surprised that fruit doesn't appear on its branches.

God Is Fully Happened, Not Still 'To' Happen

Realize that that 'connection', that oneness, that felt happening within *is* God fully happened, *is* the fruit on every branch, *is* the Lord's earth and the fullness thereof, *is* the heavenly treasure itself, evident through the unconditioned mind as unconditioned form — the "image and likeness", heaven as earth.

On the other hand, if you still make effort to heal, or pacify, or save, or hang onto anything of materiality for its own sake, then you are a house divided, identifying the forms of experience as being reality. It is as if I, looking through the window that morning, identified the beautiful morning sunlight in the trees, the flowers, the buildings, the colors and activity as being myself, and real in and of its own self. But I am I and I alone. Yes, I observe the experience before me this minute, but never mis-identify either I or it, never attach to it of its own self and never believe it of its own self. I am 'in here', 'before' and independent of that which I observe; therefore I am unaffected by it. I don't want anything of it or from it because I am already complete and whole as *I*, as spiritual being living in the spiritual universe.

I don't want anything of or for my sense of body, relationship, family, home, business, practice, finances, neighborhood, world or universe be-cause I know that it is "the Lord's and the fullness thereof", and I am simply experiencing sensed, corporeal images of that which is forever and one hundred percent incorporeal: God — therefore perfect, whole and complete, and eternally so.

I equally do nothing about the appearing pairs of opposites and their continual tug of war. They are nothing but false belief, and I know it. Only God is real and I know that too — actually I know that first and foremost. There is nothing I have to do about them — either pair of them — because nothing needs be done about that which is unreal. All I have to do is get on with the "Father's business", and then I will evidence the Father as experience.

I do not need to act in any particular way, or stop acting in another particular way. I am neutral when it comes to appearance, yet full of vi-tality, attention, interest and receptivity when it comes to God — which is every minute of my day. I live and move and rely on and am satisfied with God alone. God is what I rely on as my everything everywhere. God is my every breath, my every sight, my taste and touch and smell and thinking. God is my talent, my opportunity, my customer, client, patient or student. God is my dollar, my home, my car, my clothes and my food. God is my everything, and because I have now discovered that only God *actually experienced* is God witnessed as earthly fulfillment, I devote my self to experiencing God. Then I am worth something to the world, and I give what I am worth — I give of all the fruit I find filling my branches knowing that it itself is nothing less than God itself, for God itself.

Let God Be All

Let God be all of the life you are — all. "I of my own self am nothing . . . it is the Father within that does the works." I often wonder how much longer it will take for students to wake up and stop trying to be something of their own selves. Nature offers her example each and every day: simply rest in God, relax without belief and without thought, and *let*, and watch the miracle that takes place. Be like the vineyard, the orchard, the acres of grass and the millions of flowers and *let*. Just like nature, our only con-cern should be to stay rooted in truth, to stay rooted in God, stay rooted in the felt happening of truth within, and then watch the miracle, just as nature is able to watch the miracle. Do not do anything — just watch. Do not attempt to help God — just watch, witness. Do not believe, do not think, do not manipulate, do not persuade — just watch, witness, behold. Do not attempt to use the mind to manipulate or shape your good; never use mental effort, physical effort, material effort — just rest, relax, be open and receptive; and watch, witness, behold.

Continue to live by feeling God happening within and then — watch, witness, behold. Then you will witness the treasures of heaven as the treasures of experience, bursting forth as unstoppably as the flowers of springtime burst through the earth. Then give, and serve, and share of them, and your experience becomes like "the seed that fell on good ground, and did yield fruit that sprang up and increased; and brought forth, some thirty, and some sixty, and some an hundred".

12

Opening The Windows Of Heaven

❦

Malachi 3:10–12, the Lamsa translation, which is deemed to be the most literally accurate because it is translated directly from the Peshitta the ancient Aramaic scripture (Aramaic being the language of Jesus), is interestingly different from the King James and other translations.

These three Malachi verses are among the most beautifully poetic and inspiring in all of scripture, and also among the most commonly misunderstood:

Bring all the tithes into my storehouse . . .

A tithe is a giving of one's being, one's substance. Because all is spirit, all being is spiritual and all experience (universe) is spiritual. Therefore the true tithe is a giving of one's spiritual being and spiritual fruits.

Tithing is a miraculous act of being with miraculous 'results'. But it has been assumed that when we give a percentage of our matter, it somehow results in God giving us more or greater matter. But matter does not exist, only God exists — only God is, only spirit is — so if we are still in material belief and lacking spiritual awareness, we may hear about tithing and try to practice it, with little or no results. This was my experience when I was still attempting to get God to improve my physical body and material world — and in the particular ways I needed them improved!

So let us immediately understand that only God is, and because of that, God is *for God alone.* There is none but God; therefore there cannot be, and is not, anything but God 'happening'. When we realize this we have the key to the miracle of being. Before we realize this we not only have the wrong key, but we're attempting to use it to open the wrong door.

The true tithe is a constant giving of our spiritual awareness — the constant giving of the "first fruits" of us, the first and foremost activity each moment being that of knowing only God, serving only God in awareness and deed — first, by our keeping awareness free of belief and filled with spirit; and second, by devoting our being to the silence of the God experience, the actually felt experience of God happening, in which and through which God can 'get on with being God' as we are a nothingness of self. Then and only then are we the "presence of the Lord" in which "there is liberty" wherever that presence is. "Where the presence of the Lord is, there is liberty."

You are tithing every time you place your awareness here or there, and instead of being fixated on the way the scene appears to be and the 'him, her, it, amount or condition' it appears to consist of, and believing it, you consciously know that only God is there.

Only God is, only spirit is, only the incorporeal is, and because God is omnipresence, the whole of God is right here as this place I am observing, inclusive of all its contents.

The only being, the only thing, the only place, the only amount and the only condition that can ever present itself to me is God, because only God is.

Only the incorporeal is, and that which appears to the senses to be corporeal, of either good or bad, is nothing but a sense of that which is one hundred percent incorporeal, whole and complete, free and true.

SATISFIED WITH GOD ALONE

Forever devote your 'first awareness' to God. *Be* God awareness rather than material awareness. This is *being truthful being* and is the first aspect of giving your first fruits to God. What greater fruit do you or I possess this and every minute than the fruits of God awareness — the discovery of our true identity, and then the continual living awareness of that identity? Our being is the gift of God being, and so what greater way could we have than the continual awareness of and gratitude for that truth, the continual 'giving' of our thinking of God, our contemplating God, our moment-by-moment awareness of God to God *for* God (not for *us* and what *we* believe is needed to fulfill our experience), but God awareness *for* the fulfillment of God awareness alone? There is no greater way 'we, of our own selves' can thank God — can tithe to God.

You will notice that Malachi hears God saying, Bring all the tithes into *my storehouse*. 'My' is God, and because only God is, the only storehouse God has is God itself *being you, me, all*. Malachi is telling us to *be God awareness for God alone*, not for matter — nor for human, physical or material gain because what belief believes to be 'human, physical and material' is nothing but a false *sense* of God, of spirit, a corporeal *sense* of that which is incorporeal alone, and not reality. Bring all of your awareness home, here within — God awareness *to* God and *for God alone because all there is is God alone.*

Then we are prepared to be still enough, silent enough and receptive enough to feel God happening as our being — to feel truthful being happening as the being we are and the world of experience we are. This *feeling* — the *actually felt experience of God happening* — is the tithe experienced happening. As we *feel God happening*, we are witnessing the fulfillment of "bringing the tithes into my storehouse". It is actually happening, and of course it is and has nothing to do with 'us' as a human, personal sense of self. It *is* God *as* God *to* God *for* God, and 'we' are just a beholder of the miracle taking place in experience.

> . . . *that there may be food in my house.*

What is 'house'? Consciousness, being, I, spirit. Because only God is, the only 'house' — the only consciousness, being, I, spirit — is God's house, "my house", besides which there is "none else". So the "food in my house" is the 'happening' of God as individual being — in or as the

God "house" of individual being — individual you and me. Without God felt happening, it is as if God is not happening, and then the house of God, the being and universe of God as individual being, appears as if it is lacking or even empty of food. It is not ever empty or lacking even one grain of good. Emptiness or lack is impossible for omnipresence, and because omnipresence is the only presence, there never is emptiness or lack. But there is a lack of awareness of God being all. That is the only actual lack or emptiness experienced.

Because God is *consciousness,* if we are not *consciously* aware of — *consciously* experiencing — God happening, then we cannot see the image and likeness of God as our experience. The unconditioned presence of God as all experienced as the unconditioned mind-forms of all good — harmonious, whole and peaceful — are invisible to our senses even though they fill to overflowing every branch and pathway of life. "My house" is empty of food. It is the recognition of God as all and then the felt-happening that I know as being omnipresent God — the omnipresent one experience — that feeds the house.

Until we understand what has been said to this point, it is a waste of time reading the rest of these verses of Malachi. Without spiritual understanding it appears as if Malachi is talking of tithing the first fruits of your material good to a spiritual God.

You see, the activity of being aware of God as all, and the felt happening of God itself within, is one activity — one intermingled and continuous activity. As we first start becoming aware of truth and first begin the activity of consciously knowing — constantly being aware — of God as all, it seems as if 'our' awareness and the felt happening of God within are two different activities. But as we continue to practice God awareness the 'two' meld into one activity — one experience. It becomes one continuous activity of being, activity of awareness, to the point where 'we', and 'our' effort to know God as all, really dissolve into a ceaseless experience of knowing and feeling God happening.

Until we have understood this, there is little point in going further. Otherwise, what comes next just proves to be an unfulfilled frustration, as it did for me for many years. Malachi 3 has always been one of my favorite truth passages. It is incredibly beautiful and poetic, rich in truth — one of scripture's great treasures — and yet, because I didn't understand these first two lines, I wasn't able to witness their truth. So take time if you need it. Read and reread this chapter — one hundred times if necessary — and give yourself the gift of pondering what has been said, over and over, until its truth surfaces in your awareness. Then sit in silence for a while, even for two or three days on and off, until its truth starts to live you.

Then you are ready to move on . . .

. . . and prove me now in this.

The King James translation reads, "Prove me now herewith," but Lamsa's direct translation is "prove me now *in this.*" In what? *"Bring the tithes into the storehouse."* When being — awareness, consciousness — is filled with God, in and by both 'our' constant knowing of God as all *and* more importantly, by the actual experience (feeling) and complete satisfaction of God happening within — then "my storehouse" is full, and indeed it is proven that a God-filled storehouse is quickly then continually evident as a God-filled experience.

So bring all the tithes — all the God awareness *and actual experience* — into *my*, not your, but *my* storehouse. Fill yourself with *me*, with truth alone, with God itself morning, noon and night. 'You' are living a sense of I, a sense of your true identity, but only *I* am I. *I* am truth, *I* am being, *I* am "my storehouse". I do not *have* a storehouse; I *am* the storehouse. "The earth is the Lord's [God itself], and the fullness thereof [because only God is; God is the fullness of itself]". Being and experience (earth) is not yours or mine or Gautama's or Jesus' or Moses', but God's. *Only God is.*

"Bring all the tithes into my storehouse, that there may be food in my house." Well, God already has food; God *is itself* the food of life, and the fullness thereof. So obviously God does not need food. Therefore Malachi is referring to the *objectified* God experience — the image and likeness of God as the infinite forms of good (God) and true experience. 'Food' is a reference to the fulfilled objectified experience — the unconditioned mind as unconditioned form — the health, wealth, love, happiness, peace, harmony and fulfillment of purpose as earthly (objective) experience.

God does not have objective food in it. God only has God in it. When we seek God alone, and are satisfied (fed) with God alone, then the fulfilling God experience turns up looking like that which 'we' name food — the good and harmonious, plentiful and fulfilling forms of earthly life. God-fulfillment experienced *is* earthly fulfillment experienced.

Prove me now in this, says the Lord of hosts . . .

The "Lord of hosts" is the one God, the one truth itself, the Lord of the hosts of individual being and their experience, the 'host' of individual being, being the truth of individual being, the master consciousness, the very presence — omnipresence — of *all*, already whole and harmonious, visible and tangible, manifest and demonstrated as individual and unique you, me, all. And so the master consciousness says, *prove me.* Go ahead, prove — by bringing all of your awareness to God, and by living by and relying on and being satisfied with God actually felt happening — that when you faithfully do as instructed, then . . .

I will open the windows of heaven for you
and pour out blessings for you . . .

I will open your awareness to spirit for you, so that heaven as earth is clearly visible and tangible and real for you. Harmony, health and wealth is visible and real. It is already present everywhere you are and everywhere you look. But with your "windows of heaven" closed by material awareness, you cannot see that your earth — your experience, each and every individual — is *me* and *mine*, and full of the treasures of heaven, treasures of truth as your earth. *I* will. You cannot open the windows of heaven anymore than you can open the day with a new dawn.

But if you recognize that only *I am*, and let *me* do the work of showing you myself, then, like the lilies of the field, and like the dawn each morning, I will reveal for you — open the windows of heaven for you — such wonders, such truth, such life and harmony and peace and fulfillment on your every branch, such that material awareness will never believe.

This may be the single most important truth statement ever given the world. *I will open the windows of heaven for you and pour out blessings for you.* This is the vine, the branches of experience, filling with fruit, with blessings, with truth — awareness being filled to overflowing with truth and harmony and wholeness — the whole and truthful God experience as earth. As you and I keep knowing that all is God, *absolutely all;* and as we make our very life substance and activity that of God felt happening within for God alone, never for us; and as we are satisfied with God alone rather than with material things and material experience alone, then we discover the windows of heaven — of being — opening ever wider, revealing ever more of the goodness, the love, the infinity and the omnipresence of the treasures of heaven as earth — the truth of earth (experience).

The spiritual awareness of being opens, blossoms, and expands, and truthful identity is discovered. As spiritual awareness opens and expands, so does life's health, abundance and harmony open and expand and never cease opening and expanding. Being *is* earth; awareness *is* experience; and so because the truth of you, me and all being is infinite and omnipresent spirit — God which is God and God alone, good and good alone, infinity and infinity alone — the blessings that are poured out to and as you, never cease.

As spiritual awareness multiplies all good, experience multiplies because awareness and experience are one. Just as at dawn we can metaphorically say that as the sun multiplies its light, the experience of light on earth is equally multiplied. The 'amount' of sun and the amount of light on earth is the same one amount of light. In this very way, as God awareness multiplies or expands, and as we ever more live by and rely on and are satisfied with God felt happening within, the truth of earth and everything everywhere in it and of it multiplies. This is why, wherever God awareness as actual experience is, there is abundant life, abundant supply, abundant love, protection, happiness and freedom. The God-filled being *is* the God-filled earth. The blessings pour out and out and out, ceaselessly filling every branch with the infinity of good . . .

until you shall say, It is enough.

Indeed, the 'problem' of life becomes not lack and limitation, but how to quickly enough give away, share and serve the infinity of substance and form that we discover ceaselessly pouring through us, filling our branches as the windows of heaven are opened ever wider, and as the blessings of truth continue to pour out for us.

Do you now see more clearly what the Master has been trying to tell us? "Take no thought for your life . . . seek not ye what ye shall eat, or what ye shall drink, neither be ye of doubtful mind . . . But rather seek ye the kingdom of God; and all these things shall be added unto you." Seek to constantly — morning, noon and night — be aware of God as all, and seek as your very life and all its formation the kingdom of God, not just as an intellectual awareness, not as belief and not as thought, but as actually felt experience. And then "all these things are added unto you [your experience]" — just as light is 'added unto the earth' as the sun 'seeks itself alone' for itself alone, and never to brighten or harmonize darkness.

And I will rebuke the devourer . . .

I — I itself, God felt happening within — will rebuke the devourer. What is the 'devourer'? Belief, thought, misperceived God, misperceived earth, misperceived experience — idea, opinion, judgment about that which seems to be as being something of its own self. These false senses are what devours the experience of truth — devours the light of truth and fills experience with darkness, the blindness of material sense.

But as soon as truth is known and experientially lived, all false sense is 'rebuked' — dispelled and dissolved. God (truth) is greater than sense — "He that is within me is greater than he that is in the world". Therefore as soon as God is introduced where sense has existed, all sense is dissolved and all truth is revealed, just as — and just as easily, naturally and spontaneously as — light is introduced where dark exists, all dark is dispelled and dissolved, and instantaneously so.

So that it shall not destroy the fruits of the land . . .

The fruits of the land exist eternally. God *is*, and because God is all, the earth is God and nothing less, nothing different, nothing changed. The omnipresence that is God is the omnipresence that is earth — one and the same presence and same formation. The term 'earth' is simply the objectified mind being itself as form. God *is* mind *is* form. And because God is unconditioned and unconditional, mind is equally unconditioned and unconditional; and because mind is form, form is also unconditioned and unconditional. Only belief and thought veil the truthful earth — ever infinite, omnipresent, whole and harmonious form — from perfectly clear, natural and unconditional visibility.

The God experience felt happening *is the light of truth* which 're-bukes' all false sense *for you* and *for me*, automatically and infallibly revealing the truth of experience. Yes, you discover as we each do, that it is automatic and it is infallible because false sense is just that: *false*. Sense is not reality, just sense, and sense never is, nor ever can be, an entity. Sense has no resistance to offer truth anymore than dark has resistance to offer light. Both sense and darkness have no legs to stand on, no body, no strength, no reality. Sense is *sense* is *sense alone*, and nothing more. The minute truth arrives where sense has lived, that sense is dissolved, and because all false (discordant) experience is nothing but false sense, all false experience is dissolved. Truthful experience (heaven as earth) is revealed — the truth that has eternally been. No longer can belief 'devour' (veil or cloud) the fruits which eternally fill the land, which have never been lacking or discordant, but only ever *veiled* or *clouded* by false sense.

Neither shall your vine cast its fruit before the time in the field . . .

'The time' refers to the 'time and place' of experience. The 'time' is also often referred to in scripture as 'season'. This is not like the seasons of earth which come and go and have to be waited for. The 'time' and the 'season' is this and every moment of now and refers to the 'time of need'. There is no 'before' and there is no 'after'; there is just now, this moment of 'time', this place, this moment of experience.

Wherever you are, there God is, and where God is, wholeness and fulfillment is. Because God is all — simply experienced objectively as and through mind as earth (form) — you can see that wherever the presence of God is as actual living experience, there is witnessed the form of God, the wholeness and completeness of form. As long as we are empty of the belief and thought which clouds mind, the forms of mind are equally unclouded as experience.

Never forget the great truth: the forms of mind are always whole and perfect — harmonious, unbounded, peaceful, true and free — incapable of being made incomplete or imperfect, limited or discordant. Only belief and thought *cloud* mind, leaving perfect form blurred and distorted *to sense*, lacking and limited *to sense*, ill and diseased *to sense* — but never in reality.

Just as light fills the places of darkness at each place and 'time' darkness presents itself, so the presence of God consciousness (light) fills each place of materially-believed lack, limitation, disease or discord (dark) at each place and 'time' it presents itself.

If we were to take a cardboard box and seal it shut, dark would exist inside it. The dark is not an entity but just a lack of light. We have closed off the interior of the box to light. The box does not consist of an entity named darkness; it consists of a lack of light. Now let us take the box into the sunlight. As soon as we open it, light instantaneously floods its interior, dispelling the dark as the nothingness it was. The sun did not need a stock of light in its bank account to witness the dark dissolve to reveal light. The sun is the presence of the infinity of light. As soon as dark is brought to it, the dark dissolves to give it the experience of light alone.

We are, each and every one, the infinity and omnipresence of God being. We require no stock of life or supply or love or harmony or peace in our pockets, our bank accounts, our truck or our trunk. We *are* and *have* the infinity of God itself, and of omnipresence itself — the infinity and omnipresence of life, supply of all form, love, harmony and peace itself — and our presence itself dispels false sense to reveal the wholeness and harmony of all form, just as the presence of light dispels dark to reveal light.

The presence itself 'does the work' — do you hear that? "He performs that which you are given to do." And when does it do it? Instantaneously. *Neither shall your vine cast its fruit before the time in the field* . . . no, not before and not after either, but *at the time of the experience* — at the place and at the time darkness, material belief, presents itself to God consciousness. "Where the [presence] of the Lord is, there is liberty." When is liberty witnessed — liberty from ill health, disease, discord, lack and limitation? Instantaneously the presence of God consciousness is happening as experience — the presence of the Lord.

Jesus did not carry a stock of five thousand loaves and fishes with him, and baskets too, in case thousands of people needed food. God is spirit and God is infinite; therefore *all* is spirit and spiritual. Spirit does not change into matter to fulfill the material needs of physical people — no matter what that need seems to be. *Only God is, only spirit is, only the incorporeal is.* Remember, remember, the mind presents a corporeal *sense* of that which is one hundred percent *incorporeal.* Corporeality is nothing but *sense*, never reality. God is incorporeal and the universe of experience is incorporeal. There is none else but incorporeality.

When this truth is known, then no being, body, condition, amount or place can fool us. All is God; therefore all is whole and complete, infinite and omnipresent, and *the presence of the one being God consciousness* reveals the wholeness and completeness, limitlessness and omnipresence of all form where material consciousness was blind to it. Therefore, wherever Jesus was and is today, there was and is the evident fulfillment of experience — the God-form, the image and likeness of God consciousness, wholeness and completeness, evident as form. God, mind and form are *one* — the very same one presence, substance, form. God consciousness is God mind is God form. This is the secret of the miracles of fulfillment Jesus evidenced for everyone who came into his consciousness, and it is the same secret evidenced for anyone who today comes into the God consciousness.

Form Is Incorporeal Not Corporeal

Form is *incorporeal* not corporeal. Because it is incorporeal which is infinite, omnipresent, indivisible and inseparable all, any and every formation is forever whole and complete. It is utterly impossible for formation to be incomplete in any way, even by one grain or one second. It is just as impossible for God to be incomplete as it is impossible for the sun to be dark — lacking some of itself here or there, or limited or discordant or diseased in some way here or there. The sun is incapable of being anything but the wholeness and completeness of itself.

In this way, God is incapable of being anything but God — infinite and omnipresent, whole and complete at every point of itself simultaneously. Because God *is* infinite and omnipresent, there being nothing 'else' but God, nothing of *experience* — anywhere, at any time, for any reason, under any condition — is anything but God: infinite and omnipresent, whole and complete. There is no 'where' else, no other 'time', no other 'reason', and no other 'condition' than God itself. *Only God is.*

Experience (formation) is just a picture of God. Formation is literally and tangibly — here, now and eternally — infinity and omnipresence, therefore whole and complete and incapable of being anything 'but' or 'other'; incapable of lack or limit, incompleteness — utterly incapable.

God consciousness — spiritual consciousness, incorporeal consciousness — sees only God, only infinity, only omnipresence, only wholeness and completeness, *whereas material awareness is blind to it.* The faculties of a being in material sense are extremely foggy, unable to see, hear, taste, touch and smell that which actually *is*. Because awareness is experience, material awareness experiences material good *and* bad with much apparent lack, limitation, illness and discord — much. Oh yes! Belief is reality to the believer. Whatever is believed seems very real to the believer's experience.

But when we are aware of, living by, reliant on and satisfied with *God alone* — and as we know that *only God is, even as formation* — then the formation of God through mind is experienced as nothing *but that of God* — incorporeal, infinite and omnipresent. There is not, and neither can be, any 'other' type or category of formation. Again, *only God is.* Those three simple words *if taken absolutely literally and without exception* would lift all material awareness right into God consciousess, therefore right into God experience.

Wherever experience is happening and whatever that experience looks like, it is actually and literally a picture of God, therefore a picture of infinity, omnipresence, wholeness and completeness — utterly and absolutely incapable of being a picture of anything but infinity, omnipresence, wholeness and completeness.

Wherever awareness is, there God is — there infinity and omnipresence is, therefore wholeness and completeness of form is — because only God is; therefore only God is happening. Seven billion people in God consciousness around the globe (the 2014 population) would experience seven billion moving pictures of infinity, omnipresence, wholeness and completeness of formation — individually and collectively — and this is how each person individually experiences, or *can* experience the minute each lifts in God consciousness, the miracle of God as health and healing, abundance, love, safety, security, peace and harmony, and fulfillment of all of life. Picture by picture, place by place, moment by moment God consciousness witnesses God (fulfilled) experience (formation).

Neither shall your vine cast its fruit before the time in the field. Neither shall the wholeness and completeness — the fulfillment — of form be visible and tangible before the 'time' and 'place' of experience. How could it be? How could you see what is seen before the moment of seeing? How could you hear or touch before the moment of hearing or touching? How could gravity give you its experience before your foot touches the ground? Truthful experience is spontaneous. You do not have to walk around this earth loaded with an abundant stock of good form in order to have fulfilled experience. Only material awareness believes so and, because of that belief, is forever running short of, or out of, or lacking the quality or harmony or peace of fulfilled and boundless and invariable life, supply, love, harmony, peace, creativity, purpose, expression and satisfaction of being.

And all nations shall praise you when you shall be a land of my delight . . .

Yes, all the 'nations' of your experience shall praise you, admire you, look up to you, be inspired and lifted by you "when you shall be a land of my delight" — when you are the land, the consciousness, of *my* delight. What is *my delight?* The consciousness filled with, fed, illumined by, and being God, and God alone; the consciousness of God felt happening, empty of belief, thought, judgment, opinion, idea, desire and effort for that which seems to be. This is the consciousness of, the 'land' of, my delight.

All nations of experience shall praise you. Wherever you are, wherever you go, whatever you do or touch 'praises you' — opens its doors to you, respects you, is attracted to you and your work, gives its good and its plenty to you and to what you are doing, wants to be one with you and to benefit from your expression, your talent, what you give and share.

The world responds and reacts to you as you take no thought for it of its own self, and get on with making your business the "Father's business". All formation comes together as the complete and harmonious, whole and peaceful experience in your presence. "I am the light [harmony and wholeness] of the world [experience]."

Experience is witnessed as one, as whole and complete formation of the 'time' and the 'place' you experience as each moment. All form is witnessed to be in, or to quickly come into, divine order. "I go before you to make the crooked places straight." The multiplication of good and needed form is witnessed happening. We, the personal sense of being, have nothing to do with it. We are the window: I will open the windows of awareness — the windows of heaven — for you. *I* will; you cannot. Only *I am*, therefore only *I can*. The continual seeking and the continual experience of God felt happening within is our only involvement and only responsibility.

The only involvement and responsibility for any of life is God-involvement and the responsibility of continually feeling God happening as the very substance and form of our being. The only love we can give one another, the only good we have for one another, the only value we have to give and share with one another, the only truthful being we are for one another is that of God felt happening within and filling us to overflowing with and as itself. There is no other truth and nothing else truthful that we *have* as a being and *have* to offer our world.

If my words and if your words are not the substance, impulse and expression of God felt happening within, then our words are empty, useless, wastage, personal indulgence, ego satisfaction and sometimes lies. But when my words and your words are the expression flowing forth of God felt happening within, the expression of oneness of experience, then those words are true and valuable — *the word* rather than 'my' or 'your' word.

When our business, profession, practice or charity is the substance and expression of God lived within, not only are our words and promises of truth itself, but our product, service, treatment or teaching is the very substance of God as form. More than that, every dollar given to us for whatever we sell does not come from our customer's or patient's or student's pocket but is the fresh manna — the new form — of God happening as us. Just as God happening as the substance and form of the vine pushes through as new leaves, flowers and fruit — and ceaselessly and abundantly so — so God experienced as the substance of being pushes through as new clients, patients or students, including the dollars 'paid' or 'donated'. There is no difference, and no different 'happening' between the vine and the human. Only *one* is, only *one principle* is, only *one activity* is, and *one way* of activity is.

It may appear as if dollars are being 'given' to us 'from' our customers, patients or students, but as long as we are truly living by and as and from the actually felt God experience, and we are reliant on and satisfied with God alone, then dollars push through from within just as grapes push through the vine — and just as infinitely and abundantly, without material season but with ever-present 'time' and 'place' season. Those who give us dollars literally discover that they never lack the dollar amount they gave to us, but have an untouched amount for their own needs. The God consciousness happening as us supplies them, feeds them, protects and satisfies them, and the more they are 'connected' with us, open and receptive, the more of God's (truth's) presence is felt and witnessed by them as peace and harmony and happiness, and the more their lives are satisfied.

I can assure you that every penny you ever give to the Miracle Self is God giving of itself, its substance, its formation in and as and through my consciousness. Never does a dollar you give to me come from your pocket or your resource or by your hard work. I can assure you of that. It is God happening in and as my consciousness, pushing through as the leaves, flowers and fruit that populate my branches, including the fruit we name 'dollars' which are no different from any other form. You will notice that when you give a dollar amount to the Miracle Self for a class or donation, you are never even one dollar short of the amount you had before you gave. Somehow, not only those dollars you gave, but more, quickly find a way of getting to you and filling you with more than you had before you gave. Why? God is happening as the infinity and omnipresence of all in my consciousness, including you when you are a student of the *Miracle Self*.

In this way, as you yourself live by God felt happening, and as you rely on and are satisfied with God alone, you watch your good, your expression and your freedom multiply. And then as you give of your being and fruits to every person who comes for your light, your blessings and your talent, indeed you watch the blessings flow forth all over your land, all over your experience until you shall say, "Stop, it is enough!"

You will behold all belief and misperception dissolve: "I will rebuke the devourer so that it shall not destroy the fruits of the land." No longer does belief and false thought "destroy the fruits [visibility and tangibility] of the land [your experience]".

Know now that living by God felt happening — knowing that only God *experienced (felt) happening* is God tangibly and visibly *evident* in life — and by truly relying on and being satisfied with *God itself alone* and none else, that you are now living, being and witnessing the very truth for which you've searched all your life. The felt experience within *is* the living truth. The living, felt experience *is* truth happening as you, *is* life, is health, substance, supply — the miracle of God itself evident as every 'place' and 'time' of whole and fulfilled experience.

By knowing this greatest of all truths — the one supreme truth itself — and by devoting more and more of your every day to it and as it happening as your being, you not only will witness the miracle of truthful and vital body, health, love, wealth, talent, expression and success of expression, joy, safety, security, happiness, and fulfillment of purpose, but your spiritual presence will radiate throughout and as the universe, healing the sick, comforting and feeding the poor, bringing safety and security, joy and freedom to countless hundreds or thousands or tens of thousands.

You achieve ten, twenty, fifty, a hundred times more from your life, and you achieve it effortlessly and sometimes miraculously because what seems to material consciousness to be 'you' and 'your achievement' is nothing to do with you and everything to do with God. "I of my own self am nothing . . . it is the Father within me that does these works . . . He performs that which I am given to do . . . He perfects that which concerns me."

Material sense and belief cannot even begin to understand how all this 'work' is achieved. The 'work' is invisible, undetectable and often deemed as impossible by material sense and human logic. Nevertheless, it happens, and it happens because the whole of infinity and omnipresence — already and forever manifest, demonstrated, visible and tangible — is now *alive* as you, happening as the tangible experience of you, the life and being and substance and world of you.

The miracle of God is happening as, and pouring through you as, perfectly visible and real world experience. It defies logic; it defies the physical laws of cause and effect and of time and space. It proves that physical laws are nothing in the presence of the *one* true and supreme law, the *one* true and almighty principle that is God itself alive as individual being, the "temple of the living God" — not just God intellectually realized, but God actually experienced happening: alive, living, vital, real. That and that alone is God in action, God evident, God real here and now; the infinite and the omnipresent truth of God actual and real and perfectly visible and tangible for the world to see and be blessed and freed by.

It is impossible to feed 5,000, or more likely 15,000 people including the women and children who were undoubtedly present too, from five loaves and two fish. But that is an impossibility only to material awareness that has in it the belief of corporeal men, women and children and a certain amount of corporeal food — and usually too little of it. To *spiritual* consciousness the only being is the incorporeal being who never lacks a grain of fulfillment. Spiritual consciousness knows that appearance is deceptive, and that spirit is infinite and omnipresent, incapable of division and separation from the oneness, wholeness and completeness it is.

A lack of food or any other form of good is an absolute impossibility in spiritual consciousness. Spirit is the only — omnipresent and indivisible — so where could lack be, and what would be lacking? Only God is, only spirit is, only infinity is, only the *whole is*, omnipresent at every point of infinity at the same time. Indeed, lack is nonexistent, an utter and absolute impossibility. The false idea of lack exists only in and as false belief.

The moment you live and move and have your being in God awareness, and the moment you have a sufficiency of actual God experience which you *feel* filling your being and spilling out into your universe, and the moment you have truly given up all desire and effort for the things of matter, then you are "abiding in me and having me abide in you" — you are "bringing all the tithes into my storehouse" that "there be food in my house", and then do not be surprised when the windows of heaven open and pour out blessings for you. No longer be surprised when great sufficiency of all good activity and all good form pushes through the branches of your experience, with twelve baskets full left over.

Do not be surprised when you witness the miracle of healing not only of the body, but of all aspects of experience. Nothing of experience — nothing, right to the last grain of sand or blade of grass in your universe — need be experienced as discordant or diseased; or limited in any way whatsoever; or lacking in grace, beauty and purpose because 'it', whatever belief believes it to be, is God.

The Real Miracle

The real miracle is not so much that of beholding healed, truthful, harmonious, beautiful and bountiful form, but that of *our* finally having learned what truth is — *our* finally awakening to truthful identity and living it. Once we have awakened to truth and live by it the 'rest' is automatic and infallible because experience is simply consciousness witnessed objectively. The awakened being should not be surprised, as it peers through the belief- and thought-devoid mind, that it witnesses a harmonious universe. It is no surprise that the body is healthy, strong and purposeful; that supply of all form, including dollars, is plentiful and never absent from any activity, place or condition; that love flows and blossoms; that home is beautiful; talent is abundant and success natural.

It also should not be surprising when harmony, peace and union are reported from around the world, when groups or governments u-turn on aggressive, selfish or greedy plans of action, and even when wars cease, weapons are dropped and peace declared. It should be no surprise when corporations begin one-by-one (then two and three and ten and one hundred at a time) to feel and respond to the impulse of truth and become value- and giving-focused rather than profit-focused. It should be no surprise when the idea and need to tax the population dissolves and people begin to naturally give to and support their individual communities on a mass scale, then their country, and then their world. It should be no surprise when the millions of hospital beds throughout the world begin to empty, and the tens of thousands of hospitals begin to close their doors.

In every aspect and way of life, as truthful identity rises in awareness, truthful mind, body and world are experienced — the untruthful dissolving and disappearing from experience just as naturally as dark dissolves and disappears in light.

The Only Truth

Love, joy, happiness, purpose and freedom in all of life is the only truth and the only true way. As we each individually, and then collectively, awaken to the one truth and live by it itself instead of living by ourselves in mis-identity, we behold truth as all being, thing, activity, place and condition. We often watch life transform right in front of our eyes. The fog of untruthful awareness dissolves, and that which has always been true and forever tangibly present becomes visible.

It is wonderful to behold. People appearing stressed, unhappy, self-absorbed in the pain and misery of suffering, blossom in your presence. A little 'release' and then a smile and then a joy and happiness emerge into visibility and reality. We experience this everywhere we are, and it has nothing to do with anything of desire or effort to witness the truth of the people. *The, therefore their, only truth is God, and the evidence of their more truthful being IS being satisfied with God alone.* Then it is that their truth becomes more evident to experience. "Where the presence of the Lord is [God consciousness is], there is liberty." Wherever you (in God consciousness) are, there is liberty; there is the freedom and the fruitage

215

and the fullness of truth as all being, all thing, all condition, every step — around every corner, presenting itself to you, opening its doors to you, and revealing its being to you.

It is like flowers opening everywhere you are, for you. Everyone and everything and every place and condition is a flower, usually closed, tight, shy, dark. But in your presence, when your attention is not 'out there' but 'in here' — so much so, and so constantly so that you feel the presence happening ever more each hour and each twenty-four hours, filling you and spilling out, filling and illuminating your universe — then you witness through that belief- and thought-devoid mind the opening and the truth of people, the opening of thing, amount, activity, place and condition, the healing of the body. Whatever it may be, the blossoming of truth is witnessed; conditioned experience transforms into unconditioned experience; the fog of mis-identified awareness clears to reveal truthful being, body and world.

Do you catch the secret? You do not judge the world as it appears to be. You have no judgment, no opinion, no idea, no desire for it of its own self, nor do you make effort to either be rid of its bad or to gain its good. You are neutral towards the world of appearance — the whole of it, including every detail of it. You know that, despite appearance, all is God. You know that the full glory, freedom, beauty, bounty, safety, joy and purpose of God is fully tangible and present this minute and eternally.

Therefore, as you get about the "Father's business" of staying in God consciousness and living by the actual and substantial experience of God felt happening within, and as you are satisfied with God alone and rely on nothing but God alone, then everywhere you are, every being, thing activity, amount and condition that comes into your awareness *is recognized as God alone, I alone, spirit and truth alone.* You are "abiding in me and I in you". You are not abiding in false belief which observes itself as its world and then judges what it observes — praises or criticizes, laughs or cries, is satisfied or unsatisfied by form and how it appears moment by moment, day by day.

As you constantly abide in me and I in you, I reveals itself. It has no choice anymore than water has a choice in being wet or sunshine has a choice in being light. Principle is principle, and because God is the one supreme and ever-present principle, the moment we live that principle of truth, it is fully, gloriously and permanently real as experience. *I* can only reveal itself if you are *being it* because the you that you are, is really God being him, God being her, God being it — being now awakened to truth, *being God-being*. Where truthful being is, there is truthful experience.

Give to God

One final thing — as each day you give of your substance, your talent and your fruits, give as and to 'God', not as and to 'humanity'. If you give 'humanly', your giving is highly limited, not only in the recipient's experience, but in yours too.

If we give one to another, right there we have fallen out of truth. We are giving personally, of separation from God as all, of limitation, out of an objectified 'amount' 'we' happen to have in our pocket or bank account at this moment. There is no God in that picture; therefore there is no God as the gift being given nor as the recipient receiving it, and if there is no God, there is limited and finite, personal resource and nothing more. There will forever be inadequate resources to give to the world that needs it — the world which as yet is asleep to its truth. But when we give our fruits as and to and for the infinity and omnipresence of God — as the impulse, flow and circulation of ever-increasing God presence and God form, equally and freely shared with all of experience — then our gift is boundless and omnipresent and ever more infinite in form, not only in and for our experience but in and for the recipient's too.

The multiplication of good is automatic and unstoppable when only God is and when only God is *happening* as all of life, including all of giving and all of the forms being given. When we recognize God as all, then there is no 'me' or 'you' giving to 'another' — or 'another' giving to 'you' or to 'me' — but just God *as* God *to* God *for* God. As you give into *my storehouse* — not a human or corporate or charity or world storehouse which is how it seems to be — but *my storehouse*, then you are giving in and as truth, and the fruits of your giving, for all concerned, are abundant and perfectly fulfilling at each 'place' and at each 'time' of your experience.

SATISFIED WITH GOD ALONE

Where Is Your Awareness?

The question always is, and only is, where is your awareness? If you are in material awareness, then you will believe 'you' are giving to 'another' out of 'your resources' and in that way you have instantly limited both the gift and its value to the recipient. You have put a stopper in the flow of infinity ever multiplying the good forms of experience — the abundant fruit on your branches. But when you recognize that all is God and God happening, and you then give as God to God for God with no personal sense involved, you are bringing "the tithes into my storehouse that there may be food in my house". Then that very 'same' giving and the very 'same' gift itself is boundless and experienced as 'much more' than it appears to be for the recipient, and is witnessed ceaselessly multiplying for you, for greater giving.

Only God is; therefore all the fruits, all the giving and all the gifts themselves are that of and for God — God *as* God *to* God *for* God, not God for human or God for world, but God as and to and for God alone. Then we are *being* and *have* only infinity and omnipresence tangibly experienced. We have only God, therefore boundlessness and effortlessness; we have no amount, no measure, no limit, no 'us' with something and no 'them' we give our something to. We have only God happening, experienced objectively. Appearance no longers matters; only God matters and only God is lived.

We no longer wait for better times in which we will be able to give more substantially. All of this is purely material belief born of mis-identified self, form and experience. Even if we have but one dollar in our pocket today, we now, in truthful identity, give ten or twenty or fifty cents of it as God, to God and for God, in the realization that the whole of God — the whole of infinity and omnipresence — is the only actual presence, form, amount and condition. We start the flow of giving and of serving and sharing, recognizing that those we give to, although appearing 'human', are not 'human', but are God just as we are and all are. "Have no other God but me ... and treat your neighbor as yourself." We give, serve and share as God of God to God for God. Then that gift, service and sharing, stretches far afield and far wider than the objective act and form appears to allow, and the multiplication of good for you and for all you give to, is unstoppable and boundless.

Opening The Windows Of Heaven

Bring all the tithes into my storehouse
that there may be food in my house,
and prove me now in this, says the Lord of hosts,
and I will open the windows of heaven for you
and pour out blessings for you until you shall say, It is enough.
And I will rebuke the devourer, so that it shall not destroy the fruits
of the land; neither shall your vine cast its fruit before the time in
the field, says the Lord of hosts.
And all nations shall praise you, when you shall be a land of my
delight, says the Lord of hosts.

Well, thank you Malachi, for this wonderful lesson!

13

Truth Revealed

❦

G ood morning. We are to have, in the afternoon break, the most fruitful experience of life you can possibly have, and that is silence. I am going to sit in the break with as many of you as have a question you want answered, in the realization that the question in and through belief and thought and talk, plus any answer that can be given to you in and through conceptual understanding and words *is not it*. It will not help you, it will not reveal the fruits of your truth. But the silence of you and the silent presence of truth happening as you *is* your answer, fully embodied — and perfectly visibly and tangibly — here and now.

In the deep and secret place of being all *is*, and that which *is* — God — is fully manifest and demonstrated for you and as you. In the deep silence you *feel it;* you *feel* your answer fully embodied and manifest, welling up and springing forth as the image and likeness of God as form. Then, as you remain empty of belief and thought, and filled with God as your way of being, you soon witness the fulfilling form 'come through' in experience.

High In Spiritual Consciousness

We have lifted so beautifully high, out of material sense, out of the confusion of belief, into spirit, that truth is free to reveal itself here, there and everywhere in your life. Whether belief believes this to be true does not matter. Belief has nothing to do with truth. If belief still wants to tempt you to doubt that you've lifted effectively away from untruth into truth, then be strong, stand up to it as the nothingness it is, and tell it, Get away, you are nothing but false belief! "Get thee hence Satan!"

Simply ignore belief and get on with "the Father's business". Do it now. Fill your awareness with the glory of God, of spirit, of the incorporeal, of infinity and omnipresence, and then rest and *feel* God happening, filling your being, your universe and beyond, and there it is — all you have is the light and substance and freedom and glory of God as all.

It is only belief that obscures that which actually is, and that which actually is fully manifest, visible, tangible and forever demonstrated. God is complete, finished, whole and omnipresent where you are and as your entire experience. Never is there anything for you to do. It is already done, and completely so. As you now live the life of beholder not doer, you witness only God — the perfectly glorious conceptual experience of the kingdom of truth everywhere you are.

There will, of course, come a day when you can gather, and just through silence, hear the message, be taught of God — of God felt happening within and *as* wholeness and completeness of being. You are not quite there yet, and so God appearing to you as your teacher, whom you gather with, gives you the words of truth which you take in, assimilate, ponder and be silent with, and then witness 'coming through' your lifted being as fruits of life and love and harmony and plenty in your experience. The words you are given by teacher are *of you*. Never believe that your teacher has truth while you do not. Never believe that you have to somehow 'get' what your teacher is giving you, and before you have 'got' enough you remain out of truth and unable to witness truth in your life. Such belief is one hundred percent untrue.

SATISFIED WITH GOD ALONE

You *are* and *have* all of God this minute. Never disbelieve or doubt that truth. Only omnipresence is — there is no 'other' type or choice of presence. Therefore your presence, my presence and all presence is *om*nipresence — the whole of God. Belief cannot change that truth, and indeed does not. Belief can do whatever it wants to do, and it can do it all day and night long, but it makes not one iota of difference to the *truth* that you, this minute, *are* and *have* the whole of God, and are able to witness the wholeness, completeness, harmony and fulfillment of your entire life this day because that witnessing has nothing to do with 'you' or 'me' or even the Master Himself. "I of my own self am nothing. . . it is the Father within me that does the work."

Your teacher's words are telling you of this wondrous truth. They speak of the one truth you *are*, and *already are*. They speak of the one presence, one substance and one form you are and already are. You are simply still requiring the agency of words to hear and be lifted up into a living awareness of the truth you are. The words of truth given to you by your teacher are as a ladder into spiritual awareness, an awakening agency. But everything you hear or read is your hearing consciousness, your substance, your presence — the one being and experience we call God, truth being given as what is biblically termed 'the word of God'. It seems — to belief — to be your teacher giving you the teaching but it is actually *you* hearing the teaching, hearing and feeling the very truth of God as you.

The Spontaneity of Experience

Very soon, maybe even in a year or two, at least a good number of students will be ready to drop the agency of the spoken or written word. Then we will gather in silence, in silent receptivity, and therein will flow the message as clear and vital and tangible and real as the spoken or written word is today. When you are ready for that, you will discover the forms of good are very quickly witnessed throughout life. Indeed, as you ever more live in and as God awareness alone, and *by* God felt happening as the very totality of life and substance and 'cause' of you, and as you are ever more satisfied with God alone, you discover that *God itself alone* is ever more spontaneously *visible* as the good forms of objectified experience.

It is because belief still requires the agencies of truth — the written or spoken word — that there seems to be a delay in witnessed good, but that delay is one hundred percent only of belief, a sluggish awareness still quite foggy with remnants of believed experience rather than clear and "quick and sharp and powerful" as truthful experience alone. As you now begin to be taught of God itself — truth itself felt happening within and 'out' as the forms of experience — then, of course, the agency is no longer needed. You can literally hear the exact same message you are hearing or reading now, but without the agency of human language. You will hear the message purely as feeling within, welling up, filling your universe with and as the very form of itself experienced, and your comprehension is far greater, far more vivid and real to the point that 'human' reality is no longer real to you at all.

You still have the perfectly beautiful and true three dimensional and five-sensed experience, just as you do now, but it is no longer reality to you. You have lifted into the one and only true reality. "I am in this world but not of it." Because there is no longer belief about any of this world as it appears *in and of its own self* to be, the forms of truth you *feel happening* and *are* as your very infinity of being are quickly if not spontaneously evidenced.

We witness this quick or spontaneous visibility of truth as the consciousness of Jesus — the master consciousness so beautifully empty of belief and full of God alone. Truth was evident for the Master and those who came to him within a few seconds or minutes or within the hour.

Daughter, be of good comfort; thy faith hath made thee whole. And the woman was made whole from that hour.

O woman, great is thy faith: be it unto thee even as thou wilt. And her daughter was made whole from that very hour.

And in that same hour he cured many of their infirmities and plagues, and of evil spirits; and unto many that were blind he gave sight. . . the blind see, the lame walk, the lepers are cleansed, the deaf hear, the dead are raised.

Any delay in the evidence of truth was not of the Master's consciousness but that of the people who were still filled with, and observed with, false belief. The Master knew that although truth is spontaneously evident *to truthful consciousness* it often took some 'time' for the fog of false belief to dissolve in the people's awareness before the whole and complete being, body or condition became visible. There is the 'hour' referred to in scripture.

God, truth, already *is.* All being, body and world already and forever *is* God and God's and none else. "The earth is the Lord's, and the fullness thereof. . . the earth is full of the goodness of the Lord. . . the earth is full of thy riches. . . the whole earth is full of his glory." Only God, good, only infinity, only omnipresence, only divine perfection *is,* and is already fully manifest and visible, real and tangible. Truth is the only, and so there is nothing to heal, nothing to transform, nothing to fix, prosper, harmonize or pacify but *awareness de-fogs* and begins to see that which *is* instead of a foggy, distorted, lacking, limited and discordant *image* — experience — of that which is.

Our ability to witness that which *is* is entirely dependent on how empty we are or become of belief, thought, judgment, idea, opinion, matter as reality. Every grain of you and your experience is nothing but God, incorporeality, divine good, love, infinity, omnipresence, freedom, purpose, oneness, union, grace — every grain, every being and every particle, every blade of grass, grain of sand, every thought, every place and condition.

Even as belief believes it's experiencing something 'other' than God — truth, wholeness and harmony of all — *it is not.* It is experiencing and observing nothing but God, truth, spirit, grace, love, oneness and union of all because none but God exists. Every being, body, amount, place, condition is the one true being, body, amount, place, condition of heaven, nirvana, of truth, but belief believes not. It is that erroneous belief that throws a veil, a cloud, over the experience of that which is.

Only Truth Is

Nevertheless, truth is the only. Truth is the only visible presence, the only tangible presence and the only real presence. "The only thing that can ever present itself to you is God." If you see, hear, taste, touch or smell anything whatsoever, it is God because non but God itself exists. "If you see me you see the Father." God is perfect wholeness and harmony of all at this 'human, worldly' level of awareness and every of the infinite levels of awareness (the many mansions in my Father's house).

Yet, because the I of being and its experience is believed to be something of its own self, separate and different from God, and is operated by thought, it is misperceived. God is not changed by the misperception of belief and thought; nothing of truth has changed nor ever can be. God itself, pristine and perfect, whole and unconditionally available to the experience of every being, is right here where you are, there and everywhere, yet misperceived.

Isn't that a pity? The moment we begin to awaken to this great truth — the one truth — it is nonsensical to continue our lives by the activity of belief and thought. Let's be kind to ourselves and call it unwitting nonsense, but it really is nonsensical to act as finite, limited, lacking and discordant mental beings with physical bodies living and attempting to survive and succeed in a material world of two powers — he chaos of good and bad belief — when our truth is God itself, the unconditional oneness, infinity, omnipresence and eternity of being!

Not 'Change' The World But 'Reveal' The Truthful World

As soon as we awaken to the truth, our whole goal is not to change anything, heal anything, prosper anything, rectify anything, gain or be rid anything or anyone because all of this is of belief — of idea, judgment, opinion and concept — and there is no truth in it. Belief deals only with itself — false sense, shadows, false or discordant, limited and lacking experience. Our whole goal is to be rid of belief, to empty ourselves of judgment, opinion, idea and concept. Once that is achieved, *there God (good) is* as and through mind as perfectly clear, visible and real Godly form. It has only ever been false sense that clouds God from experience.

Remember that. God *is* mind *is* form, therefore when mind is empty of the fog of belief — thought, judgment and idea — it is the divine and true faculty of experience, a clear and flowing receptacle of God, the faculty presenting nothing but the image and likeness and wonder of God experienced objectively. In truth, every form experienced is nothing but *all that is*, God — infinite, omnipresent, unconditional and eternal. But belief and thought mis-judges and misperceives it. So as we lift out of belief into *only God is*, experience becomes the image and likeness *of* God — that which all form has eternally been but which belief has obscured.

Expanding Awareness Is Expanding Experience

Awareness flows, moves, expands and evolves. Awareness is what we call *experience*. It is for this reason that experience flows, moves, expands and evolves; it is for this reason that experience seems to exist in and of time and space; it is for this reason that existence appears to consist of cause and effect. All of experience *is awareness flowing, moving, expanding and evolving* and that is why the universe, as physicists are measuring, is expanding and evolving. The distance between planets a million years ago is greater today; the volume of the universe itself is greater today and becoming ever greater still, and this will continue infinitely and eternally.

Awareness expands, and because awareness *is* experience, experience — which is mind forever formed — equally expands. The more God-aware we individually and then collectively become, the more we witness the believed and foggy sense of I, body and world transforming into its truth, good (God) alone. "One with God is a majority," and so it takes just *your* God-awareness and God-lived experience to completely transform and fulfill every detail of your life — with twelve baskets full left over to generously give, serve and share. More than that, your truthful presence helps lift, heal and often transform many dozens or hundreds of others' lives.

You are never required to take thought for experience or any detail of it. Do not take a single thought for the state of your life, your health, your dollars, your love, your family, home and neighborhood, your work or your world. Let experience be witnessed as transforming, healing, filling and fulfilling as *you* be about your Father's business.

Do not resist by holding onto materiality. Let go of all but God — release God. Do not 'hold onto, therefore bind God' in your experience by believing your mind, body and world to be something other than God itself, and nothing but God itself — therefore forever whole, complete, perfect and free. "And God saw every thing that he had made, and, behold, it was very good."

The Joy of Transformed Experience

Let experience transform — this is the way; *let*. Never hold onto experience in any way. Let it flow and perfect itself as you stay in God and are satisfied with God alone — just as you *let* the ocean be revealed as you remain satisfied with the sun itself, knowing that the sun itself will dissolve the morning fog. You are not involved.

Do not attempt to be satisfied with God *and* still desire satisfying matter at the same time. That is the guaranteed way of failure. "No man can serve two masters: for either he will hate the one, and love the other; or else he will hold to the one, and despise the other. Ye cannot serve God and mammon [matter]."

Trust God as the utter and unconditional good of all. Trust God as mind as form (experience). You never have to fear the transforming of experience. Love has you in its arms; love is your very being and your transformer of all untruthful experience. Love dissolves the untruthful experience belief is presenting to you, leaving you with nothing but the formation of love — the truth, wholeness and fulfillment of experience.

Only belief resists the transformation of experience. It wants good — and plenty of it — but it wants it in *its* way, *its* time, fitting into *its* desired framework, fulfilling *its* idea. Belief 'outlines' the good it wants but you cannot finitize or localize infinity and omnipresence (God) which is exactly what naming or outlining attempts to do.

But as you empty yourself of belief, thought and idea, and let God be the unconditioned mind as form you witness the miracle of transformed form in experience. Form is witnessed as unconditioned as the unconditioned mind the moment you consistently remove belief, thought and idea from life. The forms and functions of body, relationship, finances, family, work and world become ever truer, freer and purposeful — infinitely *more* true, *more* beautiful, *more* graceful, *more* abundant and *more* purposeful than belief could ever design.

Leaving This World, Becoming a Being of Truth

You have come this far and are ready to be in this world but not of it. The world will not disappear nor will you disappear from it until you are ready to and want to. We do not have to walk away from our lives, our loves and our families; we do not have to sell our homes and give away our goods. It can look like that; it did for me. It was extreme for me as it became clear that I was to be the ear and servant of the Miracle Self message. I had to give up the sense of body completely; I had to give up the sense of relationship completely; I had to give up the sense of dollars completely; I had to give up the sense of children completely, which is still probably my greatest difficulty. It is much better now, but it was very hard for the first two years.

You have to continually give up and re-give up all material ties and remaining sense of material need. You have to continually 'die' and 're-die' to material sense because it — material sense, the 'master hypnotist' — enters like a thief in the night, when you're unaware, and attempts to convince you of its reality and your need of it. This is a continuous every day, even every hour, dying to matter and living in spirit alone. It is an act of awareness and of God happening as your experience. It is the spiritualizing — illuminating — of being. It is not a physical act. You do not physically cut off your comforts, desires and needs. You lift and re-lift into God alone, spirit alone, and you live ever more by God felt happening and then watch as material comforts, desires and needs drop away for God alone, and the image and likeness of God as the gift of truthful experience.

Look at the life of Jesus; look at the lives of any of the prophets and seers, the illumined ones, and you will find that they were forever presented with the temptation to believe in and rely on matter, to gain good and satisfying condition, to use the power of spirit on matter to harmonize or pacify or fulfill it. But to every temptation came the strength of spirit to say, Get thee hence Satan!

Hour-by-hour belief tries to make a believer out of us, and hour-by-hour we have to say *no* to it, and die and re-die to the belief tempting us this hour. It's an ongoing work, but a beautiful and powerful, life-changing work. When we are grounded and strong in spirit, we know exactly what is tempting us, why, and how to be rid of it. Material belief in this, that or the other has crept in as we were unaware or 'lazy' in our spiritual awareness. We have taken time away from loving God with all our being, and we've forgotten that the moment we do, the master hypnotist — collective awareness, collective belief — enters our 'open back door' and fills us again with the belief in and seeming reality of matter, and the need for its good. "Love the Lord your God with all your heart and with all your soul and with all your strength and with all your mind."

The solution is to lift immediately and completely out of material belief into spiritual. Fill your awareness with truth. Turn within, fill yourself to overflowing with *only God is;* ponder *only God is, only the incorporeal is, only spirit is, only the infinite is, only omnipresence is, and is fully visible, tangible, already wholly manifest and demonstrated, and besides God there is none else* until you feel the peace and freedom of truth welling up within, and then relax and bathe in it. Bathe in the presence of God felt happening. Then you are back; you are back home and you are safe.

Stepping Into and Relying on God Alone

When you are ready to step right into spirit and finally leave matter alone completely, you withdraw all belief, all thought, all effort, all desire and all reliance on matter in and of its own self. All of it has to be withdrawn so that you now live and move and have your being in God. You think only of God as all, and you rely on God alone for all of the life experience. You now take *only God is* as literal and absolutely practical. Your literal satisfaction now is in the God experience, not the material experience — not that you ignore or are uninvolved with material people, things and activities but that you know that they *of their own selves* are not what they appear to be but are God. In knowing their truth and the truth of all things, and in withdrawing all belief in and reliance on appearance for God alone, you witness not only the truth of you but of many others too.

And so, when you are ready to make that step, you give up all materiality for God awareness and God satisfaction alone. Your one truth and the one truth of all the world and every being, thing, amount, activity, place and condition in it, and your one life satisfaction is the God experience itself — God felt happening as your being, your world, your universe and as everything everywhere in it and of it.

As you live by and rely on God alone as the truth and substance of all, you begin to witness the miracle of infinity, limitlessness, effortlessness and true freedom of being, thing and activity — in immeasurably greater and more practical degree than belief could ever imagine.

SATISFIED WITH GOD ALONE

Abundant Fulfillment of Being

People are afraid that stepping into truth and relying on truth alone will strip them of much they love and wish to keep enjoying. This is untrue — although there is a caveat.

Let us understand this now. God *is fulfillment of being.* Truth does not lessen fulfillment but enhance, heighten and expand the experience of being in every way. God is fulfillment not nonfulfillment or sacrifice of being. What did we hear in the last chapter? What is the promise of truth? "He that abideth in me, and I in him, the same bringeth forth much fruit." Indeed, the fruits of truth are abundant and *in this way* — in your and my abundant fulfillment — the Father is glorified. "Herein is my Father glorified, that ye bear much fruit."

Each being is unique and individual and "full of the goodness of God". Your fulfillment is unique and individual just as each vine, even though it be in the same one family of vines, is unique and individual. As "you abide in me, and I in you," and as your satisfaction is God felt happening rather than matter experienced happening — God living itself as you, your body, world and every detail and fruit of it — you will watch as one-by-one and then many-by-many your branches burst forth with abundant fruit.

But, you see, belief, thought and idea does not know what fulfillment is. We think we know what we need and what we want, but we do not. "My thoughts are not your thoughts, neither are your ways my ways." We have heard and meditated on this truth yet we still think we know what we need, what we want and how it is to happen. We desire to retain what is deemed 'good' or gain more and better of it, and we desire to lose or be healed of that which is deemed 'bad' — and to be free of it as quickly as possible.

It is impossible to use or evidence spirit in the pairs of opposites. We cannot use spirit to either retain or gain more and better good, or to lose or be healed of the bad. 'Good' and 'bad' are (by definition) one hundred percent the pairs of opposites — *and one hundred percent incapable of evidencing God or being 'saved' by God.* It is impossible to witness God among them. God is not there, in that state of awareness, neither ever can be. God is *one* and can only be — and is instantaneously — witnessed among itself: one and oneness alone, God as God alone. This is why I have told you that spiritual being has nothing to demonstrate. *All already is*, and is fully finished, manifest and demonstrated, perfectly and instantly visible, tangible and real *in and to and for spiritual consciousness*.

God, spirit, truth has nothing to do with the pairs of opposites, neither *can* do anything about them. Solomon realized this and said, "Give me neither poverty nor riches." Give me satisfaction in and by and of *God alone*. It makes perfect sense that if God is all, and if God is the all-knowing and the all-wise, and if "My thoughts are not your thoughts, neither are your ways my ways" then we do not neither can know what we want or how to get it, or how to be rid of those conditions we do not want, those people or conditions which are causing us pain and suffering. we cannot manufacture it. If we continue in the way of the pairs of opposites — designing and making effort for our own lives — and if we do manage to hold onto, or gain, or improve, or get rid of, or heal or find some relief and freedom, first of all we have not understood truth at all, and secondly, all we do is set up a temporal satisfaction, for it only to collapse and crumble and give us even greater pain tomorrow — whenever 'tomorrow' is.

'Human' Sense Is Not God

The 'human' sense of God, of spirit and of truth is mis-sense — the belief that that which seems to be is something of its own self, either good or bad. So when we seek that which we believe we need we "build a house on sand". We build our relationships on sand, our health and strength on sand, our wealth and success on sand, our peace efforts on sand. We attempt to get and keep more of the good of the pairs of opposites. Even if we temporarily succeed we soon discover the nothingness of that which we gained. The health, wealth, love and peace of belief and name has no law or principle to support it or sustain it, no substance, no truth to its form. It is an image and likeness of the pairs of opposites, not of God, and of course only the image and likeness of God itself is real and upheld by law, principle, substance, body, life, love, peace, harmony and eternality itself. You discover that *that* image and likeness is not built on sand, but a rock which all the storms in the world cannot disrupt or blow down.

SATISFIED WITH GOD ALONE

Eventually we must realize that if we seek to 'get' anything at all *in and of its own self* from the world — that which we can name; that which already exists in and, therefore belongs to the pairs of opposites; that which already exists in and, therefore belongs to "this world" — we are really, in truth, stealing from people who live by and rely on the pairs of opposites for their health, their wealth, their home, their work or business, their charity, their automobile and its gas or electricity, their food, their safety, comfort and happiness. Everything we can name — everything of the pairs of opposites, everything of "this world" — is *in and of its own self* of *its* level of awareness alone, *its* world alone, *its* formation alone, and not of God. God is ever *new formation*, ever fresh, never seen before.

The vine does not seek to acquire its buds, leaves, flowers and fruit from the world of already existent form, but from within. It does not look out, it looks within. It does not 'go to market' or seek its forms of life, business, wealth, security, purpose and satisfaction from other vines with already existent buds, leaves, flowers and fruit, then 'borrow' or 'buy' these from other vines to hang them on its own branches. No! If we saw a vine acting like this we would think it mad! It and every vine under the canopy of heaven has its own and limitless source of good life formation *within*, that 'source' being God itself, the truthful identity of the vine and its entire experience of being. God — the whole of infinity and omnipresence — is the very presence, life, substance, power, intelligence and prosperous expression of the vine.

The vine witnesses its fulfillment by the image and likeness of God, not the image and likeness of "this world". And in this very way we witness our fulfillment. Only *God* is, only *one* is — only *one way, one law, one principle* is. All truthful being and expression operates in the same one way. The minute we awaken to the truth of oneness, we are privy to the secret of nature's fulfillment and realize it as the secret of our own. The way of the vine is also the way of the human.

All form that already exists in and as and of the pairs of opposites — in and as and of "this world" — can only be *circulated* among the people existing in that world. The world's existing goods are all the world *has* — not more, not less and not different. Therefore, the people of the world can only circulate and gain an individual portion of those already existent goods. Each individual vies for as much of the good of the world as he or she can get, or work for, or win, or in desperation lie and cheat for, or steal. Whatever good things and conditions the world has this day, this month or this year is 'all' its population can choose from, vie for and attempt to gain.

If I am of outer, material awareness then I will believe that wealth is dollars. I will believe that the more dollars I have the wealthier I am. Then I will set about trying to 'get' as many dollars as I can by work, business or profession or, if I'm desperate, by borrowing or even stealing them. I am making effort for what is already in the world — in this case dollars — and attempting to get a share for myself and my family and maybe, hopefully, to also give some to others who have not managed to acquire quite the same good share I have.

The One Real, Ever New Form

But the moment we awaken to our spiritual identity — the infinity and omnipresence of *God* being the infinity and omnipresence of experience — and the moment we begin to *live by God felt happening,* we witness the miracle of *fresh form* forever 'coming through' and filling experience.

We no longer seek the world's form, but the *form of God alone.* We never look 'out' for already-formed good to fulfill our experience; we forever look 'in' where — laid out before us and filling our being — we have an *infinity and omnipresence of new form* the world has not seen before. It is the one true and real, infinity of form unconditionally and equally present throughout the expanses of being — limitless, effortless, and eternal. It is experienced by the *spiritual* faculty — the pure, most truthful and most powerful of our faculties — that of *feeling.*

The material faculties of seeing, hearing, tasting, touching, smelling and thinking are those used for the *mind* experience of God — the objectified "this world" experience, the faculties of sense used for the 'human' degree of awareness, "one of the many mansions in my Father's house". But the one spiritual form itself — God itself, oneness itself — is *felt happening.* As it is *felt* and as long as it is known as the *one,* all-inclusive *truth* of being, presence and form — having no 'inner' versus 'outer' — it is quickly witnessed 'coming through' as the objectified image and likeness of itself which the five senses experience as whole, healthy, harmonious and abundant, three-dimensional form.

Literally, *new form* comes through into the world (the objective experience of God). Just as the vine witnesses *new form* coming through into the world — *new* buds, *new* leaves, *new* flowers and *new* fruit the world has never seen before — *new* and healthy organs, functions, muscles and bones come through; *new* dollars come through; *new* love and relationship comes through; *new* peace and harmony comes through; *new* idea and innovation come through; *new* knowledge and skill comes through.

Material belief cannot grasp this truth. Nonsense!, it says. But the moment we awaken spiritually, to truthful identity — the identity of *one* God, *one* being, *one* truth, *one* presence, *one* form, *one* law, *one* principle, *oneness itself being all* — we observe the expression of nature and discover the secret of ourselves. We are one with and as nature, one and the same presence 'happening' as experience, and one and the same *way* of experience because there is none else, and no other way. Only one and one-*ness is.* We are the same one law, one principle in operation — the 'inner' infinity of being — the *truth* of being — ever 'coming through' as new, beautiful and bountiful, objectively sensed form.

It is called 'birth' — the 'birth' of the new and ever greater awareness of the one truth, the one form in and as objectified experience. We witness it all around us, every hour of every day, when we are awake and alive to the truth of experience. Every new bud, leaf, flower, fruit, color and fragrance is birth. Every newborn being is birth. Every new idea, improvement, invention and innovation is birth. Every inner feeling, intuition and sense is birth. All is one and oneness — God, truth, spirit — *being born,* 'coming through' awareness as objectively experienced form.

Wherever we are and whatever we are doing, ever new and abundant form of fulfillment fills our branches of experience. We forever turn within for our good, and *feel* our infinity and omnipresence of all *happening.* That 'happening' is the *one real* and perfectly visible, tangible, manifest and demonstrated — formed — experience. Then we quickly 'meet up' with our own experience appearing as objectified imagery and likeness of God: the fulfillment we experience within, we now experience objectively 'without' — but all *one and the same form, same presence, same substance, same body, same truth:* God as, and being all.

Do you see that if we seek what is already 'out there' in the world, we seek amiss. We are doing nothing but involving ourselves in circulating already existent form rather than 'giving birth' to our own. We seek that which is not our own but somebody else's whether that 'somebody else' is an individual, organization, country or world. It is just as if the vine were to seek other vine's buds, leaves, flowers, fruit, color and fragrance. But the Master told us, "Without me ye can do nothing." Without living by and as your truth of being, you cannot witness a single grain of your truthful formation. Truth *is* form, therefore only as we live as and by the one truth do we witness our truthful form as experience.

Already existent 'outer' form is nothing of its own self, therefore when we seek, make effort for and manage to gain some it we have gained that which is actually nothing of its own self — whether it be the forms of health or wealth or love or harmony or peace. That is why it does not last. That is why it eventually fails us. The outer-focused and sought life let's us down, is both good and bad, is conditional, variable, unreliable and temporal. Truth is none of these. Truth is God, good alone, infinite, omnipresent, unconditional, invariable, effortless and eternal.

But "he who abides in me, and I in him, will bear abundant fruit" — your own and my own new, unique and individual fruit, not seen before in the world. Nothing and no person in the whole world can keep your own away from you. As you know this great, one truth and then as you "abide in me, and I in you" — the "I in you" being God felt happening in you — then your fruit is "quick, sharp and powerful" and, in fact, so powerful that even dense matter cannot keep it from coming through.

In the world we see the miracle of nature pushing through even the densest of resistance. Asphalt roads, concrete walkways and even gigantic boulders cannot stop plant life from pushing through them into expression. In this way, even the most dense material awareness cannot prohibit truth from pushing through as the abundant fulfillment of your own form when you know the truth and from the moment you begin to faithfully live *as* and *by*, and *rely on* and be *satisfied with God alone.*

"I take only what is mine, Lord," Bernie Taupin writes in Indian Sunset. 'Mine' is God, and the image and likeness of God, good, as my formation of experience — not what I of my own self can desire and attain. "I of my own self am nothing", therefore what could I desire and attain if but also nothing. Let us not seek or take or try to find security and satisfaction in other's form or the already existent world's form. Let us seek and take and be satisfied with only "what is mine, Lord" — God itself as me and mine which I quickly has no limit to it but only infinity and omnipresence to it. *Then* I am of truth and of real, new, original and even miraculous value to my world. *Only then.*

"My own shall come to me," says John Burroughs. Yes, your own infallibly and abundantly comes to you, and often at such speed that there "shall not be room to receive it" because "your own" is the very law and principle of being, the infinity and omnipresence of God as form.

At some point in our rising spiritual awareness we realize that to seek, take and be satisfied with form from the 'outer' is really little better than stealing from those who have not yet risen to their spiritual identity, their infinity of being, and who depend on outer form. We ourselves are the god of our experience — "it is written in your law that ye are gods" — the Lord of experience. We have awakened, we are aware of this great truth. Now we must *be it.* We ourselves are able to, and are meant to feed our world, be the light and the life, the water and wine of our world — *be* the good of life, not *take* it.

Give Not Take

Always seek to give to the world of your spiritual substance; never seek to take from what it already is and has. The fruit tree does not exist to consume its own fruit but to ceaselessly and boundlessly give of its fruit to the world.

Be the god — the Lord — of your experience. "The earth is the Lord's, and the fullness thereof." *Be* that Lord. "Son, I am ever with you, and all that I have is yours." If this is the truth of you and of me, and it is, what more could we possible want? Why would we seek, consume and be satisfied with daily finiteness, labor, limit, struggle and temporality when we *are* and *have* the very infinity, omnipresence and eternity that is God unconditionally available as all of experience? The 'I' that is ever with you, and the 'all' that you have is infinity and omnipresence, the very spirit — the very substance — of life-formation itself. You unconditionally *are* and *have* what God is and has, and it is your *conscious, living awareness* of this truth, and your experiential living of the 'I' and that which I has — the actual living as and by and for 'I' felt happening within and as all you are — which gives you literal and tangible and perfectly evident, visible dominion over experience.

And God said, Let us make man in our image, after our likeness: and let them have dominion over the fish of the sea, and over the fowl of the air, and over the cattle, and over all the earth, and over every creeping thing that creepeth upon the earth. . . And God blessed them [every male and female], *and God said unto them, Be fruitful, and multiply, and replenish the earth, and subdue it: and have dominion over the fish of the sea, and over the fowl of the air, and over every living thing that moveth upon the earth.*

You are the 'lord' — the god — of your experience. Wake up! Accept your spiritual identity, your spiritual lordship! Accept your spiritual dominion! *Be* the treasure of heaven *for* the world, not take of the little that already exists in the world. *Be* the beauty and the grace, the love and the life, the peace and the harmony for and of your world. *Be* and continuously give of your spiritual presence because what you *be* you *experience.* "I am the light of the world." *I* — your spiritual being — am the light of the world, the light — the substance — of all formation. Then that light must *be* the light of the world. It is of no use knowing the truth yet not being it. Only *being* is witnessed as experience; knowledge alone is not.

You experience what you *are* and *give.* "Give and it shall be given unto you, good measure, pressed down, shaken together, and running over shall men [the world] pour into your robe [your universe, your experience]. For with the measure that you measure, it will be measured to you." When you measure with (are *being*) infinity and omnipresence, infinity and omnipresence of all good form is "measured to you" — becomes your objectified experience.

Consciousness *is* experience, therefore when you are *being* and endlessly *giving* your spiritual infinity and omnipresence, infinity and omnipresence of all form is your experience.

Recognize God Alone; Live By God Alone

In this awareness, we are forever turned within, aware and alive to spirit as the one reality rather than form as reality. Our awareness is spirit-centered rather than form-centered. We continuously seek spirit for no reason than for spirit itself. We do not bring belief and thought into experience, we seek only God for God, spirit for spirit, truth for truth because when we have God for God we have all.

We ponder spirit and spiritual things morning, noon and night. "Love the Lord your God with all your heart and with all your soul and with all your strength and with all your mind." Our continuous awareness and pondering of God keeps our consciousness open and receptive to the actual experience of God — God felt happening as our being and universe. We live by that felt happening; we rest and bathe in it; we remain the stillness and transparency of being, letting it live itself as the being we are and the world we have — "I live, yet not I, Christ lives my life". We let it itself — God itself felt happening and witnessed as form, and none else but God itself — be the one and only, ever-new and abundant formation (fruit) of experience. Then we serve the world with the gifts truth serves us.

Our entire being and experience is the gift of God, the gift of heaven, the miracle of truthful being *being* and experiencing the beauty, bounty and grace of its universal formation — spiritual, infinite, omnipresent, eternal and unconditionally whole and complete, perfect and purposeful. The gift of God is the gift of you — that which you *are* and *have* and *with which* you feed experience, the world. *I am* the light, the life, the food, the water and the wine of the world, and besides *I* there is none else.

Imagine your every hour, your very life now being the miracle of truth for all in your world, for and as every being who turns to you, for and as all that touches your consciousness — yes, you; certainly as and for your family, your loved ones and loved things and activities, your talent and expression — but as and for *all* inclusively. God is all, so you and I must be all — unconditionally spiritually all, as all, and for all.

When you *have God felt happening within*, you *have all*, not so that you can consume it, but so that you *have* all *as* and *for* all. The Master did not say, I am the light of me, or my family, or my business, or my circle of friends, but I am the light of *the world*. God is God as God for God — and God is the infinitude, the simultaneous omnipresence of all, the all and equal one being, one presence, one formation.

Beginners in awakening misunderstand and think, Oh good, I can have all that God is for me and mine. No, all that God is *is for* all that God is — inclusive of you and yours, but never exclusively. If we attempt to get and have God exclusively, we fail. If we seek God for something of our benefit, we fail. It is as if God does not hear us, or even know us! "Ye ask, and receive not, because ye ask amiss." God is impersonal and omnipresent. As soon as we awaken to this truth we watch the miracle of God everywhere and equally present.

When you feel God happening within, the one infinity and omnipresence of life itself as all formation *is being and feeding the world* — equally and simultaneously. This is the true purpose of you.

"Herein is my Father [truthful being and world; heaven as earth] glorified, that ye bear much fruit."

14

You Are The Miracle

❧

You are and have the whole of infinity and omnipresence *as infinity and as omnipresence*, not infinity as finiteness and omnipresence as local presence. Knowing truth you can *be truth;* knowing truth we each *must* be truth, otherwise all our knowing will be as nothing, and will leave the world just as devoid of truth as it was before we knew.

Only *being truth* evidences truth. As you *be truth*, wherever you are, there is the wholeness and harmony of truth. You are being God consciousness, not personal or selfish, not local, finite, objectified, material being, but spiritual, infinite and omnipresent being. Now all in your atmosphere are lifted and illumined, all are supplied, all are fed, all are known as life itself, joy and happiness itself, love and freedom and satisfaction itself, not for you or for me, but as and for all equally.

You are the miracle. Do you realize why this is true? You cannot be and indeed are not less than the miracle when you awaken to, "Son-daughter, I am ever with you, and all that I have is yours". There isn't a greater miracle than that, and you watch that miracle of truth, and the miracle of you being the very presence of truth, from the moment you awaken to living as and by and for God alone, and from the moment you are *satisfied* with nothing less or different from God felt happening within.

God felt happening is the only experience you want and need, because God *is all*. Therefore as God is actually *being experienced*, the good, wholeness and harmony of all is being experienced. As God is now experientially known rather than just intellectually understood, thought and talked about, all we truly seek — and all we need to truly seek — is the actual God experience. Everything 'else' then takes care of itself. *Take no thought for your life, but seek the kingdom of God instead, and then all these things will be added unto you — good measure, pressed down, shaken together and running over.*

God experienced, inclusive of God pushing through as abundant good form — God felt and witnessed happening — is the only experience we wake up for each morning, the only experience we work for, and the only being, talent and form we *have* to give. There is nothing else truthful about being or experience. If we seek and are satisfied with anything 'else', then we've missed the truth of truths, and we are really doing nothing but stealing from the world — taking from the good health, relationship, wealth, home, harmony and happiness the world already has in it, and in and of which the people of the world need, and rely, and find their satisfaction.

Let's put it like this. Imagine God walked into your room right now and asked *you* for something. Bear in mind, God is *the* infinitude itself, inclusive of the infinity of experience — all one, all the same one infinity and omnipresence of experience. Yet, God asks *you* for something. Of course, if God were to ask you for something, you'd give it, and give it immediately — without thought, without reason, without hesitation. Imagine that. Now let us think. Firstly, why would God, the omnipresence of infinity, ask for something finite and local?

Secondly, if you were of material belief you would now lack that which you gave to God. Imagine the infinite asking something from the finite, leaving the finite lacking even the little it had?

Thirdly, why on earth would God ever want or need something of the finite or, better stated, why would God ever want or need something of earth — that which already exists in the world of corporeal sense?

SATISFIED WITH GOD ALONE

Whatever you could possibly give to God, no matter how much of it you were able to give, God already has — and an infinity and eternity more, never ending, ceaseless and abundant in its flow. God *is* the life we experience formed; God *is* the water, the wine, the fruit of all experience — infinitely and eternally. God already *is* whatever it is, and, not only that, *is* and *has* an infinite infinity of that very form you gave. So how could it possibly be true that God would ever ask you for it?

Why then, would you or I ask a human being or ask the world for anything whatsoever? From the very day we awaken to our truthful identity we would not. "It is written in your law that ye are gods." You are the god of your experience — the whole universe of it. You *are* and *have* all that God is and has. "I am that I am. . . Son-daughter, I am ever with you, and all that I have is yours. . . I and the Father are one. . . The works you see me do, you can do also, and greater than these you can do." God is your truthful identity. Infinity and omnipresence is your truth, your reality and your greatest practical experience. Therefore, do not continue to ask a person or the world for anything it has. Whatever he, she or it has is finite, local, temporal *and needed* for all those who are living a finite, local and temporal belief of existence, and those who do not yet know of their own infinity and omnipresence. Once we have awakened to the truth of being, to our infinity, we must never seek or be satisfied with anything finite. Surely this is clear.

The Presence Of God

It is true that "ye are gods" but we are only the actually evident and practical presence of God when the 'we' we have thought we are, the personal self, is relinquished, and when God lives our being as itself, by itself, for itself, to itself. *As itself, by itself, for itself, to itself.* This is the key.

There is no room for a 'you' or a 'me' or a 'world' — the personal, local, finite, corporeal sense of self and world — in God. Yet, the paradox of truth is that as soon as the personal self is relinquished, and God alone is what we live, and what we live *for*, individual life is fulfilled.

When we are devoid of belief and thought, when we know that only God is, and when we seek nothing but God, and when we live by, and are satisfied with the experience of God actually happening within and as our being and world — which makes it just as impossible to seek or take anything from a person or the world as it is impossible for us, even humanly, to seek or take something that belongs to a child — then indeed we are the presence of God, and where the presence of God is, there is wholeness and harmony of all. "Where the presence of the Lord is, there is liberty."

When we have finally shaken off the majority of the personal sense and exist as a living awareness of God as all; when only God is desired; when our whole purpose, our whole devotion as a being, as a life, is that of the revelation of God, the presence of God made visible, tangible, manifest and real in every day, practical ways that benefit not only 'us' but all who touch our presence, and when we literally live by and rely on and are satisfied with God felt happening as the very life-blood and formation of experience, then we are the presence of the miracle that is God. It has nothing to do with 'us' or anything 'we' are doing, but is the nothingness of the personal sense and our awareness that only God is, and our emptiness — the window of being — that enables God (truth) to be evident. Wherever 'we' are, the fruitage of God becomes evident, and abundantly so. We cannot do anything to block it or stop it from flowing forth as abundant and ever-new fruit filling every activity and place of life anymore than we can stop the sun from shining.

All we have done is relinquish belief and thought, relinquish the personal sense of being and experience. With personal sense relinquished, God is perfectly evident. The fog of false sense is dissolved, and *there God is* perfectly clearly, beautifully, bountifully and unconditionally evident as all.

God is. As I withdraw the senses of belief, and rest my sense of being — giving all of the being I am to God — I quickly begin to feel truth happening within.

The presence I feel happening within is truth itself, God itself, infinity and omnipresence happening as itself as me. What more could I want or need?

I am whole and complete and satisfied with God alone. Nothing 'else' is, therefore I need nothing else.

As we withdraw and relax from, and abandon the material sense of God — the personal sense of self and world — completely letting God be God as being and world; and as we are satisfied with God alone as all the formation of fulfillment we could ever want or need, our experience "bears rich fruit".

Withdrawing and relaxing from, and abandoning the material sense of its own self does not mean we are poor in 'material' good. It means the opposite! Material good becomes rich and abundantly so. Remember forevermore that material experience is simply a material *sense* of spirit, a corporeal *sense* of the incorporeal, God. Sense is not incorrect, 'evil', wrong or erroneous and does not produce erroneous experience. Sense alone is innocent. Only *belief* in the sensed experience *as being something of its own self* is erroneous. The falsity is belief, and it is belief, not sense, that leaves us with the pairs of opposites experience — the multitudes of good and the multitudes of bad, and every degree of both. Belief itself *is* the pairs of opposites, and this you can prove anytime you wish to by realizing that every belief has an opposite.

There is nothing at all wrong or incorrect or untrue about the material or corporeal sense of God — the sense we call 'human' and 'this world'. Oh, if you can truly grasp this you will walk into your freedom this day! The very moment we drop the belief in sensed experience as being something of its own self — in form, name, category, character, nature, condition, amount or place being an entity in and of its own self — and realize, rest in, and rely on God felt happening as being the totality experience, rich and fruitful in every way, we are free.

As we thoroughly live the God life it looks, from material sense, as if we are ever more creative, busy and productive. It appears as if we have unusual energy on little sleep, that we have a quiet wisdom and knowledge about us, that life presents opportunity after opportunity, that we are doing something very clever or effective in our life. Indeed we are, but it has nothing to do with *our* doing it or being it or achieving it — other than our willingness to go with the flow truth perpetually presents.

People may say of us, He or she is so productive, so busy. But we are none of these; we are riding the wave of God; we are the willing animation of God itself, the almighty truthful being 'happening' as the being we are. *We* do not work yet we are witnessed working; *we* do not perform yet we are witnessed performing; *we* are not creative, productive or successful yet we are witnessed being creative, productive and successful and there is only one reason: we now know that only God is, and we are finally *enabling* God *to be God* as us and our experience.

"I perform that which you are given to do". . . or stated even better,

"I perform you". . . even better, "I *am* you". . . even better, "I am". . . even better, "I". . . even better. . . (silence).

The Rich Fruits of Silence

In the silence and sanctuary of God felt happening, the fruits of experience are rich, abundant and rewarding. Never be confused about the truthful life and its rich fruits of fulfillment. Never believe that living truthfully means you have to sacrifice good and abundant experience. Experience becomes *more* abundant and *more* treasure-filled, not less so.

We do not live like beggars. "I have been young, and now am old; yet I have not seen the righteous forsaken, nor his descendants begging bread." The 'righteous' are the people living in God-as-all awareness, and living by and relying on God itself experienced happening as the substance and form of all. 'Descendants' refers to the branches of experience. The God-aware and God-living person is not forsaken, and all the descendants or 'extensions' of experience are not in poverty but are filled with the "rich fruits' that "glorifies the Father".

No, we do not live in a state of poverty, under the guise of 'holy poverty'. *But* we have lost our materially-believed life in order to gain our spiritually-true life. Anytime you read of 'poverty' or 'sacrifice' in scripture it refers to that of material belief and reliance, not that of true life.

All we have to do is observe the illimitable beauty and bounty of the vineyard, the orchard, the forest, the mountain, the valley and the field forever bursting with grasses, shrubs, trees, leaves, flowers, berries, fruits, colors and fragrance to realize that truthful life is not that of poverty but ceaseless and boundless, rich expression.

But we now know the *truth* of form, therefore we seek *it itself* rather than the objectified forms of it which appear as and through mind. We have discovered the secret: the more of truth itself we experience happening — the more of truth, God, spirit itself fills our being and universe — the more good and plentiful forms of truth we have in our world. We have lost interest in gaining the things of the world for their own sake. We have little more interest in material health, wealth and relationship than we have for shadows on the ground or clouds in the sky, because we now have infinity itself. Why would we seek finite, objectified forms one-by-one throughout life when we have the whole of infinity itself at every step, which — when sought for itself alone — illumines our whole being, presenting us with unlimited forms of every good thing?

Ah, the reason is that we have believed that infinity and omnipresence are what *God* is and has, but not what *we* are and have. Right there is the problem, and in fact, the *only* problem — the *belief* of there being a difference between God *and* man. The moment we awaken to the truth of God as one and all — incorporeal, infinite, eternal and omnipresent — we seek God alone and find ourselves surrounded with an abundance of good matter.

Let us awaken to the truth that we are life itself — eternal and invariable — and cease from seeking a little improved life, or even healing. Let us awaken and realize that life does not need healing, that life itself is whole and perfect and eternally so, and that only poor *sense* needs healing.

The Work

The work now, each individually, is to one-by-one withdraw from wishing anything of this world — in and as and for its own self, its own form, its health, its wealth, its amount, its result, its love, its happiness, its success — and to literally now seek God alone as all, *for* God alone as all.

I want nothing this hour, this day but to God aright, and to feel God happening within me, as me, and as my universe.

The rest of my experience, I know, is incidental. It is nothing in and of its own self and yet it is the fullness of God. Experience and all the forms of experience are, of their own selves images alone, shadows alone, false belief alone, yet as the truth of God as all in known, all formation is witnessed as, and indeed is, God and nothing less, nothing different, therefore infinite, omnipresent and eternal and unconditionally free to and as experience.

I no longer desire just physical health, vitality, beauty and energy. If I do still desire these things and conditions of life, I still do not understand; I am still mis-identifying what God is and what I am.

No, I now desire only God as body — the incorporeal, the spiritual, the eternal one body that is God being individual me, and all being.

As I now desire and am satisfied with nothing but God as all, and as I rest and relax in God, I feel God happening, and then I tangibly have God as actual experience.

As you consciously live by and are satisfied with God felt happening, life is no longer temporal in experience, but eternal. Now the body can never die and can never be born, but is eternality itself. To material sense the body is believed to one day die, but to you and me in spiritual identity and living God awareness, the body is life and eternity itself because there is no other.

There is no dying and no being born, but continual spiritual transformation as the ever more pure, graceful, and divine body of truth, individually and uniquely expressing as you, ever more joyous and free, purposeful and giving.

I do not seek dollars, nor am I satisfied with dollars alone. I seek and am satisfied with God alone — the incorporeal, the infinite and the omnipresent itself. God and 'dollars' are not 'two' different things or forms or states; the 'two' are the same one. "I and the Father are one".

Dollars are simply objectified forms of infinity, appearing objectified only because mind forms infinity into appearing objects, amounts and activities. But all form is all of God — infinite and omnipresent.

Therefore, I seek God alone, and as I do, and as I am satisfied with the infinity of God as all — God felt happening within and as all of me — I am filled with the abundance of all forms of infinity.

The dollars we use in three-dimensional experience are simply conceptually perceived forms of infinity — but never separate, never different, never needing to be increased. That which is already infinite and omnipresent cannot be increased, nor ever needs to be. Only poor *sense* needs to increase (spiritualize, illumine, rise) to become truthful sense.

If we seek dollars for their own sake, we mis-identify and mis-perceiving what dollars actually are. If we know them as the very presence of God itself — infinity and omnipresence itself — we are in truthful identity and truthful awareness, and we can rest and relax in the midst of that infinity and omnipresence and watch all the dollars we need at every step seeking us. The days of seeking and laboring, and sometimes having to struggle for a sufficiency of dollars are over the moment we awaken to the infinity and omnipresence — the already present presence — of all form, including the form we call dollars.

Hear it well: you need never seek, labor or struggle for that which is already present. It seeks you the moment you know it is present, and then open yourself to receive it in experience — just as when you know the sun is already present, all you have to do is open the drapes to experience all the sun you need or want seeking you.

Seeking The Kingdom of God

Again and again, I turn within, I seek and ponder within, I seek and ponder the spiritual things, the kingdom of God rather than the kingdom of matter:

What is God? What is this that wells up within me, despite me — so lovingly, tenderly and unconditionally that even though I have been remiss in knowing God many times this day, still its presence fills me?

As I have fallen down a thousand times again this day, tempted into believing I need something of the world of health or finances or love or harmony or safety or security, nevertheless, as I turn within and as I give what I actually am half a breath of a chance, then there it is, welling up within me, filling me and my universe of awareness with all its love, all its life, all its wealth and all its harmony.

God is the only wealth I want. I do not want to 'sell' whatever I have to people; I do not want to persuade people; I do not want an agenda each day other than God-agenda.

I do not want to make a profit from the world. What is profit other than theft from the moment I have awakened to my truthful identity, my God being? If I set out to make profit from the world and the world's people, I have not awakened! I am the god of my experience, the Lord of my earth. I have come to give and serve, not to take, not to profit. "Whosoever will be great among you, let him be your minister; And whosoever will be chief among you, let him be your servant: Even as the Son of man came not to be ministered unto, but to minister."

I come not to profit from the world but as the prophet of my world. I am prophet — p-r-o-p-h-e-t. Why would I seek profit from the world, when I am, as true being, the true prophet itself?

I am the infinity of all form and all of experience — infinite being, infinite body, infinite amount — because the 'I' I am is the 'I' God is. Therefore, life, love, purpose, success and prosperity is the very presence and purpose of me, and is abundantly evident as I let God itself live itself as the being and world I am.

I do not 'do' anything — 'I' is all, and 'I' does all. Do you think Moses himself had anything to do with the miracle of the parting of the Red Sea? Was it by his ability, his effort, his doing, even his 'spiritual' doing? Of course not. Do you think the feeding of the four and five thousand men — plus women and children too — was anything to do with the man Jesus? Of course not. Jesus himself tells us this: "I of my own self am nothing. . . it is the Father within me that does these works."

No, the parting of the Red Sea and the multiplying of form is not achieved by man. How can man or woman part a sea or multiply form? Humanity has been trying and failing to do such works for thousands of years. But when it is realized that all form is God, therefore already and forever infinite and omnipresent; when it is realized that all being is God, therefore already and forever in harmonious, peaceful, safe, joyous and satisfied experience, and then when, in that awareness, we withdraw to our withinness and live the fulfillment that is God — feel the fulfillment of truth living, happening, experienced within — then *there* the miracle of safe, harmonious and plentiful form is witnessed. The disease, lack, limitation or disharmony dissolves to reveal the healthy, harmonious and plentiful form that has always been there but clouded by false belief.

God Is Changeless; Experience Harmonizes

As we observe the fulfillment we are experiencing within, through the unconditioned (belief-free, thought-free) mind, experience is witnessed changing, harmonizing, healing, pacifying and prospering. God is not changing; God is forever whole and complete, but awareness is lifted and illumined, and witnesses itself changing, harmonizing, healing, pacifying and prospering. Awareness moves, God does not.

Nothing *actual* is taking place. Awareness is lifting, being illumined, becoming more spiritual, and because awareness is experience, as awareness moves, experience moves; as awareness becomes whole and harmonious, experience becomes whole and harmonious.

Your arm cannot move by itself, but as awareness of your arm moves from here to there, your arm moves from here to there. The form follows awareness because form is not something of its own self, but is awareness alone. The arm itself is a dead piece of flesh — nothing of its own self. Awareness is what it is; therefore only awareness moving is the experience of the arm moving.

In this same way, as awareness is spiritualized, lifted and illumined, filled with the actual 'happening' of God, that awareness is experienced as the image and likeness of itself as form — the good and truthful forms of health, wealth, happiness, harmony, abundance and peace. Great miracles are often witnessed, and equally great 'natural' harmony and peace and joy is witnessed. No matter what 'name' or 'category' we give it, it is God — God experientially happening as individual you and me.

God is the miracle; you and I are simply beholders of God as experience, beholders of the miracle in experience. The miracle is within, and is experienced within, then beheld through mind as the miracle of form — God, mind, form — all one, and now *experienced* as one.

This is how miracles are witnessed. This is how the abundant fruits of God are witnessed — the complete withdrawal from wishing to gain, improve, heal, prosper, pacify or harmonize anything of form, or equally to be rid of, reduce or avoid anything of form — and then the living by and reliance on the God experience alone. There's the miracle, and there's the miracle happening as you, and as every person and thing that touches your being.

Be satisfied with God felt happening within as all. It's all you ever need. Live it; don't visit it, but actually live as and by and for God felt happening within. Let it be your life in all and every way; let it be the new and fresh you 'born' into experience each morning, each hour, each moment.

Let it reveal the truth of experience here, there and everywhere; let it be life; let it be love; let it supply; let it be all, without a single effort made by you — not even the effort of knowing truth and expecting what you know to appear as good experience. Only God is, therefore let God be God as God as you as all. Then you will witness the earth and all its good seeking and finding you.

You Are The Miracle

Serene, I fold my hands and wait,
Nor care for wind, nor tide, nor sea;
I rave no more 'gainst time or fate,
For lo! my own shall come to me.

I stay my haste, I make delays,
For what avails this eager pace?
I stand amid the eternal ways,
And what is mine shall know my face.

Asleep, awake, by night or day,
The friends I seek are seeking me;
No wind can drive my bark astray,
Nor change the tide of destiny.

What matter if I stand alone?
I wait with joy the coming years;
My heart shall reap where it hath sown,
And garner up its fruit of tears.

The waters know their own and draw
The brook that springs in yonder height;
So flows the good with equal law
Unto the soul of pure delight.

The stars come nightly to the sky;
The tidal wave unto the sea;
Nor time, nor space, nor deep, nor high,
Can keep my own away from me.

John Burroughs

16

The Way Of Healing

❦

PART 1

Dissolving False Sense

Spiritual healing is real and scientific. The body's healing and sustained health and vitality is the experience of *principle* — one hundred percent real and scientific — just as the principle of gravity, aerodynamics and math is one hundred percent real and scientific. When we come to the momentous point of realizing that with belief and thought withdrawn, *there God is*, our awareness is open and we quickly begin to experience the true body.

Healing of the false sense of body has begun. When we have finally given up the attempt to heal, pacify, harmonize, prosper or transform that which appears to be, in the living realization that, despite appearance and suggestion, only God is — forever whole and perfect, therefore never in need of healing — then we have arrived at the point of being free of the struggle we have put ourselves through in awakening to truth.

When we first hear that God is life, false belief assumes that spiritual meditation and silence will heal the physical body: "Oh, good! God consciousness can heal my body; God can bring health, strength and vitality to my body; God can transform my illness or disease or injury to health and wholeness." God does no such thing and anybody who has tried to get God to heal his or her's or another's body has discovered the futility of such effort.

God cannot heal a human body anymore than math can heal 2+2=3 or aerodynamics can heal a broken airplane. The incorporeal cannot heal or even influence the corporeal no matter how many hundreds of hours of meditation and silence are put into attempting it. Why? Because only *God is;* only the *incorporeal is.* The physical — the corporeal — is *sense* alone, not reality. The physical is not an entity but just sense — a corporeal *sense* of the incorporeal, the infinite, the true. There is only *one,* therefore only the *one* body and *one* condition, that being *God,* the *incorporeal* body and condition — the *spiritual* body and condition.

God which is incorporeal cannot give birth to a corporeal being with a corporeal body; nor can God create a corporeal universe for his corporeal beings to live in, and then heal it all when it goes wrong. If you can catch this truth, you are free of the material belief that binds. With the truth that God is all, and that God is incorporeal, you rest and relax in *is,* not wishing for the corporeal to heal but for the revealing of the image and likeness of the incorporeal. In this state of awareness, restfulness and relaxation, you behold false sense dissolving to reveal truthful being, body and world. You now expect and are satisfied with nothing but the *God experience itself as the tangible form and presence of all good.* In this spiritually elevated state of being, you will not only be able to 'heal' but heal rapidly.

Realize that all failure in spiritual healing is the attempt to have an incorporeal God heal a corporeal body and world. As soon as you realize that only God is — which means only the incorporeal is — you have the truth that the corporeal is nothing but sense. Anything of corporeal experience is sense not reality. The whole pairs of opposites — both the good and the bad — are sense not reality. God — the incorporeal — cannot be ill, weak or dying; *neither* can be healthy, strong and vital because all of these are corporeal states of being, the bad versus the good. The incorporeal does not contain corporeal states of being. God is God alone — pure and invariable. There is nothing to heal in God and nothing different 'out there' for God to heal. Spiritual healing is not the act of changing matter from ill or diseased to healthy and vital, but that of *illuminating sense*. As quickly as sense is illumined, the image and likeness of body — the body form — is experienced as healthy, true and vital.

A False Sense of Truth

We live with a false sense of truth, a false sense of identity. Our one truth of being is God, spirit, incorporeal being experiencing his or her glorious incorporeal universe — whole and complete, infinite and omnipresent at every point of experience at the same time. This is the first great truth: only God is, only the *incorporeal* is — forever whole, perfect and complete; alight with joy, purpose and freedom.

But sense is experience. Whatever sense is collectively believed *is* collective experience, and if the individual is mesmerized by collective belief, collective belief is experienced individually. This is the explanation for all the good and bad of human experience, both collectively and individually — all the wonder, beauty and majesty of the world *and* all of its disease, disaster and suffering.

Being *is* its own universe of experience. Whatever an individual's sense of identity is, *is* his or her experience. Nothing happens 'outside' of being. There is no 'outside'. All is one and oneness; all is being experiencing itself — its consciousness (universe) of sense. If we live with a multitude of beliefs about who we are, what the world is, and what every 'he, she and it' in the world is — as we have been taught to do by our collectively influenced parents, education system and society — then we live a mesmerized sense of experience. But "one with God is a majority". As soon as we awaken to the truth of God as the one and only existence, false sense dissolves to reveal truthful experience — the experience of one and oneness, wholeness and completeness.

Healing a False Sense of Body

We have been raised to believe that the body is physical and personal, subject to either healthy or unhealthy physical condition. Because sense is experience — and because experience is 'reality' to the one who believes it — the 'physical' body seems to be very real to one whose discernment is limited to physical sense. To that individual, it really seems as if the physical body is real, but it is not. Only the spiritual body exists because only spirit is.

You do not have a physical body. Belief believes so, but belief is nothing *but* belief. Only spirit is; therefore only the spiritual body is, and because spirit is forever whole and perfect, it is never in need of healing. You cannot heal that which has no need of healing! This is why all attempts to use spirit to heal a physical body and a material world fail. Sense is what needs healing, not the object *of* sense. You cannot heal that which does not exist but you *can* heal the false *sense* of existence. The reason humanity forever struggles with what it terms 'health' and 'healing' is its belief in — and attempts to heal and keep healthy — the objective body. The great secret of individual and mass healing is the healing of individual and mass *sense*, not object.

If you hold onto the belief of an incorporeal God and a corporeal man and universe, populated with corporeal things, activities, amounts and conditions, and then reach out to God to heal that corporeality, you cannot succeed. There is no spiritual truth or principle to the corporeal — either its good or bad. Corporeal experience is sense alone and is not, in and of its own self, real. That is why all attempts to heal the physical body and material world *by God, spirit and truth* fail. If the object of disharmonious or diseased sense is believed to be, of its own self real, then all attempts to bring healing and health to experience are focused on the *it*, the *object itself,* therefore on sense instead of reality. In this way, focus is turned in exactly the wrong direction. Belief has succeeded in convincing sense that *it*, not God, is real. "Ye ask, and receive not, because ye ask amiss."

If we still believe in the corporeal, we have not understood the truth that *only God is* even if we have heard it a thousand times. There is no such thing as a corporeal body or any other corporeal form, place or condition in all of God, which is the only. Only God is, only the incorporeal is. The incorporeal, which is the only, cannot heal or do anything else about the corporeal experience, which is just sense. Ah, but therein lies the secret. As soon as it is realized that ill, diseased or disharmonious form is actually ailing *sense*, then focus turns towards healing (illuminating) sense. As sense is spiritually illumined, the forms of sense are revealed to be whole, healthy and harmonious. This is spiritual healing.

It is only when we have incorporeal God and incorporeal man — incorporeal God *as* incorporeal being — that we witness the miracle of truthful being with his or her truthful body. Through spiritual — *incorporeal* — consciousness the sublime and eternal body of spirit emerges as the image and likeness of itself as our sensed 'physical' body. The perfect spiritual body exists eternally. This minute your body, and all body, is the perfect spiritual body. None else exists. But the fog of false belief disguises it from sense, making its experience discordant, disharmonious, ill, diseased and eventually dead. *All* of this variable, pairs-of-opposites experience is false belief alone, never reality. Reality exists eternally undisturbed — perfectly and *tangibly* real, whole and vital, unrealized amidst the fog of false belief — and can be awakened to at any moment; and because awareness is forever formed, the awakened body awareness *is itself* the healthy, vital, beautiful, purposeful and eternal body *form* — the 'physical' body healed and transformed in experience.

Healing is infallible once, first, we cease from attempting to heal the 'human' body and instead realize that only God is, therefore only the God-body is; and second, when we realize that only *God-felt-happening* is the actual body. Then the experience of body transforms from false (corporeal) to true (incorporeal), and it is whole and well.

Healing a False Sense of Supply

It is the same with supply. We've learned in past teachings that God is supply. . . God is the infinite storehouse of all good including dollars. . . . God is infinite and omnipresent abundance. This is all true, but if we assume that incorporeal God has, and somehow sends us, an abundance of corporeal dollars, we will continue to struggle with lack and limitation.

The truth of life, including that of wealth, has been given us 2000 years ago by the Master, then again by Mary Baker Eddy, Joel S. Goldsmith and now by the Miracle Self, but because humanity lives with a false sense of identity, it misses the secret. Humanity believes its identity, and the identity of all of experience, is corporeal when actually it is incorporeal. This false belief is the reason for all of humanity's struggle and suffering, including that of wealth and sufficiency in all its forms including dollars. The belief in the corporeal being real is so deeply ingrained that when human sense hears the word 'supply' or 'wealth' or 'prosperity' or 'abundance', it immediately assumes 'dollars' or means of 'gaining' dollars. For years, I was stuck with the same ingrained belief. For the life of me, I couldn't grasp what was meant by "God is supply", nor could I lose the idea that somehow God had to be evident as the dollars I needed to pay my way in this world. The belief in corporeality was too deeply embedded.

Corporeal sense cannot see that which is. It senses separation, incompleteness and need. But truth is one, complete and omnipresent — not just 'in God' but in and as *all*. There is only one, therefore only one presence, one form, one experience. Where corporeal awareness sees lack and therefore need, incorporeal awareness sees wholeness and completeness, and therefore no need. It sees that which *is* instead of a false *sense* of that which is — the false sense which makes oneness appear to be a multitude, separate and apart, lacking and limited, incomplete and needy, subject to the pairs of opposites.

Understand that *all* is spirit — the incorporeal — omnipresent and whole at all times, incapable of being partially present, locally present, incomplete and therefore in need. Experience which appears to lack any good form or quality of or quantity of completeness, *is not*. Form is forever whole and complete and is incapable of being partial or incomplete. That which appears to be lacking is a *lack of true sense* which makes *experience* seem to lack good, complete and omnipresent form. *Lack is never an object of lack but is a lack of incorporeal awareness.* As soon as incorporeal awareness becomes greater than the corporeal, then wholeness and completeness of experience — that which this minute and forever *is* — is witnessed.

God does not 'do' anything — either for you, me or the Master! God *is*, not 'will be'. God is finished, whole and complete, one and omnipresent. And because God is *the only* — the finished infinite that is *all* without even a grain left over, or left out — nothing anywhere, at any time, for any reason or under any circumstance is incomplete, partial and in need. Only God is, and God is finished, whole and complete as all. As individual awareness begins to realize and live this wondrous and principled truth, we begin to experience it as the completeness of form.

As you awaken to this truth when it comes to dollars, the 'objects' named 'dollars' and the multitude of objective needs dollars pay for, fade from concern, no longer seducing your attention, and are replaced with an ever-increasing desire to seek and experience the one reality, the *incorporeal* — the infinite and one omnipresent wealth that is God itself as all. Belief dissolves, objects of sense fade, and truth emerges as the one incorporeal reality of being and world, always and forever complete, whole, harmonious, peaceful and fulfilled.

Healing a False Sense of Love

God is love. Immediately belief hears this truth, it has the idea of 'human' love, 'human' relationship, 'two' in a loving relationship 'together'. God is love becomes the bringing together or the healing or joy of 'human' love, 'human' relationship.

In believing this, being and love is still mis-identified. Mis-identity is the reason truth does not 'work'. Truth cannot be evident as or through human, physical, material, corporeal, local or personal identity any more than math can be evident through a non-mathematical mind. God is perfectly tangible and visible as and through the God-mind, but perfectly *intangible* and *invisible* to the non-God mind! God is *incorporeal.* It is only when we are awake and aware incorporeally — incorporeal being aware of its incorporeal universe (experience) — that we witness the miracles of truth as universal form. The forms of experience *appear to come together,* become whole, complete, loving and harmonious.

Existing love is experienced healing, transforming, blossoming, becoming ever new, more joyous and purposeful, or new love is discovered. But these objective experiences are nothing more than the image and likeness of oneness awakened to — the *oneness* of incorporeality experienced as the oneness of mind appearing as the oneness of whole and harmonious form. Form appears more beautiful, wondrous, affluent, graceful, peaceful, purposeful and harmonious; but realize that form is not 'changing' — even though it appears to be — because it forever has been, and is, whole and complete; now though the true and eternally perfect form is more *evident*, more visible and more tangible to your experience because *you* are recognizing its truthful identity, which is incorporeality.

All is one, that one being eternally fully finished, perfect, whole, manifested, demonstrated, visible and tangible, and incapable of being less or different. So the experience of wholesome, happy, abundant, loving and peaceful form eternally *is*. The only experience you can ever have — the only experience you are having this minute — is actually, despite your sense of it, whole and perfect, and fully visible and tangible too. But a low spiritual *sense* makes the one whole and perfect form appear to be incomplete and imperfect. It is not, but it *appears to be*. The perfect and already-existant form is evident only by the degree we are *being* true oneness, true spiritual being, identifying only the *one* as all.

Truth is witnessed when truth is known and lived. It is fully present all the time, but it must be known and lived to be evident. When we have stopped believing in form being something other than God-form, and equally, when we have stopped attempting to gain more good form and lose more of the bad in the realization that all already is God-form, then we are free of belief and able to evidence truth throughout experience.

Truth is witnessed only when we realize that only God is — literally and tangibly, despite appearance that tries its best to tempt us otherwise — and only as we live within, with our attention, interest and reliance seated firmly with God and none else.

I am interested in the spiritual I that I am, not a false sense of it, but it itself, the one true I; the I that I really am.

Why would I not be interested in the true I from the moment I realize that only God is? Therefore, I seek the spiritual I of me, the spiritual body of me, and the spiritual universe of me, which has nothing to do with sense, but only of reality itself — God itself.

We must cease from seeking an improved or healed physical experience — whether it be of the individual sense of body; or the body of our family, home, business, money; or of union, peace, justice and harmony of the world body. We must stop seeking an improved or healed or enriched or pacified sense of experience, and seek the truth itself — the truthful, spiritual identity of being, world and universe. We must rest and retire belief, and seek awareness of I itself as all that is. 'Our' understanding is "foolishness to man" — to 'human' sense.

Go within and be taught of truth itself; let truth itself spring up as a living felt-experience within, and blossom and become the awareness of it itself alive as you — greater, greater, greater each time; more and more vivid, more tangible each time we go, and we rest and feel and bathe in that happening within. Rely one hundred percent on it itself alone. Then watch, just watch.

Expectation

If God is all, which God is, what do you expect of God? What do you expect of God-awareness, meditation and silence? Many students still expect God to be what God is not — corporeal, objectified and personal. How can that which *is*, and is the *only*, be something it is not? How can the incorporeal, which is the infinite and omnipresent only, be corporeal finite and objectified for a personal you or a personal me or even a personal world? Of course it cannot, and all attempts to get God to be what God is not will continue to fail. If only the world could awaken to this truth, we'd see all suffering and pain, all lack and limitation, wiped from earth in a moment.

Expect God from God, and then you will discover you *are* and *have* the whole of God as the whole of your being and experience, and not only 'yours', but with enough for your whole community and beyond.

Yes, indeed, as God is experienced through the mind as form, there is the abundance and rich fruitage of God as the formed image and likeness. Yes, the abundance and love and miracle of experience is infallible, but only so as we are *being*, and are satisfied with, God alone — God as God, for God, and to God, with no 'human' or 'world' or 'personal condition' in consciousness.

God or spirit — the incorporeal — does not become corporeal, objectified, finite, personal or local. God is sensed as and through the three dimensional and five-sensed mind as formation, but nothing of formation is 'changed' God, 'lesser' or 'less of' God, 'different' God or 'differently experienced' God. Remember, nothing is capable of changing or reducing God one iota because there is no being, no presence, no power, no law or principle other than the *one* that *is God* and God alone. Only God is. Nothing of truth has changed as we experience form. Form is God; God *is* mind *is* form. "All things [forms] were made through him, and without him nothing [no form] was made that was made."

Only truth is; therefore, "the only thing that can ever present itself to you is God", but if we observe experience with belief that it of its own self — its own appearance — is real, then God is not real as our experience. Only God — incorporeality, infinity, omnipresence and eternity itself — is what you are, what you have, what your world is and has. Only God. It doesn't matter that we observe God through the 'finitizing and objectifying glasses' of sense. Our sense makes no difference to God, to truth, to the one principle and presence of life. The only life, being, body, form, amount and condition is God.

Everywhere you observe, and every being and thing you observe, is God for there is none else. Sense does not change that one truth, nor can it, just as sense does not, nor can, change anyone or anything *other than the senser's experience*. It takes a believer of sense to experience sense as 'reality', but as soon as belief is removed, truth itself stands perfectly visible, strong and eternal as all form.

Withdraw Belief

All we are doing is withdrawing belief or fixation from that which appears to be, and giving our love and our interest — our devotion — to that which actually is. Turn within, to what you sense as your physical withinness, and there gently and joyously and freely begin to ponder truth.

Remember, all good *already is*. You do not have to 'make' your good become real for you; it already is real and standing right where you need it, as perfect fulfillment, perfectly visible and tangible. Know this truth, and therefore ponder gently, without effort or urgency. This is the key. Stay in a rested and relaxed state of being as you ponder the truth you've learned throughout these pages, realizing that the truth you are pondering is already true and real. Your attention and contemplation, now on truth, quickly dissolves the clouds of belief previously held.

In other words, you leave appearance alone. You make no effort toward either the problem or the seeming solution. All 'human' or intellectual belief is dropped, and you now abide here within, pondering truth until you feel a peace welling up. "As you abide in me..."

Then stop pondering, and let truth itself 'take over'. Let God itself get on with being entirely what *it is* as your being, with nothing of 'you' present to cloud it. Become a nothingness, a vacuum, an empty vessel, a puppet with no personal presence or effort or desire. Give up personally, and *let God be God as itself as you.* Simply sit as a nothingness and behold God 'happening' as you — but not the 'you' you are familiar with, rather the God-being you actually are. Be free in allowing God to be whatever God is as you in truth. In that way, you will discover your infinity and freedom of being here and now. But if you continue to cling on to the personal sense of self, you never will.

Give yourself entirely to God, and trust that God is the perfection, wholeness and intelligence of the being that he-she is as you and your experience — as indeed God is. Be rid of all personal self, all personality and everything of it — all its traits, needs and desires — and let God completely take over. "I live, yet not I, Christ [God, spirit, truth itself] lives my life."

As you let God take over, you feel a deep restfulness spreading throughout you, a blissful state of rest and relaxation welling up from within or *as* the very essence of your being. This is truth being felt, truth being tangibly experienced. As you sit, as a nothingness, experiencing truth 'happening', the 'happening' is universal and omnipresent. Although it may feel as if it is happening only 'within you' or 'as you', it is not. It is happening as the entire universe of you and every grain of it.

All is good, God, the moment you feel God happening. Remember, you cannot divide or separate or localize or personalize God even though belief may sense God happening only personally or locally, within. God is infinite and omnipresent, indivisible and inseparable. The only God there is is infinity and omnipresence, equally present at every point or place of itself, infinitely, at the same time. Be assured that as you feel God happening, you are experiencing the infinity and omnipresence of the finished kingdom of every grain and condition of your *whole* experience.

Seeking, finding and experiencing God are 'achieved' the minute you start feeling truth welling up within, and sitting with the experience, letting it live you. You have now tangibly witnessed the miracle of God as you, or 'in' your experience, and you are now very satisfied with that experience alone (for there is none else).

I remember the very day I first experienced the miracle of God 'taking over' my whole life. I was sitting in my tiny, cubby-hole office, personally helpless, with no hope anywhere on the horizon, my life draining away, and just enough money left for a little food. My situation was so desperate that I laughed at its hopelessness. It was late afternoon and I'd spent the day reading truth. Nothing was helping, nothing was talking to me.

Then I suddenly felt the impulse to give up all 'my' sense, 'my' effort, 'my' need. I put down what I was reading, and gave the whole of my being, body and world to God. I realized that what I thought of as being 'me', 'my body' and 'my world' was not; it was God. A deep, blissful, total rest and relaxation quickly spread throughout me as, for the first time, I let God be the whole presence, being, body and world *of itself* as the being I was, instead of 'me' and 'mine'. I realized that the being and body and world of 'me sitting here' is not in any way what I sense it to be, but is God. The very presence of 'me' is actually the entire presence of God, the finished kingdom, the whole of the infinite, and all that the infinite is and has, omnipresent here as 'me'. "Let God be God as itself as me," I realized. Get 'me' completely out of the equation. I had never before felt as relieved and rested and cared for as I did that magical moment, and from that day onward life changed.

This is the great key or *way* of experiencing truth. Be rid of the personal sense of self — completely rid of it. Realize that the presence of you, which means the entire consciousness of you, your entire universe of sense, is actually God. Therefore, *let God be God as itself* as 'you' — never 'for' you, never to benefit 'you', never to heal or prosper or pacify or love 'you' — but *as and for and to itself alone*. Then all you have to do is *behold* the miracle of truth 'happening' as and throughout your experience. It is as a surprise, a gift — a miracle of good — because your attention and effort is no longer on 'you' and 'yours', but on God *for* God alone. This is the way of healing.

The Form of God Experienced

God felt happening 'within', or as the essence or presence of being, *is* the experienced truth of being, body and world. When self is empty

— truly empty, a nothingness, a vacuum with no personal agenda, desire or need remaining — and God is felt happening as the presence of being, *that experience is itself* the manifested and demonstrated, visible and tangible, and very real wholeness of God as all. The clouds of false sense have dissolved, and God is fully revealed and real. When you know this truth, you are free in the goodness and completeness of all experience. If you do *not* know it, and expect something 'else' to happen in or for or to experience in and of its own self, experience stubbornly refuses to budge from its inharmonious state. You know now that 'it' is not refusing to budge, but *you are* by hanging onto the belief that form is separate or different from God, and that the experience of God happening within has to somehow translate to the experience of good happening in form.

The miracles of truth are witnessed objectively — the image and likeness of God as form — when you know ("Know the truth, and that very truth will set you free") that God experienced *is good form experienced* — infinite and equally present good form. God experienced within does not 'produce' good form, but *is itself* the good (God) form because God *is* mind *is* form. God does not pour 'through' a faculty called mind, which in turn 'produces' or 'creates' mind-form. God *is,* and because God is infinite and omnipresent, all is God.

Contemplate God:

God is God — infinite, omnipresent, indivisible and inseparable; mind is God — infinite, omnipresent, indivisible and inseparable; form is God — infinite, omnipresent, indivisible and inseparable because there exists nothing in the whole of the infinitude but God itself.

God *is* the infinitude and everything everywhere experienced 'in' it. Nothing at all is 'produced' or 'created' or 'made' manifest. All is, and the all that *is* is infinite, omnipresent and eternal; therefore cannot be and is not local, personal, finite.

God can no more be local *as* or *to* or *for* you or me or even the Master, any more than math can be local. When you know that $8 + 8 = 16$, you know it universally. You know that '16' exists as the truth of $8 + 8$ everywhere equally and at the same time. Seven billion people on earth could calculate $8 + 8$ this minute, and math would not in the slightest be depleted of '16', and in fact would have an infinity of 16s left over — "and there were twelve baskets full left over".

And so you see, as God is felt happening within, the whole universe, in fact the whole of infinity, is simultaneously feeling — tangibly experiencing — the whole of truth 'you' are experiencing. "I and the Father are one." And because there is no 'unmanifest' God, the fully manifested and perfectly visible and tangible forms of God are — the very minute you are experiencing God happening — filling your experience with their good, their wholeness, their harmony and their peace.

This truth is easy to grasp when it is realized that God is *spirit*, and that the universe of experience — consciousness — is *spiritual*, not structural, physical, material. You are, and your entire universe is, spirit; therefore perfect, whole and harmonious — every grain of it. The structural experience of being and universe is simply a material *sense* of that which is one hundred percent spirit.

When this is known, and when it is deeply enough realized that God is, therefore all is, one, infinite, omnipresent, finished, perfect, whole, harmonious, peaceful, purposeful and fulfilled — despite the way it may appear to be at any moment ("Judge not by the appearance. . .") — then it is also realized that the moment God is felt happening, the whole of God is tangibly experienced.

The peace experienced — felt happening — is the presence of God tangibly witnessed, and that tangibility is omnipresent, not local; infinite, not personal; and all-complete, not partially complete. Do you catch this? It is impossible for God-felt-happening to be the health and vitality of our body but not of our finances and relationships. God is *one, all* — infinite and omnipresent — the universal *whole* already and forever perfect, complete, fulfilled.

Know this great truth, and then completely rest and relax, and bathe in the miraculous experience of God felt happening as the whole universe of you and all that is in it. You will behold miracles indeed. A great peace fills you and becomes the essence of you and your world, ever more clearly witnessed as the beauty, bounty and freedom of form. Burdens drop from you, fear dissolves, the intellect rests, and human effort is put away. No longer do you live with desire or need, but in the living awareness of *God is*.

People remark, "You are so peaceful; you are so calm; your eyes are full of light. I feel calm and relaxed in your presence." Certainly, when you are devoting your being to God, the very presence of God shines peace and harmony into the world as a lighthouse shines light. The presence of God shining — living — within reveals the universal good, truth of form. In this way you see that form is not healed — even though it appears to be — but *sense* is healed.

Once you understand this great secret, you never again seek to heal or harmonize form in and of its own self, but forever seek God itself felt happening within, letting the felt-happening fill and 'heal' your senses — lift and illumine, sanctify, pacify and harmonize your every sense — until you are so filled-full with living God awareness that your whole universe is alight and sings with joy of the harmony, peace and freedom it truly is.

16

The Way Of Healing

❦

PART 2

The Works Which I Do

T ruly, truly, I say to you, he who believes in me shall do the works which I do, and even greater than these shall he do." What works? The works of healing bodies, feeding and prospering those in lack, pacifying wars and harmonizing conditions? No! God's kingdom is in perfect order; God's being is perfect spiritual being; God's world (form) is here, now and forever perfect, complete and harmonious, there being none else.

The "works which I do" — those works which you shall do too — are the works of experiencing truth happening: the one, infinite and omnipresent experience of God-felt-happening within or *as* being. Once God is known as all, as one — God as mind as form — then only one work is true and needed: the work of feeling truth, feeling God's presence, feeling God happening. Once the *feeling*, the *experience*, is taking place as your being, *all* of God is visible and tangible, *all* of your experience is witnessed as the truth it is — the God, good, it truly is. In this way — and no other — does the fog of false belief dissolve and the senses heal, revealing form as the good and completeness it always has been in truth.

We must live as and by truth, as and by God felt happening within as all. "I live, yet not I, Christ [God] lives my [my universal] life." The amount and consistency of the experience of God felt happening within *is* the amount of fruitage — good and harmonious form — witnessed. It's as simple and as straightforward as that. God itself felt happening is the *only all* — the *only* life, the *only* being, the *only* body, the *only* activity, the *only* business, the *only* place, the *only* home, the *only* amount, the *only* love, the *only* relationship, the *only* world.

When you have a relationship with God felt happening within — without 'doing' anything more, without understanding even a thing of what's happening but truly having a relationship of oneness with that felt happening within — the whole universe cannot keep life, love, abundance, peace, purpose and fulfillment from your experience; the whole universe cannot keep you from gently and undetectably being the light of the world: feeding the hungry, comforting those who are suffering, fulfilling and enriching those who are poor in spirit.

As you establish your relationship with, or more accurately stated, *as* oneness — with and as God felt happening — you behold form and experience transcending the laws of the earth, the laws of matter, physics, including all mental and physical barriers put up by man. All such barriers — all those mountains, those beliefs, those impossibilities, those overwhelming circumstances we may come up against — are of belief alone, without a single law or principle to uphold them. They are as insubstantial to spirit as dark is to light. All human, mental and material barriers fall down and away, melt or crumble or dissolve, fight among themselves and destroy themselves, when we are the established oneness of truth — when we have established our relationship of oneness, of allness, with and as God actually felt happening within. Once we have God as actual experience, our very presence is, and has, all that God is. We are *consciously one* with and as God, truth, and all is well.

True Awareness

We learn to train our awareness to be true instead of untrue. It is a learned discipline or way of being. We train our awareness to keep attentive to, interested in, trusting and rested in *God as all* rather than appearance as all. Belief has consumed our attention, interest, trust and effort for so long that we have to train our way out of it. Nothing will do it for us; there is no miracle solution, and so we *learn* to use our awareness truthfully.

Let us take four major aspects of experience — health, relationship, money, and peace — and learn how to drop belief in, attachment to, and effort for the good of these experiences. One by one, thread by thread, let us drop the attempt to manage life as it seems to be mentally, physically and materially. Let us lift into truth and live there, as a true and practical relationship of oneness, allness, as the very being of oneness — the being of God only, truth only — happening as individual experience.

Let us realize that our *sense* of life has nothing at all to do with the truth of life; therefore, the 'we' who believe we are experiencing lack or limitation, discord or disease must be entirely dropped out of the equation. If we sense 8 + 8 as being 15, we must entirely drop that sense instead of attempting to have math 'fix' it for us. There is nothing to fix in math, and math certainly cannot fix our poor sense. Equally, there is nothing to heal or harmonize, prosper or pacify in God, and God certainly cannot come to where a problem is experienced and heal it. Nor are 'we' involved in the God experience happening as individual us. Only God is, and we must get 'us' out of the equation so that the being we truly are, existing in the perfect and fulfilled universe of spirit, can be tangible to our senses.

We are not assistants to God. It is only when we completely give up the sense of self that believes God requires assistance, that truth can begin to 'get through'. It is only as we drop all personal effort to know and witness truth, and let truth itself — in and as and through the nothingness, the vacuum and receptivity of being — be itself as itself for itself as us, that we witness the truth of God as complete and harmonious form.

SATISFIED WITH GOD ALONE

Healing of the Body

Let's begin with the body. Let's say we find ourselves with an injury or illness or disease, or we start experiencing pain somewhere in the body — or that our loved one does. What are we to do?

The first thing we must learn to do is recognize the *nothingness* of the 'it' itself'. We must realize that any experience we can name, good or bad, is not God — not true, not of truth, but of belief alone — and if not true (not God), then having no law or principle to support or sustain its presence in our experience. The 'it' of good or bad experience is like a shadow which has no body in and of its own self — no law to support it, nor principle to sustain it. The shadow, either 'good' or 'bad', is not an entity but rather a *lack* of entity — a lack of light. Equally, an experience of illness, disease or injury is nothing in or of its own self. It is a *lack* of entity — a lack of God-as-all awareness. Where there is a lack of God awareness, there is 'dark', and because whatever we believe *is* our experience, our lack of God awareness is experienced as some form of discord, illness, disease, lack, limitation, poverty, suffering or pain.

It is only the *belief* that a he, she or it, good or bad, is something other than God — a real existence, an entity with its own presence and power — that first enables a 'lack' to enter our experience, and then remain as a discordant form.

Any and every discord is experienced only because collective false belief has found an unwitting believer in which to nest for a moment. In fact, every aspect of false experience — the so-called cause, the 'it' and the effects of it such as pain and suffering — is nothing of its own self. It is all an experience of false belief alone, of no actual entity, of no reality whatsoever — anymore than the '15' (or any other incorrect number) of 8 + 8 is unreal, a nothing, of no reality or entity whatsoever. Because the form of false belief is not an actual entity, nothing has to be done about 'it' of its own self.

And, again, remember our disclaimer: If you are not ready for this, then do not attempt it. But when you are ready — which you will be one day — then you rest in and rely on truth one hundred percent. I think you could not be engrossed in this message if it were not your time, or very near to it, but your time of readiness is not my decision; it's yours. So — very importantly and very seriously — only go this far when you are ready.

'Until that time, take all the necessary medicinal and medical steps to soothe and pacify, rectify and heal any condition you need help with.

But when you are ready, you have to, at every temptation to do something to help an experience of illness, disease, injury, pain or suffering, say, *No, no. Only God Is. Yes, I am having this experience; there is no denying it, and no need to deny it. But it most certainly is an experience of belief alone, a false experience of that which is true — that which is God alone.* After realizing the falsity of the experience, turn within: ponder God; ponder truth, but not in terms of the body and not in terms of health or healing. If you do that, ingrained belief cannot help but think in terms of, hope for, and attempt to bring about an experience of physical healing via truth — and as you know well by now, that is guaranteed to fail. The physical is sense alone and not an actual entity; therefore, there is no entity to be healed of something it is believed to be suffering. This is why all attempts to have God heal the physical fail. Go to God *for the experience of God alone* — God experienced happening as your being. That, and that *itself alone, is itself* the experience of health and wholeness of body which is, stated in material terms, the *healing accomplished.*

You cannot go to God for a healing of the physical body. Only God is, and only the wholeness and truth of God is. The entire experience of both good and bad physicality is sense alone. And so you see that only sense is in need of healing — illuminating, un-darkening — in the same way as a dark room only needs light. God has nothing to do with our sense of body, either good or bad, healthy or sick, strong or weak; yet, because sense is form, as sense is illumined, the forms of experience are illumined, giving us the experience of whole, healthy and strong formation — body.

Always go to God as god for God. Realize, to paraphrase Saint Paul, "We do not know what is right and proper for us to pray for; but the spirit prays for us." I cannot go to God to heal my or another's body because my sense of body, and what may be wrong with it, is false, and if false, I indeed do not know how to pray or what to pray for. I can only go to God as god for God — the incorporeal as incorporeality for incorporeality; spirit as spirit for spirit.

SATISFIED WITH GOD ALONE

The Experience of God Is Itself the 'Healing'

The kingdom of God is finished, forever whole, perfect and complete; and because God is *all*, infinite and omnipresent, the kingdom of *all* is finished, forever whole, perfect and complete. Indeed, the kingdom of the body is forever whole, perfect and complete. It is only false sense — false belief — that leaves us with an *experience* of illness, disease or injury, old age, incapacity and eventual death. But even while the experience is happening, being and its body is actually, truthfully, in its eternally perfect form, function, purpose and freedom.

An injured, sick or diseased body, a degenerating or even dead body, is experienced only because we have not known our truthful identity. Our belief and, therefore, attention and effort have been towards the mental and physical rather than the spiritual. The experience of healing is a 'healing' of the *sense* or *awareness* of body — a lifting into the living awareness of the truth of body. The moment the *senses* are lifted into truth — filled with the light of truth, just as your room is filled with the glorious light and warmth of the sun — the body is witnessed whole and healthy, healed.

As you know this truth, you only have to sit still and silent and receptive, *feeling* truth happening, *feeling* God happening, knowing that as you feel truth happening you *are experiencing* your tangible, truthful, whole and perfect body. This is healing, and has nothing to do with focusing on, and healing, the physical. Healing is one hundred percent the miracle of healed (spiritually illumined) *senses* which — because sense is experience — is experienced as the whole and healthy, perfectly naturally healed physical experience of body.

Any way in which you feel God happening within — as a peace, a deep relaxation, warmth, heat, light, bliss, spaciousness or just a welcome calm — *is itself* the tangible experience of your whole and healthy body. The 'type' or 'intensity' of feeling does not matter. As you feel truth happening in any one of an infinite number of possible ways, you *are experiencing* your tangible, real, healed, whole, healthy and vital body. Only be careful not to believe that the experience, the feeling of God happening 'within', is *different* from, or *separate* from the 'physical'. No! All is one and omnipresent, in just the same way as the sun is one and omnipresent as the whole body of universal light. You may feel as if God is felt happening 'only within' and not in and as the 'physical' body. Do not be fooled by such a belief! It may also feel as if there is no connection whatsoever to that which belief believes your body requires in order to experience its healing and health. Again, do not be fooled! When you know the truth, and then sit still and silent and receptive in it and as it — like a vacuum, an emptiness, a nothingness, a sponge is receptive, letting God get on with being God as itself alone, and for itself alone — you can be sure you've succeeded. You 'have' your healed and healthy, vital and strong body.

Go to God with wide-open arms — a wide-open and empty being — and say:

Take me. Be everything you are as this being I am. Dissolve every belief I have about me, and fill every sense of me with you, and you alone. I do not know who I am or who I am supposed to be, and I cannot ever know. "My thoughts are not your thoughts, nor are your ways my ways, says the Lord." All I can know is you, God, happening as what I know as me — your presence, your being, your body, your awareness, your experience, your thoughts, your ways.

Indeed, along with Saint Paul (and every illumined being), I do not know what to pray for or even how to pray, what to hope for or how to hope, what to be aware of or how to be aware. What is truthful awareness? Of what should I be aware? What is the God experience? What experience should I expect? I do not know — other than its usually being a peaceful feeling, a deeply restful and relaxed and protected and safe feeling, a warm feeling, or a feeling of blissful release and freedom. More than this, if I believe I know what God is, or what the God experience is, I believe amiss and will have to continue to live without God or the 'healing' experience.

The way is straight and narrow. We know the truth, then sit without a trace of personal self, and let God get on with being God as itself and for itself while 'we' sit and observe or witness whatever 'happens' as an experience of being. Because there is no personal self in the God experience, nothing 'personal' is being asked for, prayed for, meditated for, or expected. Just the God experience itself for itself — whatever it will be this minute, this hour, this day — is expected. This is the straight and narrow way, and the infallible way of tangibly and visibly experiencing

God as being, body and world.

Only as we become a complete vacuum of being, a vacuum of consciousness, do we — because God abhors a vacuum — tangibly and visibly experience God filling our senses, illuminating our awareness, until we are so full that it spills 'out' and becomes very tangibly evident as the formation of our world and every aspect of it.

There cannot be, and never is, an actual vacuum in God. So when we make a vacuum of our *personal sense* of self — when we have nothing or very little of self and its needs remaining — we discover God existing where false sense existed. Where false sense — false belief — existed, clouding the visibility of God from experience, now stands God in perfect visibility and reality, being everything of our being, inclusive of (one *as*) the image and likeness of itself as formation (experience).

Fulfilled With and By God Alone

It is often hard to begin with, to know and trust that God felt happening within *is* the healing and health of the body — that because God is one, infinite and omnipresent, all is 'healed' when the senses are filled with the loving light-form of truth. It is hard, especially for the beginning student, to realize that the feeling of God happening within *is* truthful formation.

The fog of the false experience of form *is* dissolved the very moment God is felt happening within — not 'will' be dissolved, not leaving some other or additional activity of truth still to take place, but *is* dissolved. There is a battle for your belief, attention and effort — a battle between spirit and materiality, between that which is real and that which seems to be real. It is hard for a short time, but if you can now, somehow, muster the strength of spirit to believe nothing but the truth that God alone is, and keep your attention on God morning, noon and night, and stay fulfilled with and by God-felt-happening and nothing less or different from that happening (that experience), then you will quickly see the fruits of spirit as healed and harmonized form.

Every time your belief and attention is tempted back to matter, disallow it. Temptation to believe in, and react to, that which appears to be, happens all day long. You find your belief and attention darting right back to that illness, that disease, that lack, that pain, that suffering, that threat to one's life or safety or security, and the desire for spirit to heal, pacify or prosper it. Constantly dismiss belief and bring attention back to God alone. Withdraw your attention from 'out there' and bring it home, here 'within'. Again and again ponder God as and for God — not God as or for body, but God as and for God itself alone. As you ponder truth in this way, and the more you ponder, you begin to feel the welling up of peace, of light, of freedom. Live for that peace or light or freedom — bathe in and as it, rest and relax in and as it until you are fulfilled by its experience. The fulfillment of truth actually felt happening — the re-lease and joy and freedom of spirit actually felt happening — *is* your truthful body being experienced.

If you can grasp this, healing of the body is evidenced very quickly. If you can grasp that the 'physical' experience of the body is a physical *sense* of that which is truthfully one hundred percent spirit, and then seek and be satisfied with the spiritual reality of the body tangibly experi-enced — as peace or light or freedom or joy or harmony and fulfillment 'within' — then healing is "quick, sharp and powerful". Sometimes it takes just moments, sometimes hours, sometimes days or a few weeks, but it rarely takes longer.

One time I started feeling a pain in the sole of my left foot. It started becoming sharper and more tender. Day by day I ignored it as nothing. Then one day, I decided to feel it and there was a tumor. It was painful, and beginning to be very tender and uncomfortable when I walked. There was pressure and pain where the tumor was. But, you see, I knew what it was — collective belief 'passing through' my experience, tempting me to believe it and to do something about it — even to do something 'spiritual' about it, to seek truth for the healing of 'it'. And my response? (and yours too now?), "Get thee hence, Satan [belief]."

Held In or Held Onto Belief

In experience, untruth works itself out of our being. We have been very good at holding on to untruth, holding in material belief, suppress-ing the effort and struggle of living unnaturally (untruthfully), suppress-ing the pain of the misperceived experience.

The being of belief, living by the pairs of opposites, is a bundle of held-in trouble. As we release it and let it go by rising in truth, and as we begin living ever more by truth, all remaining belief works itself out. Belief 'washes out'. It is as if, as we rise in and soak ourselves in truth, we are washing the dirt from our clothes. It has no choice but to dissolve, or wash out as the felt-presence of spirit fills us, pacifies and comforts us. "And all unclean and evil-smelling things shall flow out of you, even as uncleannesses of garments washed in water flow away and are lost in the stream of the river."

"Unclean and evil-smelling things" (belief, desire, effort and reliance on the pairs of opposites) often do not dissolve without first 'coming through' — usually as some form of lack, limitation, discord or even dis-ease. It is as the dirt, hidden in the clothes, first becomes *more* visible and tangible because, and as, it is being washed out, so hidden belief, being 'washed out' by the light of spirit often first becomes more visible and tangible than it was before we lifted in spiritual awareness.

Hence, very often, for most if not all of us, each phase of spiritual lifting and purifying is accompanied by a temporary troublesome experience. It is nothing to be concerned about. It is natural and good. The experience of trouble coming through as we lift in spirit is *the very sign of spiritual progress*. We never need be concerned, rather *happy*, that remaining belief is finally being dissolved in the light of spirit. As we do not react but stay in spirit and continue to rely on God-actually-felt-happening as the one truth and body of experience, remaining belief dissolves quickly and naturally.

Think back to the incident with my foot. I knew this and so wasn't concerned — interested, but not concerned. I ignored it, then completely forgot about it. It probably was a week or two later that I realized there was no longer any pain, no sensitivity whatsoever, so I decided to reach down and feel the area and the tumor was completely gone.

This is it, do you see? We do nothing about that which appears to be illness, disease or injury of the body — nothing — because that which is experienced as *bad* is nothing more than the opposite of that which is *good*. Both the bad of experience and the good are nothing to do with God but just the experience of belief — one or other of the pairs of opposites. There is only one thing to do with the pairs of opposites and that is to ignore them — not react to them, and make no effort to replace the bad with the good of them *in and of their own selves*.

The Way Of Healing: The Works Which I Do

We keep our awareness in truth as and for truth, and we go to God for the God experience. We never go to God for a reason or result we can name because all reason and result is false sense, not God itself. We go to God as god for the God experience alone. The God experience — as long as we are completely satisfied with it itself and never desire anything 'from' it — *is the tangible experience* of our fully-embodied and manifested truth. The God experience is itself the life, health and vitality of the body. Once we 'have' the God experience and as we are satisfied with it itself as all, then we have the healthy, vital, strong and purposeful body. We never did have to do anything with or about the false sense of body — the physical sense — either to heal the bad or acquire the good of it. We never have to do anything with appearance; all we have to do to experience the fullness of life and the health, vitality and joy of life's body here and now is to turn to, live by, and be satisfied with the true body of spirit.

What Are We to Do In Relationship?

The same truth applies to relationship. When something is discordant in a relationship, what are we to do? If our loved one, or we, make a frustrated or hurtful comment, what are we to do? If our loved one, or we accidentally slip into belief for a moment (and believe me, I sometimes do as well; we all do; we're all still by degree caught by belief), what are we to do? Here we are listening to our love or ourselves saying something out of truth and immediately thinking, Why did one of us say that? It's too late now; it's been said, but why did I, or she or he, say it? What do we do?

Immediately we 'do' nothing; we say nothing; we react in no way whatsoever except with the silence and presence of love. We must uphold truth. We must *be* a consciousness of love with no reaction, no comment, no judgment or complaint. Even though a comment made towards us may have hurt, we do not react anymore than light reacts to shade. We judge not and react not, which includes giving no *sign* of reaction or dismay. Oh, how good the human being is at giving a sign! I won't say anything, but if you take a look at me, you'll very quickly know how unhappy I am! The human being is masterful at this, so we have to be neutral in reaction, yet full of love. As far as we're concerned nothing has happened. Just as the sun is undisturbed by the shadow, we are undisturbed by comment, opinion, judgment and deed.

True love remains undisturbed, and being truly loving means being love alone — non-reactive, non-judgmental, non-idealized. True love has nothing to think or say about that which seems to be. True love is not hurt, does not react, does not teach lessons. *Do you know, my dear, you shouldn't say things like that.* Or, *You should not act in this way.* Or, *Go and read this book on true love and then come back.* No! Love has nothing to say, has no reaction, has no advice to give.

Then we come right back here, home, within, and start feeling the presence of truth happening. As we do this, any remaining temptation to say something to our loved one, or to judge, melts in the light and love of truth. All discord and temptation melts in love felt happening. Then we awaken to the truth that, of course, our loved one *is this love* felt happening within — pure and gentle, wondrous and true. It was only belief — the ego, the personal sense of self — that commented or reacted in a moment of untruth. Knowing this, we bathe in love felt happening, and all is made well. We and he or she are soothed and comforted, lifted in spirit. Sense is healed.

When we feel filled and fulfilled by this love, it fills our universe. All we are, and all we have for our world, is love. Then we get on with our day and do you know, one of these moments, or tomorrow morning or afternoon, our loved one will come to us, either with words, or with a loving glance or hug and let us know that all is well.

And if, despite all the truth we can bring to our relationship, our loved one is just not of the same consciousness, then we let that relationship go. It never is our responsibility to try to make another know his or her truth, and it is most certainly untruthful to remain in a discordant or limiting relationship. How can we *be* and *serve* truthfully and freely if our significant relationship is discordant? Our responsibility is one-fold: that of "being about the Father's business" — to *be, give* and *serve* truthfully. We have no other responsibility in truth. Therefore, if we experience, as I did, that our marriage or relationship is not or is no longer true, we let that relationship go. Our responsibility begins, continues and stops with us. It is we who must remain in truth, seeking ever new and more illumined ways of being and serving and giving in love. Then the whole universe cannot stop true love from walking into our life.

The Way Of Healing: The Works Which I Do

Healing of Supply

The same principle applies to money. If you are experiencing a lack of money, the first thing to realize is that form — in this case, the form of dollars — in and of its own self is simply a finite, material *sense* of the infinity of form actually present. If you believe that numbers of dollars are real and valuable *in and of their own selves*, you are duped or mesmerized by collective belief.

Remember, only God is; only infinity and omnipresence is. Therefore, the only form that ever presents itself to you is God — infinity and omnipresence. The only form you experience, handle, exchange and give is God — infinity and omnipresence. In fact, the only *you* and *experience* there is, is God — impersonal, infinite and omnipresent.

If the omnipresence of all form is true — which it is — what causes lack in experience? Why do so many around the world suffer a lack of dollars, and a seeming lack of the means to experience plentiful dollars? The answer is this: because only God is, the only form is *God form* — the one, spiritual, incorporeal form. Material belief searches for material form which, unbeknown to that belief, is nothing but a material *sense* of spirit; a corporeal *sense* of that which is actually incorporeal. As soon as matter is believed to be an entity in and of its own right, the one believing it is subject to limitation, lack and disharmony.

Belief and focus are finite and objectified rather than infinite and omnipresent. As soon as the reality of God — spirit, infinity and omnipresence — stirs into awakenment within you, you understand that the only lack there ever is, is a lack of *spiritual awareness.* Spirit is all; therefore if anything of good and harmony and plenty seems to be lacking, the lack is not of the objectified form that it seems to be, but of spiritual awareness. As spiritual awareness increases, so does all good and plentiful form. "As I be lifted up, I draw all men [all of earth, matter, experience] unto me."

When a need arises in our experience — just as a need presented itself to Jesus when there seemed to be a lack of food for the hungry crowd — we must immediately remember: the only thing that ever presents itself to us is God. The seeming needed form or amount is, despite appearance, God. Therefore there is, literally and tangibly, an infinity of the very form that seems to be finite and insufficient, and the infinity of it is omnipresent right at the point of seeming need.

Knowing this truth, we withdraw all attention and desire for food or dollars or for whatever form seems to be needed. Make no effort to fix or fulfill the appearing problem mentally, materially or physically; make no effort whatsoever to resolve the problem-form by bringing about its solution-form. If our belief, thinking and effort are still fixated on the appearing problem and its deemed solution, all we are doing is thinking in terms of manipulated pairs of opposites and we'll not witness God. God, the good, perfect and plentiful form — *even though standing right where the need seems to be* — is not visible in the pairs of opposites. The fog of belief is too dense.

Instead, we immediately turn to the "secret place" within, and knowing that the good, perfect and plentiful form — in this case of dollars — is right there where material sense experiences a lack, we become still and silent, transparent, and let God do the work of revealing the truth of experience. We quietly, peacefully and patiently wait for the feeling of God happening within to fill us as dawn fills the earth with light.

We know that only God is; therefore, we wish for nothing but the God experience — for the God experience itself. We do not wish for the God experience to produce dollars or food or other good form because we know that these nameable forms are just images of the one real form which is God itself, as God itself.

We know that there is nothing but God, and so it would be foolish to seek something other than God itself, for God itself. "Ye ask, and receive not, because ye ask amiss." Continuing to seek God *for* something is the reason thousands of students miss the God experience. The very belief in form being something of its own self, and the continual seeking of God for more of the good form and less of the bad *is itself the lack, limitation, discord and disease of experience*. It is the sensed separation from God, or sense of being different from God, from oneness, from truth, that leaves experience devoid of harmony, plenty and peace. As soon as we have God 'and', we suffer — we lack, we want, we need. But as oneness, we are and have all.

Morning, noon and night, turn to God *for the God experience itself*, not to God for anything 'else'. Morning, noon and night, be *satisfied* with the God experience itself, and nothing else. God is the only and the all, and the fullness of all — "The earth [experience, form] is the Lord's and the fullness thereof". As we continually turn to God for God, never, even secretly, wishing for or hoping to use God for what *we* believe is needed to fulfill experience, all fulfillment becomes ours.

Turn to God for God and nothing else.

I do not know what to pray for, and I do not know how to pray.

Even if I did know what to pray for, which I never will know, even then I could never know how to pray for it. Therefore, I go to God for God alone . . . God for God itself alone . . . God for God itself alone.

Be satisfied with God felt happening within, to the point where nothing else satisfies you. Be more satisfied with God felt happening than if $1,000,000 dropped through your letterbox, for truthfully God experienced happening is worth more than all the wealth the world could ever witness and will always be with you, wherever you are and whatever the need seems to be, in exactly the right form, amount and quality.

When you live by the wealth and satisfaction of God happening as your being — when you are filled with God felt happening rather than materiality felt happening; when you are more conscious of God as all than you are of materiality — then you *have* the wealth of God filling every minute, every place and every condition. You radiate the presence of God as your being and world; your presence *is* the radiation and the wealth of form. It is 'through' the presence of being — the presence of truth "happening" as being — that God is visible, tangible and real to experience. You are and have greater God *experience* when you are being greater God *presence*. The greater and more fulfilling God experience you are being, the greater good and plentiful form you have as tangible experience.

'Being greater God experience' means *feeling* God happening ever more often each hour of the day and night. With more God experience felt happening, you are *being* greater God awareness — greater God presence. You then discover yourself *having* more of the forms of God — the forms of good — filling your life because God-felt-happening and form are one. Before you know it, the form of dollars flows into your experience and the sense of need is fulfilled, often with "twelve baskets full left over".

In this way, you have discovered the *real* wealth, the wealth that never runs dry, is never lacking and can never let you down. You have discovered real wealth by your refusal to attempt to fix the sense of lack by mental effort and material means. You have turned to God itself and relied on the God experience alone as actual wealth. That is the real wealth — the wealth that is infinite, omnipresent and unconditional; the gift of truth.

The wealth that is God — abundance itself, omnipresence itself — is not conditional to, or subject to, or dependent on anything of material existence. The experience of God-wealth filling your day, in all its rich formation, has nothing to do with gaining more of the world's already-existing dollars, anymore than new fruit coming through the vine has anything to do with gaining fruit already existing on the vine, or on other vines. New and more abundant 'material' experience is new and more abundant imagery — formation — of infinity experienced 'happening' as individual being. "I am come that you may have life, and have it more abundantly."

Matter is not something of its own self. It is not an entity. It has no laws to uphold it. Only truth is entity — the one entity, there being "none other". *I am the Lord* [the Entity], *and besides me there is none else.*

Truth is Not Conditional to Anything Physical

The experience of truth as the fulfillment of this world is not conditional to any already-present or available thing, amount, condition, avenue or activity. Equally, fulfilled experience is not stopped or hindered by the *non-presence* of any material thing, amount, condition, avenue or activity. God *is* — and proves itself so when one lives in and as *is*, rather than materially. Then the experience of the omnipresence of all good and plentiful form — including that of dollars — defies material conditions, avenues and activities. It defies everything the intellect can understand. "My thoughts are not your thoughts, neither are my ways your ways, saith the Lord." We let God reveal itself as our abundance in its own way, not ours. We have nothing to do with the way abundance reaches our experience. Let God be God as all, in its own way. "God moves in mysterious ways, His wonders to perform."

But again, if we skip to and fro between truth and material belief, then we fall back into an experience of lack and limitation, or ill health, or unhappiness and struggle — or we never lift out of it. Whereas, when we stay in truth, simply *observing* discordant experiences, knowing they are flushing up simply to be dissolved; when we stay in truth and are undisturbed by these experiences of temporary discord or lack, even though they may be hard for a few days or a few weeks; when we persist in the discipline of staying in God alone, being vigilant in knowing that the only true experience and form is God felt happening within, then one-by-one each aspect of false experience breaks and dissolves to reveal harmony, plenty and peace.

God Itself Is the Only True Form

There is not any other form, there is not any other body, there is not any other amount, there is not any other love than God itself experienced as all of life. By persisting in the discipline of God consciousness and none other, we witness the end of all lack, limitation, discord, disease, hate, loneliness.

The same principle applies to peace. There is not a single sane person alive who does not desire peace in mind, body and world. Every person wants mind and body peace, family peace, neighborly peace, business and economic peace, community, country and world peace. Peace is the only truth and the only actual presence, form and activity. But belief in the pairs of opposites instead of the realization of God as all presents the world with experiences of stress, discord, disease, lack, limitation, war and insecurity.

How then is peace made tangible? We must refuse to do anything mentally, materially or physically to bring about peace. We must leave appearance alone. We must recognize that the only peace is "My peace" and, therefore, vehemently stay in that secret place where the whole universe of My peace is, remembering that peace is the one *universal and omnipresent* peace — not personal, not selfish, not 'for' anything we can name or desire, but for and as *all.*

When you turn to the secret place of My peace and begin feeling peace happening, you *are being*, and *have*, the universal peace, and all is well. Live by that peace felt happening. Trust it and rely on it itself and nothing else, and then watch your mind, body and world become ever more filled with, relaxed and free in true peace.

If only enough students around the world would realize this great truth — *be* truth, live as truth — we'd watch every war stop within days. We'd watch every soldier drop his weapons, climb out of his tank, refuse to fire another missile or launch another bomb; refuse to fight or kill another day. Peace is the truth of all beings, all nations, and of all of our world and universe. There is no antagonistic behavior in truth. Only peace is. Peace, harmony, love and union is the truth of the atoms, cells, organs and functions of the mind, body and world.

If in false belief, aspects of the body are experienced to be fighting among themselves, in the presence of peace all antagonistic experience quickly drops its weaponry of unhappiness, illness, disease or injury. The body stops fighting with itself and loses its false sense of destructive power just as quickly as frost dissolves in the warmth of the sun. This experience is what we call 'healing', but the real healing is not of that which seemed to need it, but of the *senses* which were falsely experiencing the one and forever-present truth.

Living in Love

The same principle applies to relationship. As we live in love, live in peace, then we watch the antagonism, or argument, or differences in our relationship dissolve to reveal truthful relationship. But this is only tangible to experience when we leave the scenery alone, leave every him, her and it alone, desire nothing of or from the good or the bad as it appears to be. We do not desire the world's idea of love, but love itself. We do not wish to be taught love by the world. The only kind of love the world has and can teach is temporal love, conditional love, and variable love. The world's love has let us down. No, we wish to be taught love by God. Be taught of God. "For ye have been taught of God to love one another." We want only God as love. Then we have love itself, and we can rest our effort and simply behold love in action and serve the love we find ourselves filled with, to and for our loved one, our family and our community.

Only by *my* love is the world of love experienced. Only by *my* omniscience, *my* peace, *my* life, *my* body, *my* plenty, *my* form and *my* spirit is truth experienced — the truth of our mind, body and world; the truth of our love and union among all; the truth of one divine being, all acting and interacting as one for the one good of God alone.

Only by living as and by and for truth itself felt happening within, and only by being fully satisfied with the God experience — not partially but fully satisfied with God felt happening — is truth alone witnessed as experience.

17

The Kingdom Come

*Henceforth I will not eat until it is fulfilled
in the kingdom of God.*

*I will not drink of the fruit of the vine
until the kingdom of God comes.*

Here is the measure of our progress in truth, each and every one: to leave the believed experience — this world with all its good and bad, the whole pairs of opposites — entirely alone. Here, in these two statements of the Master, is revealed the measure of our God consciousness and our ability to *literally* let God be God as experience rather than believe we must 'help' God, assist God, somehow be involved in the God experience on and as earth.

I am able to measure my truth consciousness by the degree I no longer desire or attempt to partake of the fruits of earth — "the fruits of the vine" — until the kingdom of God experienced happening within is then witnessed pushing forth the fruits (forms) of good and plentiful life; my own branches of life, the branches of experience, filling with the good and plentiful forms of good.

Each aspect of life is a branch, and each aspect has endless other branches growing forth from it, and I — just like the vineyard or the orchard — refuse to partake of the fruits of those branches, the good of life, until the kingdom of God *lived within* is experienced. Before I do anything — before I eat even a bite, before I commune with my family, before I take a step into the world or go to my business or talk to my client or student — I turn within, become still and silent, and wait for the kingdom of God to come into my awareness; wait until I feel God happening as my being, mind, body and universe. *Then* I partake of the fresh manna, the new fruit, that comes through as visible and real on the branches of worldly experience. But I do not partake of the world and the fruit until I have experienced the "kingdom of God come". When I have, I needn't be surprised when the miracle of God is witnessed throughout my world. "As in heaven so on earth."

Then, and only then, is experience true. Only then are mind and body true. Only then is each step, is each hour and is each day filled with the ways and fruits of truth. Only then is the light, the substance and the form of truth filling experience — the one truth filling experience.

Once you have "the kingdom come" as the substance of your life, your body is healthy and safe forevermore. Even if some discords flush through your experience, never is there anything to fear or even be disturbed about. Once you know and experience the truthful body, you live vitally, your skin glows, your eyes are alight, you have and live by purpose and truth. Truthful body and all truthful form c the forms of "the kingdom come" — are omnipresent and eternal. They are above and beyond anything of belief, of mentality, physicality, materiality; and none of belief, mentality, physicality, or materiality can touch them, affect them, or destroy them. The body is the Lord's and the fullness thereof. Because the body is the Lord's, I will not partake of it — I will not involve myself with anything of bodily activity: satisfying, pacifying, or pampering — until I have experienced the kingdom of God coming, filling my senses, being the *I* I am and the body I experience. Then I have the truth and freedom of body. I am body; I am the body — not my sense of 'I', but I itself is body, sensed as the 'corporeal' body form. As I know this wondrous truth and live by it — live by "the kingdom come" — I am free.

Live by The "Kingdom Come"

As I live by "the kingdom come", I find myself being animated in new ways of body, new ways of exercise, new ways of food. These ways are the visible fruits of the kingdom *coming through* into and as conceptual form and activity. We almost stand by and observe our body enjoying new ways of activity or exercise, preferring lighter, purer foods. These changes are not mental, but an impulse of truth. We live by the kingdom come, almost observing an outer shell of experience doing its thing, but doing its thing ever more purely, ever more beautifully, ever more truly.

The density of mind, body and world diminishes day by day. The body transforms right in front of us as purer body; more illumined, spiritual body; more beautiful body. Our food becomes purer, lighter, truer. Our portions tend to become smaller and purer, more spiritually fulfilling. This all occurs because as we live by "the kingdom come", we no longer need or have reliance on the material or the physical. Yet the material and the physical are witnessed becoming vital and fulfilled with very little "outer" need.

Spirit is what we are and what we have and what we are fed by, so we do not require as much of the material agency of food, and we find ourselves eating lighter and less as we are fed directly with spirit. "I have food that you know not of." Spirit is the one reality, therefore the one true food, the real food. The agency is a poor, temporal image. As necessary, delicious, and nourishing as nutritional experts say it is, it is a poor and temporal image of the true food — the "word" or presence of God itself, "the kingdom come", the feeling of God happening within. That's the real food.

Not only do "I have food that you [belief] know not of," but *I am* the food — the presence, the substance and the form. Remember, God is one and all, whole and indivisible. Therefore, God is *the* one and all, whole and indivisible perfection of being, body and world. Only belief can have a separated sense and say, "Over there is plenty, but here there is lack or insufficiency that leaves me unsatisfied, hungry or even starving." Food is one and omnipresent, whole and indivisible. Therefore, as I know this truth, then feed on the experience of God happening within me and as my entirety — the kingdom experienced "coming" or "happening" — I am fed and satisfied. Then, not only am I satisfied, but as many as require food are also satisfied. The *I* of me feeds the world, not only itself.

Eventually, as we rise in spiritual awareness and our body-sense becomes ever less dense, the physically-sensed body is no longer experienced, nor its birth, age, decline, decrepitude, illness or disease, and finally death. The true, spiritual body emerges as the one, eternal reality, no longer requiring sense to be experienced, but existing simply as the body of *is*. The one true body is God, spirit, the incorporeal body, experienced as the body of *presence* or *awareness*. This is the body of Christ.

The body of Christ — of Buddha, of spirit, of consciousness — does not have an 'agency', an imitation, an image-form, a corporeal equivalent. The one true body is pure spirit, pure awareness, pure consciousness, and is ageless, eternally vital, strong and perfect, carrying out the divine purpose of spiritual being. This is the truth and reality of your being and body here and now, and when you know it and live it — which means when you live by the experience of God-felt-happening-within, "the kingdom come" — then all of life's purpose and fulfillment, *all of it*, is witnessed coming to you, happening for you, and for the fulfillment of purpose without your having to make effort for it.

Waiting for "the kingdom of God to come" is what we witness every day in nature. The orchard looks out at its world of branches, refusing to 'help' or interfere with nature: "I refuse to get fruit from out there somewhere, and hang it on my branches to fulfill myself." Can you imagine the orchard going to other orchards, borrowing or buying others' fruit, and pinning that fruit on its own branches for fulfillment?

Thinking of the orchard doing such a thing is truly ludicrous, yet the human being acts in just this way to survive and satisfy itself! We seek and rely on satisfaction from the outer, not realizing that the whole kingdom of God — boundless and unconditional good, in infinite and unlimited form — exists within.

SATISFIED WITH GOD ALONE

I refuse to partake of my hour, my day, my family, my business, my customers, clients, patients or students — any aspect, form or activity of my life — until the kingdom of God has come; until I have turned to God, the truth of all, and become still and silent, and have felt God happening within.

Then I will partake, but not before then.

When I have experienced God happening, how do I then partake? How do I partake truthfully? By *giving.* For what single true purpose do I have life, and for what purpose are the fruits I find filling my branches as I live by and am satisfied with God alone? *Giving, serving, sharing, benefitting* all in my world, particularly all whom I witness coming to me.

The fruits of "the kingdom come" are not mine, but God's. "The earth is the Lord's, and the fullness thereof." The forms and fruits are the Lord's, and the fullness thereof. Well, what does God 'do' in experience, twenty-four hours a day, eternally? Give of itself.

Please, have these fruits from my branch. They are for you. I have an infinity of them. Please, take them for your fulfillment, and as many as you need. Take them. They are my gift of love to you.

I am infinite. You may not yet know of your infinity, so take of these infinite fruits I witness on my branches. It's my pleasure, it's my privilege, it's my purpose of being, my only reason for being.

My only reason for being is for you to be fulfilled, satisfied and freed.

I refuse to spend dollars until the kingdom of God has come. And as I live by the experience of God happening, I find my life always filled with a plentiful supply of dollars for every need, every step and every project. In truth, I have no right to spend a single dollar until I've turned to God first thing in the morning, until I've devoted time to pondering God (truth, spirit, omnipresence), until I've stilled myself sufficiently, made a nothingness of myself sufficiently, so that I feel God happening within. I feast there; I devote my being, my purpose to God- happening-within, knowing that this life is not about me, knowing that as I — and *only* as I — devote this moment, this hour and this day to God- felt-happening-within am I being truthful being, beholding God happening within and as every aspect and form of my world.

This is my only gift to life, my only reason for being alive. I have no right, in truth, to do anything of my own, or for my own self until the kingdom of God has come, and come abundantly — not just for a quick five minutes so I can get on with my busy life, but to feast there, to stay there with Christ, with Buddha, with God, with truth, feeding the world, not just a quick dip into truth so that I feed just myself (which is impossible).

After thirty minutes, one hour, two hours, three hours or more of being at one with Christ, with Buddha, devoting the being that I am to that which is true — not to myself, but to that which is true: the one, the all-in-all — and when I feel as if that devotion is complete for this moment, then the kingdom has sufficiently come in my experience. Now I can get up and go into the world. I am ready. I have truth filling me and my branches. I have substance, I have love, truth, spiritual presence and formation to give to the world and to every person who touches my consciousness.

When Has The Kingdom "Come" Into Experience?

How do I know that the kingdom has come this moment? *It* tells me. *It* feels satisfied *as me*. *It* does the work. "The Father within me, He does the work." Spiritual satisfaction does not come in, or by, a time set by man. I can't watch the clock and limit the time in which I expect the kingdom to come — be felt — in my experience. I must make space for the kingdom. I must make all the time I need to unhurriedly devote myself to God and experience the kingdom of God coming.

I know that many of us have family, work and social commitments. Sometimes we do need to look at the clock. I do too. But on the whole, we have to learn to live by *truth*, not by the clock. "Wait patiently on the Lord." Patience and the clock are mismatched partners.

Let us not be confused about the one reason we are alive. True life has nothing to do with our personal sense of I, me and mine. You did not form your life, your body or your world. God is the only; therefore God is the only life, mind, body and world you are and experience. You are God's life; I am God's life, the life of *one* and *oneness, wholeness and union.*

We have not recognized this truth. We have separated ourselves in sense (not in reality) from truth. We have believed that we, our mind, body and world are entities in and of their own selves, entities separate from and different from God. In so doing, we have thrust our experience into that of belief. And because every belief has an opposite, we have the bizarre and utterly untruthful experience of each good having an equal and opposite bad, and each bad having an equal and opposite good.

As we awaken to truth, and as we devote the life we are and have to that which it truly is, truth itself, without personal agenda — the one universal and unconditional good without opposite, equality without condition, selflessness and divine purpose without creed or greed, and rely on "the kingdom come" for all purpose and fulfillment — then we are ready to get up and partake of life in all its ways. But without "the kingdom come", we are running on empty — spiritless, substanceless, truthless.

What of Truth Do I Have?

What do I have for my world if I haven't first and foremost devoted myself to truth and the actual experience of God happening? What do I have for my loved one, my family, my students, my business and customers, my neighbors and my world if I am not first and foremost devoted to truth, not only intellectually but in actual experience? I have nothing.

Truly, I only have the right to step into and partake of my world, to go to the market, to be with my loved one, my family, to pay my rent or mortgage, to do business, to travel, even to talk to my neighbor, when I have experienced the kingdom of God coming — the actual experience of God felt happening within, filling my senses and flowing out, flooding my universe with the light and peace of truth itself.

As a truth devotee, I have no right to partake of life before the kingdom of God has come; I have no right to offer my services, to sell or teach or even to sing or dance, before the kingdom of God has come. What will I do with all the people, all the places and conditions I meet throughout my day if I haven't waited for the kingdom of God to come, and experienced it filling my senses, filling my world? How will I recognize each person, place and condition as the presence of God if I'm not filled with the light of God? What will I be able to be and do for them? How will I serve them? How can I benefit them? All I can offer is emptiness, nothingness, the unwitting deceit of human endeavor and material promise, a personal 'me' with personal agenda.

I can only be and operate and offer myself as an unillumined, personal being if I am not devoted to truth, and if — this day, this hour — I have not waited patiently in silence until the kingdom of God has come and filled me with truth; until I have feasted there within, with Christ, with Buddha, with truth; until I have devoted myself to the presence, the activity, the truth of Christ, of Buddha, of illumined self. But when I have, and when I remain centered within, continually seeking and feeling the presence of God happening, then as I go out into my world, I am the living presence and substance of truth. Then I shouldn't be surprised at the wonders and harmonies witnessed. "Where the presence of the Lord is, there is liberty."

As I am filled with the presence and substance of truth, I recognize all as God being, and God form. Only God is; therefore every person is God, experienced as individual being; only God is he and she; only God is the activity, the life, the shining eyes, the dancing children, the loving couples and families, the colors, fragrances and fruits of life. As I am filled with the awareness of light of God, I know this wondrous truth, and I know the oneness and unity of all of life.

I Am, I Have, I Give

As I am consciously filled with the presence and substance of God, I give of that presence and substance. I give of truth awareness; I give of the presence pulsing within and radiating from me; I give of spiritual love and recognition; I give of smiles, kindness, compassion, time, attention; I give of the forms of God with which I find my experience filled — the gifts of love in the form of flowers, food, dollars, letters and cards of gratitude, and any other form of gift and kindness.

Giving time and attention is a wonderful gift to give. When I speak with you, you are, for the period of time we are speaking together, the only person in my universe. If I have another person, thing or condition on my mind as I am talking with you, my attention is not wholly yours. That would mean my attention is not wholly on, and for, God because "I and the Father are one". My awareness of God *being all* would be dull. That is a mistake!

When I am tending my garden, let me give it one hundred percent attention. If I have something or someone else on my mind at the same time, or if I am texting or answering my phone at the same time, I am not giving any of these activities my full attention. Therefore, I am not giving *God* my full attention; I am not *practicing the presence of God*. Instead, I am practicing the presence of multiplicity, and because God is *one*, not multiplicity, I am keeping myself out of the conscious awareness, therefore experience, of the presence of truth. If Brother Lawrence were working in his monastery garden today, or in the kitchen preparing the monks' meals, would he simultaneously text or answer his phone? You know not! "My day-to-day life consists of giving God my simple, undistracted attention."

It is too easy to fall into the intellectual trap of multitasking. But in oneness there is no multiplicity, nor multi-task. There is just *one*, therefore just one *task* — the giving of oneself to oneness, God. It is unnecessary, in fact untruthful, to entertain multiplicity; therefore it is equally unnecessary to multitask. The belief in multiplicity and the activity of multitasking are great distractions which steal our awareness of God.

As we each continue to rise in truth awareness, and as the recognition of God being all becomes ever more real and tangible, we find ourselves filled with greater peace, feeling more spacious and relaxed, slowing down, giving our *whole* attention to each moment or activity of experience — never combining, never multitasking. Whether we are with our love, a friend, a student or a customer, a flower, an insect, the garden, the valley or the mountain, a dew drop or the ocean, the sunrise or sunset, or whether we are simply peeling potatoes for today's meal, our whole attention is with and as God *being all of that experience*.

It is when we are wholly aware of and attentive to the presence of God as moment-by-moment experience, that the windows of our being are open. And because God abhors a vacuum, the whole of God rushes through to evidence ever more harmonious, peaceful, abundant, loving, free and purposeful forms of experience.

Know That the Presence of God Is All

If Jesus or Buddha or any of the great masters walked into your home this hour, would you give him or her your entire attention? Would you continue to check your phone, respond to emails and texts, or allow family, friends, colleagues or clients to interrupt you? Of course, you would give all your attention to the master.

When you observe any master at his craft, you observe devotion, focus, absorption in the one activity. The whole mind-body is absorbed in, attentive to, and giving of his or her particular craft, art or expression — *one* with and as what is being expressed. One is one*ness*, not multiplicity. Therefore in the living expression of oneness (truth), there is nothing 'else' in awareness, nothing 'else' distracting us, nothing 'else' than this one moment and its experience.

I watch my gifted son as he writes music. He is absorbed in his own universe, the universe where music and he are one. Nothing 'else' is happening but his hearing the music and bringing the form out into conceptual experience. I've shared with you before that he refuses to learn to read music. He always has. It drives his music teachers crazy! But as he says, "I don't need to read other people's music. *I hear the music.*"

This is what every master experiences — the hearing or flowing forth of his or her truth of self and talent from within. All great artists, musicians, athletes, painters, writers, designers, inventors and innovators are at one with their truth of self and particular expression, almost beholding it living them and expressing 'through' them. "I live, yet not I, Christ [truth] lives my life."

As we continue to awaken to the truth that all, literally, is God, we find ourselves treasuring every individual him, her and it more. We pay full attention to whatever it is we are doing at any and every moment. In that way, every experience is filled with greater God awareness and is richer, more abundant, more beautiful, more meaningful, more satisfying, even miraculous. Everything and everyone, every interaction, every activity, every form we bring forth, everything we do, is richer in experience, more purposeful, more abundant. "I am come that they may have life, and have it more abundantly."

We find ourselves becoming more spacious. We cannot be rushed, cannot be disturbed. We treasure stillness, silence, spaciousness. Every hour is filled with the urge to be still and attentive, and to listen. Truth cannot get through a rushed or multitasking mind. It's impossible. So we find ourselves, quite naturally, becoming more unwilling to cram our hours full of activity or discussion, to have deadline after deadline, to have the hubbub of that life surrounding us. We become peaceful and spacious, and we live devoted to and attentive to truth. In this way — in this way only — are we able to feel and witness truth happening as our very being and universe. Truth cannot be felt nor evidenced in a materially crammed consciousness. Truth can only be felt and witnessed in and through peace, spaciousness and attentiveness. "God abhors a vacuum." Therefore, in that space, vacuum or nothingness of self, *there God is felt and witnessed as real, tangible and perfectly visible formation*. Our entire desire and impulse each hour is to be peaceful and spacious, attentive to God deep within and everywhere about.

The whole of God *is* what you are. Your mind *is* God, your body *is* God, your universe and every grain of it *is* God. There is none else. God is forever and fully available as experience because God already *is* the one and only true experience. You are having that experience now, but because God awareness is not your only awareness, that one, true experience is sensed falsely. As you empty 'yourself' of everything but God awareness, the one experience that is God, good, becomes ever more visible and tangible as your reality.

Be peaceful, be spacious, be a nothingness — an emptiness of self, a truthful self devoted to loving and beholding God and nothing 'else'. Then, in and as that peacefulness, spaciousness, emptiness, love and attentiveness to God, you *feel* the presence as the whole being, body and universe of you.

Make it your one primary desire, your one primary urge and satisfaction to *feel*, to *experience*, God. As you feel God, your whole universe is tangibly alight with God.

Good, life, love, harmony and peace are tangibly *alight* and *being* everything everywhere. All is *felt* whole and harmonious, peaceful and true, free and fulfilled; all are fed, employed, joyous, purposeful and happy; all are safe and protected, housed and secure; all radiate and have love; all are awake and alive in truth. The *feeling* of God 'happening' *is* the spiritual universe experienced — the wholeness and completeness of truth tangibly experienced. There is none else, and nothing else required.

Hear this, my beloveds! You and everything of you is free and whole as you *feel* God happening. Know this, trust it, and live with the strength and freedom of your truth of being, freely giving of your spirit and talents to everyone and everything everywhere.

The Kingdom Come

Henceforth I will not eat until it is fulfilled
in the kingdom of God.

I will not drink of the fruit of the vine
until the kingdom of God comes.

18

The Word Fulfilled

❦

And they shall be all taught of God.

Every man therefore that hath heard,
and hath learned of the Father, cometh unto me.

Not that any man hath seen the Father,
save he which is of God, he hath seen the Father.

Do you see that being "taught of God" *is* truthful formation (experience) revealed? God *is* mind *is* formation. As soon as God is felt, truthful formation is evident. God, mind and formation are one; the God experience *is* the experience of truthful formation just as the sun *is* the experience of light and heat. You cannot have God (the felt experience of God) without God formation (wholeness and harmony) becoming evident.

Being "taught of God" is *experiencing* God happening — *feeling* the presence. As you feel God happening, the kingdom of truth *is, right now,* visible and tangible, real and practical, laid out in front of you, palpably present throughout your consciousness, fully embodied, manifested and demonstrated. When God is felt, the whole universe of truth, including everything everywhere in it and of it, is evident — omnipresent, invariable good, indivisible and inseparable oneness; whole, harmonious, peaceful, infinite and eternal, needing no agency, no vehicle, no thought, no word and no activity to 'make' it tangible. God *is*, not will be, so as *is* is realized, felt happening, rested in and relied on, it becomes tangible and real to the senses, and all is beheld good.

The Word

Only God felt happening within is God awareness, God presence, God formation, God tangibly and visibly experienced, the actual manifestation and demonstration of God witnessed as formation. Only God felt — experienced — happening within or throughout one's being is what is described in scripture as the Word.

"The Word was in the beginning and that very Word was with God, and God was that Word." Let us understand 'was' in this statement as meaning *is* (not as in the past but as ever-present) — the *essence, purity, oneness, withinness, silence.* "The Word *is* in the beginning — the *beginning* being the essence, the purity, the one, the withinness, the silence that is All-in-all — and that very Word is with God, and God is that Word."

The Word, the awareness, the feeling of God happening does not *become* flesh, formation; it *reveals itself as* the true flesh, the true formation — the image and likeness of God as formation. God-felt-happening is itself the fully manifest presence of truth, God; is the fully demonstrated image and likeness that is God as perfectly formed experience. The experience of God *is* the full embodiment of the finished kingdom revealed — revealed as the harmony and wholeness of any and every degree of awareness you have at this moment. No matter 'where' you are in spiritual awareness, you *have* complete and unconditional harmony of experience as you *feel* God happening.

At any and every level of awareness, God itself is the only formation, the only being, body and world, the only it, condition, amount, place and activity, the only experience. Wherever you 'are' in experience, no matter how good or how hopeless experience seems to be, God, truth — which is complete and unconditional harmony and wholeness of all — is present and is instantly available as individual, real and tangible experience. But this truth does us no good and remains undetected by sense unless and until we *experience God happening* rather than just *think* and *talk* about God. God cannot be experienced in or through or by the use of the intellect — by belief, thought or talk. "My ways are not your ways, says the Lord, and my thoughts are not your thoughts."

No matter what your state of experience or spiritual awareness is at any moment, *only God (perfection) actually is.* And God is unconditionally and forever, here and now, the full embodiment of itself as experience, the finished kingdom of perfection, love and grace — harmonious, whole, abundant, peaceful and divinely purposeful — conceptually experienced as individual God (good and complete) mind, body and world. You or I can have the 'worst' degree of spiritual awareness on earth; yet, if we can be still and silent and receptive enough, the whole of God — harmony and wholeness — shines through revealing the image and likeness of itself as our experience.

It often seems like a miracle to beginner students! Indeed, God witnessed *is the one miracle of life.* Suddenly, harmony, health, peace and plenty fill the student's life — the *truth* of that which seemed inharmonious, unhealthy, agitated or lacking. How? God is the only actual and ever-present formation (experience), the one and only real, with nothing 'else' to hinder it, obstruct it, resist it or delay it. *Only God is!* It is simply false and busy *belief* that clouds perfection — the real and only *actual* presence (God) — from our experience. The moment belief is stilled, and being becomes silent and empty of self, truth is able to reveal itself. The clouds of belief dissolve revealing truth everywhere about.

In the relinquishing, or sacrificing, or nothingizing, or the dying of, the dropping of the personal sense of self, truth itself billows up within as greater awareness of the fully embodied finished kingdom (experience) of God.

The Word Fulfilled

The Word Is Itself Formation

The Word of God — the feeling, the awareness, the presence of God — is itself the visibility and tangibility of truth. As the fogginess of belief dissolves, truth is revealed or exposed. Indeed, the experience of God-felt-happening within *is itself* the dissolver of the fog of belief just as the sun is itself the dissolver of the early morning mist, revealing or exposing the true splendor of earth.

Awareness of God happening *is itself* the flesh of experience. God awareness does not produce harmony and wholeness; God awareness is itself harmony and wholeness of form. Do you catch that? Formation has been misunderstood to be material, physical, corporeal. But these are simply *senses* of the one *spiritual* form — concepts or beliefs *about* the one spiritual form. The one and only true, actual spiritual form is God itself. And the *experience* of — or manifested or demonstrated form of God — is God felt happening.

All already *is*, and that *is* is infinitely, unconditionally and divinely perfect, beautiful, whole, peaceful and true. The Word becomes the embodied awareness. As awareness illumines, the image and likeness of God as formation — experience — becomes perfectly visible and real.

That is the flesh of truth, and its visibility in experience is entirely the 'work' of God itself. As we drop and make a nothing of the personal sense of self, we quickly begin to feel the presence, the happening, of God (the 'work' of God). The feeling of the presence *is itself* the flesh, the form, the image and likeness experienced. "It is done; it is finished."

God is in actuality doing no work whatsoever. The kingdom of God is finished, still, silent — and this stillness and silence is the only reality of being, body and experience. But as we give up the false sense of a personal self, we create a nothingness, an emptiness, a vacuum of being, and in and 'through' that emptiness or vacuum, the true presence of being, God, is felt happening ('working'). Thereby there is no remaining false sense to falsely interpret the image and likeness of God. The harmony of God-as-all now becomes perfectly visible as the formation of experience. It was present all the time, but now the transparency of being enables it to be perfectly visible and real as tangible experience.

SATISFIED WITH GOD ALONE

God Seeks Us

It seems as if God seeks us and indeed *in experience* God does. But this terminology is archaic. God has nothing to seek because God already is the only and the all. *Only God is;* therefore what remains to seek?

Who or what could possibly attain more God, or more attributes of God when God already is the fullness of all? Who, where, what and why? All is God; God is all; nothing exists but God itself as all, and because God is forever whole and indivisible, all is the omnipresence, completeness, infinity and eternity of God.

Rather than this archaic understanding, truth is experienced in dropping that which is false *sense*. Truth is experienced in the same way as opening the curtains and finding our house filled with sunshine. This experience *could* be described as the sun seeking our house and filling it. But the sun is doing no such thing. The sun simply *is* and does nothing different as we open the curtains. It is our act of opening that which blocked the sun that provides us with the experience of light and heat in our homes. Such is the experience of God. It is 'our' dropping the personal sense of self, the making of our sense of self a nothing, a vacuum, a transparency, that enables God, truth, to be seen tangibly as the reality of our experience. Experience is filled with the formation of truth just as our homes are filled with the light and heat of the sun.

No man hath seen the Father, save he which is of God, he hath seen the Father.

He which is of God is you or I who experience — feel — God happening within or throughout being, in the stillness and silence and nothingness of self.

All any problem has ever been, whether individual or world problem, is *false sense believed*. Belief is itself the whole pairs of opposites, the 'devil' in scripture — the belief that experience in and of its own self is real. As soon as it is realized that only God is, and as soon as it is realized that God is tangibly evidenced only by the *feeling* of the presence happening, freedom of experience begins, and begins in a rush.

The Word is itself the flesh; the Word is itself the embodied experience of that which is true. In experience, each moment of felt presence is a miracle of good formation revealed. One moment of the Word experienced — then the living by God-felt-happening, truly lived, truly being the one primary experience we seek — that one moment of truth experienced is enough to heal not only 'your' body, but the body of every person who turns to you for help. The one truth you experience happening is the formed image and likeness of God as body — the healthy, whole and vital body evidenced.

Truth experienced is not personal, nor should it be believed to be personal. It is the one whole truth experienced, the one universal, omnipresent formation of truth individually experienced as body. It is the 'knowing of truth' and the truth experience that heals the experience of that which appears ill, diseased, injured or incapacitated.

Then as we walk throughout life, acting truthfully throughout our every day, ceaselessly giving of the abundant fruits we behold filling the branches of our life, we find ourselves fulfilling the truth that we "live and move and have our being in God". We live as God-being, for God, to God. We recognize that all is God. We "practice the presence of God", not for some profit or other benefit of 'ours', but for the glorification of God as all. "Let your light so shine before men, that they may see your good works, and glorify your Father which is in heaven."

We discover our experience filled with the infinity of resource, everpresent wisdom, intelligence and direction, a divine strength and purpose that streams through our very veins, pushing through and animating our entire being and expression with ceaseless service to man, woman and world as God, for the fulfillment of God revealed.

Build the House . . . Prove Me Now in This

Remember the words of the prophet Haggai: "Go up to the mountain, and bring wood, and build the house; and I will take pleasure in it, and I will be glorified, saith the Lord." Remember that. I, God, will. The personal self cannot; only God can because *only God is*. Bring "wood" — spiritual realization, substance and experience — into my house, the truthful house, the consciousness of God; not a 'human' house, not a human mind, not a human or material or worldly condition. No, bring spiritual substance into *my* house. And then we again hear Malachi, "Prove me now, in this, that I will open the windows of heaven for you," the windows of your very being, your every sense, the windows that reveal the heavenly presence of you and your world, the windows that pour out blessings for you until you say, "It is enough!"

The miracle of God opens and blossoms as you live truth, recognizing only God, spirit, truth as the very presence and form of all, *experiencing* the presence happening, giving ceaselessly of the abundant forms of truth with which your life is filled. "Feed my sheep" with the boundless substance and forms, the fruits of good and fulfillment that blossom and fill your every branch of experience.

But remember, feed *my* sheep — not the world's sheep, not human sheep, not corporeal, physical, separate-and-apart sheep, but *my* sheep. Feed your entire experience — every him, her and it, every place, condition, amount and activity — *spirit to spirit*, not spirit to human or material. Then indeed, you are feeding *my* sheep and the wonders of truth quickly become, and then are continually evident, abundantly being and filling your world. "I am come that you may have life, and have it more abundantly. . . the earth is full of the goodness of God."

The good, the fruits of truth, often don't appear to come directly from, or as a result of, you and your truth activity or mine. As you and I devote ourselves to truth, the fruits appear not just 'locally' but all over the earth, and sometimes in space. They burst forth all over the land, yet that bursting forth of good is the one, universal present being witnessed by every you and me sufficiently devoted to truth to regularly each day sit as a nothingness experiencing — feeling — God happening as universal formation.

You read about it in the newspapers; you hear it reported in the news; you witness it in the neighborhoods; you hear about it by email, on the web; you receive telephone calls; you hear it discussed in the markets and on the street corners. All over your land, and even in space, the omnipresence of God as beautiful, bountiful, harmonious and purposeful formation bursts forth unstoppably like a trillion new flowers in springtime.

All we are doing is all we can do, and all we were ever required to do: that is being aware of God as the truth of all, seeking God alone, and then devoting our lives to beholding God as all — beholding *God happening* as the very presence and formation of all. God-felt-happening within *is* the finished kingdom of all, *is* the infinity and eternity of being, *is* the heavenly presence itself, *is* the rich harvest, *is* the abundant fruit, *is* the life, *is* the love, *is* the glory and wonder of God tangibly evidenced.

I am the life of the world. Do you truly see this now? *I am the life, the bread, the water — the formation of the world.* As *I am* is increasingly felt happening within, then the entire world springs forth as greater, tangible truth. This is the one, true reason for being. It is the one, true purpose and fulfillment of being. *I am the light of the world*, not the light of a material world or a human being. The statement is better understood as, *I am the light which* is, itself, *the truth of the world.*

You and all individuals are the infinity of being, the light of the world. Therefore, as you continually and ever more devote your being to feeling, experiencing, the happening of God within, indeed that light you are now being illumines the world, revealing its truth. Truth springs forth all over the world; wholeness, harmony, peace, love, beauty and bounty are revealed filling the earth.

My peace I give unto you. Yes, because as we each devote more and more of our being to feeling truth happening within — and as we know that this experience is itself the omnipresence of truth, not a personal truth but omnipresent truth — then indeed *My peace* becomes your peace; you begin to experience the universal peace which is brought forth into tangibility by the peace *I am* being.

As peace is regularly experienced happening within, we *have* an infinity of peace to give to each other and to the world. If we are not living with and by peace felt happening, we have nothing of truth to give each other or the world. Our oneness of being in experience — our vitality, our talent, our purpose, our work and our world — is dead and dying, drying up, closing its petals, losing its color, fragrance and flavor.

But as we devote ourselves to truth, then we are and have the life of God itself, springing forth, filling and *being* all. Truth is revealed where the consciousness of truth *is happening.* "Where the presence of the Lord is, there is liberty."

SATISFIED WITH GOD ALONE

I am the life, the love, the light; I am the bread, the wine, the water, the formation. I am that; I am all; I am all as all, for all.

I am the presence of peace welling up and springing forth, pushing through and bursting out as the formation of the world and every grain and detail, thing and place, amount and activity of it.

I am the omnipresence *of God, spirit, truth.*

Remember, the whole of the infinite is present at every point of itself simultaneously. But in order to tangibly experience this great truth as actual and visible reality, I have to *feel* it — *feel* God happening. Then I am the presence of God, and I am able to behold God as my entire world.

Then, "Very truly I tell you, whoever believes in me will do the works I have been doing, and they will do even greater things than these." When we devote our being, our body, our life and our every activity to letting God be God as us, then we are able to "do the works I have been doing" and eventually even greater works.

The Master was able to tell us this because the works are not ours but God's. Our 'ability' to behold the truth depends entirely on how much we devote our whole being, our whole life and purpose, to the actual *experience* of God happening, and knowing that *that experience itself* is the entirety of God as all. There is no other demonstration to make, no other experience to have, because there is no other aspect of or about God. God is silence; therefore as silence is experienced happening, the whole of God is 'released' in and as and throughout experience. The formation of God — the wholeness and completeness, life and vitality, harmony and abundance of God — is visible and tangible the moment silence is experienced; the Word — which is God, silence — is fulfilled as it is being experienced.

The All- and Self-Inclusiveness of Life

Individuals who want to, or believe they need to become ascetics in order to have the full God experience, do not understand the literal and all-inclusive oneness of being. "I am come that you may have life, and have it more abundantly," more beautifully, more thoroughly, more joyously, more naturally, more effortlessly. Our life and purpose here and

306

now is true. You will witness truth bursting forth as your talent, your purpose, your joy, freedom and fulfillment. You'll watch God itself animating and directing you — the presence of silence and peace filling you, your body and your world — doing beautiful works, fulfilling your true purpose of being. *I perform that which you are appointed to do*, because I am that which you are; I am your being and the body and purpose of your being, and I lift you, animate you and fulfill you. I am, and I act. "I live, yet not I, Christ [truth] lives my life."

You are filled with the presence, the body and the impulse of God happening within and as your being and activity, without labor, without effort, without exhaustion. No one and nothing in the universe can hinder you, because the presence and impulse filling you is the whole infinity and omnipotence of God happening as you. Nothing in the universe can stop truth from being evident, if only because nothing but truth exists. Nothing other than truth is; therefore nowhere in the whole of the universe is there an obstruction or resistance to God-presence, God-formation and God-expression. Nothing can hinder; nothing can obstruct; nothing can resist, delay or stop God. One with God is a majority. One with God is the one presence. One *as* God is God formation, God expression, God revealed.

It is rare, as we make our abiding place in God, and as we feel the presence filling us, and living us and our world, that we do not find ourselves with new talent, new expression, new and greater ways of giving and of service. It is rare that our lives are satisfied by sitting under a tree, silent without expression. Was Jesus an ascetic? Was Gautama? No. We have joyous and precious, long periods of silence — yes, yes — pure devotion to God, to experiencing the kingdom without objectivity. Certainly we do, and our periods of isolation and silence become more precious, more regular and longer. Certainly. It is in and as these periods, isolated from the hubbub of the world, that we are filled and refilled with the presence, power, wisdom and body of God, the 'fuel' of God — the Word. But then, when we are filled full of God, we find ourselves lifted right out of that silence and animated with expression, talent, and service to man and world.

God lives us. God exists as the wisdom and service-impulse of our minds, the light of the atoms and cells of our bodies, and the very work of our hands. We find ourselves working — 'working' is the wrong word

— we find ourselves joyously animated from morning to noon to night. We sleep less; we hardly become tired. We can't stop serving, giving, being truthfully creative. We do not want to do anything else, because what we find ourselves doing is filled with truth, and is our fulfillment — the fulfillment of God as us.

Never believe that living the life of truth takes us out of the world. No! It *fulfills* our place and purpose in the world! Never believe our earthly life diminishes, and we spend the rest of time walking around in poverty, satisfied with nothing but feeling God happening without expression. No! The whole of God and everything God is and has becomes visible and tangible and real as our being and everything we do because now it is no longer 'we' attempting to be and do, but God. 'We' have got rid of ourselves sufficiently to be a transparency for God. And because "God abhors a vacuum", our nothingness of self becomes the everythingness of God happening as our being and our world. Everything God is and has is then fully available for us to give to the world — to feed, bless, give life to and love to the world.

Feeling God happening *is the whole experience of God, is the whole manifested and demonstrated truth experience.* Oh, if you catch this one truth, you have the keys to the kingdom, and the kingdom itself! The experience of God 'and' the formation of God (the healing, harmony, peace and plenty) is one, not two. It is simply that we have an objective or form experience of the one presence, the one happening, the one fulfillment. But the seeming 'two' or 'different' experiences are one and the same, and happen at the same instant of experience. It is as our senses are filled with the one experience of God that our whole earth is 'also' and instantaneously filled with the one formation of God. The feeling or experience of oneness embodies the formation.

All is one; oneness does not *produce* whole and harmonious form; oneness experienced *is itself* its own formation — the "image and likeness" of itself, the image and likeness of God. Then, as we discover our experience filled with the rich and abundant forms of truth, we give of them, serve with them and share them. We give and serve and share of the talent and limitless resources with which we find ourselves filled and overflowing. In this way — as described in the Master's parable of the talents — we are the presence and fulfillment of God on and as earth, with the love and wisdom of omniscience, and the resources of the infinite at our disposal.

All of being, inclusive of all experience, is God happening as God, for God, to God. We are never doing anything 'ourselves' for a 'human' or for 'earth'. We are never giving to or serving a human or this world. We are giving and serving as God, to God, for God because there is none but God. In this way, we never run dry. In this way, we cannot stop the flow of good, of life, of love, of abundance and harmony pouring out from us. We can never stay the endless outpouring of giving, sharing and service we feel filling us, pushing us and animating us. Then we are the very living presence, the infinity, the power, the activity and the formation of God on and as earth.

I am come that you may have life, and have it more abundantly.

It is *I coming* that we are seeking, that we are devoting ourselves to, and that which we experience.

I refuse to partake of life, body or earth until the kingdom of God has come. And then, in and as the *silence and receptivity of being*, it comes — I and my whole universe are now filled with life and life more abundant, the *experienced* presence, very presence of God *as* God *for* God.

Devotion to Truth

I am devoting my entire life to truth, to God, and the serving of God as, primarily, silence and secondarily, as *The Miracle Self* teaching and healing activity. Do not think of this as any kind of hardship or martyrdom! It is the greatest honor any individual can have, the greatest privilege and fulfillment. Nothing of life is as wondrous or purposeful. Nothing is as miraculous as witnessing God revealed as healthy or healed, harmonized, peaceful and abundant being, condition, activity, amount and place; and yet, as God is known and sought as and for God alone, this very truth is witnessed time and time again, each and every day.

I can give no greater love to my wife, my friend and neighbor. I can give no greater gift to you, and I can *be* no greater gift for you. There is no greater gift I can give to or be for my children and all children, to my business, my customers, clients, patients or students; my community and my world. It is joy and bliss. I have felt this devotion ever since January, 2008, when *The Miracle Self* came through as the first of our books.

The reason I tell you this is that it makes no difference what 'my' particular expression looks like, versus 'yours'. *All is God.* Whatever you discover to be your passion and talent, and in whatever ways and forms you give and serve it makes no difference. There is no difference between 'The Miracle Self' expression and 'yours'. Whatever you do, realize that God is it, and it is expressing as and through you as unique and individual God fulfillment.

Start here and now, today. There is no activity, no work, no place or condition that is not God, and the fullness of God, in the most practical and real way. It is just that we have believed our experience to lack God or be different from God. You now know that such belief is nonsense. *All is God.* You can never be out of or away from or separated from the fullness and practicality of God as real and tangible experience, and every good form thereof. And so begin where you are today, and with whatever it is you do as work or art or profession or charity today, and realize that God is it. Then, devote yourself to, and be satisfied with, God alone. Live as and by *God-felt-happening*, realizing that *that* one experience alone *is* the very presence and formation of God as experience.

In this way, you can be just as devoted as I am or any illumined individual is. Many of you are. I know that. I feel bathed and surrounded by, and in companionship with the most beautiful love and friendship of so many of you, so many around the world. I treasure you and your love and devotion, and how your presence is lighting the world.

As we continue our devotion and expression together, each in our own individual way, the entire world is lifting, being filled with the light and formation of spirit, love and truth. "As I am lifted up, I draw all men unto me." The earth filled with the light of spirit changes the course of history. We observe it. We witness it every day, and we'll see it ever more. We will watch disease dissolve and disappear from the consciousness of earth, we'll watch poverty, lack and limitation, unhappiness, hate, loneliness, injustice dissolve and disappear from collective belief. We'll watch anger, greed, war and atrocity melt from individual and collective experience to reveal that which is true and loving and eternal: God as individual and collective being, world and universe — the kingdom of earth as it is in heaven; the kingdom of God coming into awareness.

Nothing can stop the kingdom of truth coming — perfectly visibly, tangibly and real in experience — for all in the community or town of even *one* who lives by, and is satisfied with, God itself felt happening. No person, organization, condition, place, time or space can inhibit or stop it from coming through. The almighty light and presence of truth dissolves all untruth — all individual and collective belief, no matter how dense it may be — to reveal itself alone as mind, body and world formation. Always remember, truth finds no resistance because truth already and forever is all; it has nothing different through which it would have to work or struggle. Truth *is*, and *already is*, and is the *only*. *Only God is.*

As we who are devoted to truth — we who can hear and live by truth, we who can devote sufficient time each and every day to silence happening — now live truth and live by truth and live for truth and endlessly give of the rich and abundant forms of truth that fill our branches, we are not surprised to witness truth springing forth as the formation of earth and all its people; as peace, harmony, beauty, bounty, purpose and freedom fulfilled for all; as *love* being the one all-in-all substance and form, mind, body and expression.

Let us root out of belief the idea of anything but God, and of any needed process or method or means of 'getting' God as experience; of anything that truth has to 'work through' before God is witnessed. No, no. Nothing but God — truth — exists. Remove belief of anything and everything but God itself and there, immediately, stands truthful formation as every him, her and it, every activity, amount, place and condition.

The only requirement is to know what God is (Know the truth, and that very truth will set you free) — that being *silence* — and then to allow or enable God itself, silence itself, to *be* your being, the body you have and the world you experience, inclusive of absolutely everything everywhere in and of the world, by and 'through' your nothingness or transparency or vacuum of self, your selfless self, and your *feeling* God happening.

Live by that feeling happening. Live *as* and *by* silence experienced, knowing that silence experienced is your all-in-all.

Allow or enable silence itself to be and to live you, and be entirely *satisfied* with the God experience alone.

Then watch the miracle.

Printed in Great Britain
by Amazon.co.uk, Ltd.,
Marston Gate.